AF411712

Jury Trial Innovations

G. Thomas Munsterman,
Paula L. Hannaford, and
G. Marc Whitehead,
editors

© 1997 National Center for State Courts
Library of Congress Catalog Card Number: 97-65255
ISBN 0-89656-174-7
NCSC Publication Number R-193

Cover design by Lori Hampton Bearfield

This report was developed by the National Center for State Courts under a grant from the State Justice Instutute (No. SJI-93-12K-B-263). The points of view expressed do not necessarily represent the official position or policies of the National Center for State Courts, the American Bar Association, or the State Justice Institute.

Advisory Committee

Hon. Richard M. Bilby
U.S. District Court,
   District of Arizona
Tucson, Arizona

Hon. B. Michael Dann
Superior Court of Arizona
Phoenix, Arizona

Prof. Shari Diamond
American Bar Foundation
Chicago, Illinois

Curtis E. von Kann, Esq.
Ross, Dixon & Masback, L.L.P.
Washington, D.C.

Prof. Stephen Landsman
De Paul University College of Law
Chicago, Illinois

Prof. R. Hanson Lawton
South Texas School of Law
Friendswood, Texas

Hon. Howard McKibben
U.S. District Court,
   District of Nevada
Reno, Nevada

Hon. H. Lee Sarokin
U.S. Court of Appeals, Third Circuit
Newark, New Jersey

Table of Contents

Acknowledgments

A large number of individuals contributed to the development of this manual. Their contributions were reviewed and edited by persons representing differing perspectives. Materials prepared by jury consultants were reviewed by judges and litigators, for example, while materials prepared by judges were reviewed by attorneys and academicians. Our intent was to offer a balanced presentation of these techniques and innovations, based on what is known through formal evaluation and practice, without endorsing their use by trial courts in every instance. Because of these considerations, individual authorship is not given except by chapter. Rather, we have listed those individuals who contributed to each section and let their specific contribution be taken with the whole.

A number of individuals, however, gave more than modestly of their time to this project. They include Judge Thomas Barland, Eau Claire County Circuit Court (Eau Claire, Wisconsin); Judge B. Michael Dann, Superior Court of Arizona (Phoenix, Arizona); Professor Shari Diamond, American Bar Foundation (Chicago, Illinois); David B. Graeven, Trial Behavior Consulting, Inc. (San Francisco, California); Curtis E. von Kann, Esq., Ross, Dixon & Masback, L.L.P. (Washington, D.C.); Professor Nancy King, Vanderbilt University School of Law (Nashville, Tennessee); Professor Stephen Landsman, DePaul University College of Law (Chicago, Illinois); Professor Nancy S. Marder, University of Southern California Law School (Los Angeles, California); Judge Howard McKibben, U.S. District Court, District of Nevada (Reno, Nevada); Peter G. Pappas, Esq., Adams, Kleemeir, Hagan, Hannah & Fouts (Greensboro, North Carolina); Vicki Smith, Ph.D., Gary Siegal Organization, Inc. (Lincolnwood, Illinois); and Judge Leslie Brooks Wells, U.S. District Court, Northern District of Ohio (Cleveland, Ohio).

We would also like to acknowledge the organizational skills of Ginger Herbst Church and Jan Kuczaboski, Popham, Haik, Schnobrich, Kaufman, Ltd. (Minneapolis, Minnesota); the publications expertise of Dawn Spinozza and Joseph Kueser; and administrative assistance by Karin Marks Hughes, National Center for State Courts (Williamsburg, Virginia). A grant from LEXIS-NEXIS provided the editors with access to statutes, case decisions, and periodical literature necessary to prepare this publication. Finally, this project would not have been possible without financial support by the State Justice Institute (SJI).

Introduction

In June 1992, the Section of Litigation of the American Bar Association and the Brookings Institution cosponsored a symposium in Charlottesville, Virginia, entitled "The Future of the Civil Jury System in the United States."[1] In attendance were judges, litigators, researchers, trial consultants, and representatives of insurance and consumer groups. During the three-day conference, the attendees developed recommendations to improve civil jury procedures based both on their unique perspectives and on the findings of commissioned papers that were presented at the conference.

One paper, "Recent Innovations in Jury Trial Procedures," highlighted innovations that state and federal courts were introducing in civil jury trials.[2] The authors acknowledged the lack of consensus over the relative merits of some of those innovations, but stressed the importance of a forum in which to exchange and evaluate new techniques and procedures.[3] This manual, a joint effort by the Jury Initiatives Task Force of the ABA Section of Litigation and the National Center for State Courts, is intended to be just such a forum.

With funding from the State Justice Institute (SJI), many individuals from the American Bar Association and others interested in the improvement of the jury system donated their talents, time, and expertise to prepare this manual. Additionally, a videotape illustrating some of the techniques described in this manual is in the planning stages.

Before we proceed further, an explanation of the manual's organization and format is appropriate. Contemporary understanding of how jurors individually and collectively process information has benefited greatly from the insights of social scientists and psychologists. Drawing on their expertise, Chapter I describes how jurors conceptualize evidence and testimony to arrive at their verdict and why innovations in jury trial procedures are so necessary.

---

[1] *See generally* the Brookings Institution, *Charting a Future for the Civil Jury System* (1992).

[2] H. Lee Sarokin & G. Thomas Munsterman, "Recent Innovations in Civil Jury Trial Procedures," in Robert E. Litan ed., *Verdict: Assessing the Civil Jury System* 378 (1993).

[3] *Id.* at 395.

There is little disagreement among social scientists (or even among most lawyers and judges) that traditional trial procedures have largely failed to take account of how jurors process new information. Recognition of this shortcoming, and the need to modify existing trial procedures, is the first step toward improving the effectiveness of the jury as an integral component of our justice system.

Subsequent chapters of the manual describe various techniques that better accommodate this more accurate understanding of juror decision making. The chapters progress in a more or less sequential order through the typical stages of a typical trial. The format, which, as one of our contributors observed, is neither elegant nor eloquent, merits some explanation. Each innovation is featured in a subsection beginning with a description of the technique ("Technique") and a brief list of the more frequent questions and policy debates ("Issues") that its use often provokes. Next follows a brief discussion of the techniques ("Procedures"), including instructions for their implementation, advisory warnings about traps for the unwary, and reports of success or failure from individuals and jurisdictions that have attempted them.

The sections entitled "Advantages" and "Disadvantages" highlight the technique's primary benefits and detriments with respect to jurors' ability and willingness to fulfill their legitimate role in the justice system. In articulating these characteristics, we have attempted to identify only those arguments for and against each technique that have some legitimate basis in fact. In some cases, these determinations were admittedly subjective. In all cases, however, readers should consider the advantages and disadvantages in light of the experiences of other judges, lawyers, and court staff as reported in the "Procedures" section.

Furthermore, it was our intent that the Advantages/Disadvantages sections focus on each technique's tendency to increase juror comprehension and satisfaction with jury service, thus improving the effectiveness of the jury's factfinding and decision-making process. Readers should also note, however, that many of the techniques have benefits (and detriments) that affect other individuals in the trial proceedings—namely, the parties, their attorneys, and the judge and court staff.

New ideas rarely appear fully formed out of thin air. It is even more rare that they are immediately enacted as legislation, adopted as court rules, or formally recognized in case law. Indeed, as anyone familiar with legal precedent knows well, new law is almost never "unprecedented," but only "previously unrecorded." Thus, it should surprise none of our readers that the relatively few references to legal authority tend to repeat the commonly voiced phrase that "matters of trial procedure lie within the sound discretion of the court." The references cited in the "Authority" section do not provide a comprehensive, state-by-state listing of relevant law for each technique. Rather, they are intended to be illustrative of existing case law and court rules relevant to these innovations.

The section entitled "References" identifies the scholarly and practical literature relevant to each technique. Many references contain a more comprehensive treatment of the implications of the technique on the various actors in the trial proceedings. "References" are distinguished from "Studies" insofar that the latter are reports of methodologically sound, empirically based evaluations of the effectiveness of the referenced technique. Although the scholarly articles listed under "References" often incorporate the findings of empirical studies to support their respective positions, the studies themselves are first-hand reports that include a description of the methodology, the precise findings, and the implications of the research for jury systems. Obviously, few of these innovations have undergone rigorous evaluation. Indeed, if we waited for all of them to be conclusively proven or disproven, little progress toward an improved jury system could be reported here—or perhaps could even be possible. As one participant at the Brookings Symposium quipped, "Some things are so obvious that performing an evaluation would be an insult to our intelligence."

A final word on the overall tone of the manual is also in order. We have attempted to present these innovations and techniques in a neutral and objective fashion without specific endorsement or criticism. We found this task to be more difficult than we imagined, given our enthusiasm for many of these innovations. Some of the individual techniques, reported for the sake of inclusiveness, provide the reader with a broad view of the variety and resourcefulness of suggested improvements to our jury system. Other techniques appear to conform more closely to the contemporary understanding of how jurors process information (discussed in Chapter I). While we assume responsibility for this license, we welcome any reactions or comments by our readers. We especially welcome any suggested innovations to be included in our next edition.

Innovations in jury trial procedures are both necessary and long overdue. The institution of trial by jury is not fatally flawed, as some critics have suggested. Rather, the problem lies with rigid trial procedures and evidentiary rules that reflect false assumptions about jury comprehension and decision making. We believe this manual contains worthwhile and practical suggestions for remedying these problems, and we welcome the opportunity to contribute to the continued expansion and strengthening of the institution of trial by jury.

G. Thomas Munsterman
Director, Center for Jury Studies
National Center for State Courts

Paula L. Hannaford, J.D., M.P.P.
Research Analyst
National Center for State Courts

G. Marc Whitehead, J.D.
Chair, Jury Initiatives Task Force
ABA Section of Litigation

Chapter I

How Jurors Make Decisions: The Value of Trial Innovations

CONTRIBUTOR

Vicki L. Smith, Ph.D.
Deerfield, Illinois

Recent interest in the American jury system raises important questions about how to maximize the quality of decision making in trials. Debates over the competence of jurors to decide cases have prompted some commentators to argue that judges should assume more decision-making responsibility. Others advocate reforming the trial process to make the jury's task more manageable.[1] Empirical research on jury decision making has revealed that in many cases juries perform their duties quite competently.[2] When problems arise, it is often the quality of the presentation that is implicated, rather than inherent deficiencies in jurors' abilities to process the information provided. Thus improvements in jury performance can be achieved by improving the quality of communications with the jury.[3] An important step in realizing such gains is to understand how jurors process information and make decisions—specifically, how well jurors perform various tasks, what kinds of problems arise, and what factors influence the quality of their decisions.

The research literature indicates that in relatively uncomplicated cases, juries are efficient and accurate fact finders.[4] Memory of the evidence is reasonably good among individual jurors, and juries have the advantage of pooling individual recollections in group discussion. This pooling significantly improves the recall of evidence in two ways: (1) gaps in individuals' memories are often filled by the other jurors and (2) errors of fact are generally discovered and corrected in group discussion. In one study, deliberating juries recalled an average of 90 percent of the evidence presented.[5]

Jurors do have more trouble with complex evidence. Scientific and technical evidence is especially difficult for jurors, and statistical evidence is often

---

[1] *Compare, e.g.,* Warren A. Burger, "The State of the Judiciary," 57 *A.B.A. J.* 885 (1971); Richard O. Lempert, "Civil Juries and Complex Cases: Let's Not Rush to Judgment," 80 *Mich. L. Rev.* 68 (1981).

[2] *See* Joe S. Cecil, Valerie P. Hans & Elizabeth C. Wiggins, "Citizen Comprehension of Difficult Issues: Lessons from Civil Jury Trials," 40 *Am. U. L. Rev.* 727 (1991); Phoebe C. Elsworth, "Are Twelve Heads Better Than One?" 52 *Law & Contemp. Probs.* 205 (1989); Reid Hastie, Steven D. Penrod & Nancy Pennington, *Inside the Jury* (1983).

[3] *See, e.g.,* Cecil et al., *supra* note 2; Shari S. Diamond & Judith N. Levi, "Improving Decisions on Death by Revising and Testing Jury Instructions," 79 *Judicature* 224 (1996).

[4] Elsworth, *supra* note 2; Hastie et al., *supra* note 2.

[5] Hastie et al., *supra* note 2.

misused.[6] However, jurors are not alone in their confusion. Judges also have difficulty with this kind of evidence.[7] Despite jurors' difficulties understanding complex evidence, there are reasons to be optimistic about the competence of juries as decision makers in complex cases. First, improving the clarity of evidence presentation can improve jurors' understanding and use of complex evidence.[8] Second, other aids to juror understanding and recall are also available. In one study, reviewing a trial transcript before choosing a verdict improved the quality of jurors' decisions in a complex medical malpractice case.[9]

Learning the law is perhaps the most challenging task jurors face. Jurors must learn complicated and generally unfamiliar legal concepts from a series of complex instructions. Then they must effectively integrate these newly acquired rules with the facts presented. Jurors do, in fact, have considerable difficulty understanding the judge's instructions of the law, often scoring at chance levels on tests of comprehension.[10] However, changes in the method of presenting the instructions can make the task more manageable. Linguistic changes, such as presenting the instructions in simpler language,[11] and procedural changes, such as presenting the instructions before the evidence,[12] can significantly improve jurors' understanding and use of the law.

These findings illustrate that creative attention to trial management and presentation strategy can improve jurors' performance. Achieving these gains

---

[6] David L. Faigman & A. J. Baglioni, Jr., "Bayes' Theorem in the Trial Process: Instructing Jurors on the Value of Statistical Evidence," 12 *Law & Hum. Behav.* 1 (1988); William C. Thompson, "Are Juries Competent to Evaluate Statistical Evidence?" 52 *Law & Contemp. Probs.* 9 (1989).

[7] Faigman & Baglioni, *supra* note 9; Neil Vidmar, "Assessing the Impact of Statistical Evidence, A Social Science Perspective," in S. E. Feinberg ed., *The Evolving Role of Statistical Assessments as Evidence in the Courts* (1989).

[8] Cecil, *supra* note 2.

[9] Martin J. Bourgeois, Irwin A. Horowitz & Lynne Forster Lee, "Effects of Technicality and Access to Trial Transcripts on Verdicts and Information Processing in a Civil Trial," 19 *Personality & Soc. Psychol. Bull.* 220 (1993).

[10] Amiram Elwork, Bruce D. Sales & James J. Alfini, "Juridic Decisions: In Ignorance of the Law or In Light of It?" 1 *Law & Hum. Behav.* 163 (1977); Vicki L. Smith, "Impact of Pretrial Instruction on Jurors' Information Processing and Decision Making," 76 *J. Applied Psychol.* 220 (1991).

[11] Elwork et al., *supra* note 10.

[12] Smith, *supra* note 10.

requires considering the psychological factors that influence the quality of people's information processing and decision making. Armed with an understanding of these influences, judges and attorneys can work together to structure trials in more effective ways and evaluate the likely impact of proposed trial innovations on jury performance.

BELIEFS AND EXPECTATIONS

Jurors bring to trial a host of beliefs and expectations about people, places, and events. These beliefs include theories about how the world works, how social interactions operate, and how the justice system functions. Some of these theories are correct, some incorrect. Regardless of their accuracy, such beliefs may affect jurors' performance at all stages of the trial, including their interpretations and evaluations of the evidence, the attorneys' opening and closing remarks, and the judge's instructions. This situation can complicate the communication process. However, careful attention to people's beliefs and expectations can help shape effective communication strategies. For example, misperceptions about jury service may be alleviated by providing citizens with information about jury trials before they are called to be jurors. Providing this information may be accomplished in a variety of ways, including public education programs or juror orientation via cable television.

The fact that jurors bring beliefs and expectations to trial is not in itself a problem. One of the primary functions of a jury is to serve as the conscience of the community in the administration of justice. To that end, jurors are supposed to rely on their common sense notions of the world when rendering a verdict. Beliefs and expectations become problematic when they impair a person's ability to be fair and impartial, and voir dire is designed to remove from the jury individuals with such beliefs. Thus, jurors surviving voir dire are not free of beliefs and expectations, only those that are believed to impair impartiality. As a group, members of the jury bring a variety of beliefs and expectations to trial, and it is in this variety that the jury ideally represents the community. Indeed, many trial innovations, including the use of additional source lists and stratified jury selection, are designed to enhance this representativeness.

Preserving the variety of community beliefs, theories, and expectations does create a challenge for judges and attorneys in optimizing their communication strategies. Jurors' beliefs influence their information processing in several important ways. First, information that is consistent with one's beliefs or theories is quickly and easily processed. Theory-consistent information requires no interpretational effort or transformation, which speeds the processing of the information. Second, theory-consistent information is generally better remembered than inconsistent information.[13]

Third, ambiguous information tends to be interpreted as theory-consistent.[14] It is easier to incorporate ambiguous information into our existing beliefs than to reevaluate the beliefs themselves. Thus, our beliefs and expectations filter incoming information and provide a context for determining its meaning. The result is that people with different beliefs can interpret the same stimulus or event in markedly different ways. For example, in one experiment, pro-Israel and pro-Arab students watched a 36-minute compilation of actual news coverage of the 1982 massacre of civilians in Lebanese refugee camps, and then evaluated the news coverage.[15] Partisans on both sides perceived the media coverage to be hostile to their position. Pro-Israel participants indicated that the news coverage was biased against Israel; pro-Arab participants perceived a bias in favor of Israel. These perceptual differences even influenced participants' judgments about the content of the news coverage. Pro-Israel participants estimated that only 16 percent of the references to Israel were favorable and 57 percent were unfavorable. In contrast, after viewing the same news clips, pro-Arab participants estimated that 42 percent of the references to Israel were favorable and only 26 percent were unfavorable. Thus, the prior beliefs of the participants produced a powerful bias in their evaluations of the information presented.

Fourth, information that is *in*consistent with our beliefs and expectations is more carefully scrutinized and more likely to be rejected than consistent information. For example, in one experiment participants who held strong beliefs either favoring or opposing a deterrent effect of capital punishment read reports of two research studies on this issue.[16] One study indicated that there is a deterrent effect; the other study indicated equally strongly that there

---

[13] Anne Locksely, Charles Stangor, Christine Hepburn, Ellen Grosovsky & Mariann Hochstrasser, "The Ambiguity of Recognition Memory Tests of Schema Theories," 16 *Cognitive Psychol.* 421 (1984).

[14] Albert H. Hastorf & Hadley Cantril, "They Saw A Game: A Case Study," 49 *J. Abnormal & Soc. Psychol.* 129 (1954); Robert P. Vallone, Lee Ross & Mark R. Lepper, "The Hostile Media Phenomenon: Biased Perception and Perceptions of Media Bias in Coverage of the Beirut Massacre," 49 *J. Personality & Soc. Psychol.* 577 (1985).

[15] Vallone et al., *supra* note 14.

[16] Charles G. Lord, Lee Ross & Mark R. Lepper, "Biased Assimilation and Attitude Polarization: The Effects of Prior Theories on Subsequently Considered Evidence," 37 *J. Personality & Soc. Psychol.* 2098 (1979).

is no deterrent effect. After reading both reports, participants were asked to evaluate the quality of the studies and to indicate their current opinions about the deterrent effect of capital punishment. The results revealed that regardless of whether their initial belief favored or opposed a deterrent effect, participants judged the study supporting their initial belief to be more convincing and better conducted than the study opposing their initial belief. Evidence supporting the initial belief was accepted with little scrutiny; opposing evidence was harshly criticized. Even more surprising was the impact of the evidence on participants' beliefs. After reading one study confirming their position and one study contradicting their position, participants were *more* convinced of the correctness of their beliefs than they were before reading any evidence. Logically, mixed evidence that supports two opposing positions with equal force should not result in a polarization of beliefs. Such evidence should reduce confidence in one's position, not increase it. These results indicate that the tendency to scrutinize and reject information that is inconsistent with an individual's beliefs and expectations can result in judgment errors.

In general, we try to maintain consistency among our beliefs, theories, and expectations, and, when possible, we will interpret incoming information in a way that achieves consistency. This does not mean that our beliefs or theories are immutable, only that there is resistance to change. The tendency to interpret new information in light of our expectations usually occurs outside of our awareness. We do not deliberately shade the meaning of incoming information so that it is consistent with our theories; this process operates powerfully behind the scenes to influence our judgments.

During voir dire questioning, many potential jurors express beliefs or attitudes that suggest they cannot be fair and impartial. To "rehabilitate" such jurors, judges often ask them if they can set aside their beliefs and base their decisions solely on the evidence and law presented at trial. This question strongly implies that competent and cooperative decision makers can accomplish this task. It is not surprising, then, that many people say they can set aside their prior beliefs. However, such claims should not be taken at face value. In most instances, people do not have accurate insight into their own decision processes, especially for complex decisions.[17] Beliefs and expectations are not simply factored into the decision process before rendering a judgment. As we have seen, they have pervasive effects on information processing, influencing the interpretation of evidence, judgments of its credibility,

---

[17] Richard E. Nisbett & Timothy D. Wilson, "Telling More Than We Know: Verbal Reports on Mental Processes," 84 *Psychol. Rev.* 231 (1977).

and the likelihood of retrieving it from memory. These processes are not easily controlled. Thus, assurances by jurors that they are able to set aside their beliefs and expectations should be viewed with skepticism, even if confidently asserted.

ATTITUDES AND BEHAVIOR

Considerable effort is expended in voir dire trying to discover whether potential jurors harbor attitudes that are inconsistent with fair and impartial decision making. This effort is based on the assumption that attitudes are good predictors of jurors' verdict choices. Do we in fact gain insight into how a person will evaluate the evidence and decide the case based on that person's general attitudes? Intuition suggests that people's behavior is largely determined by their attitudes. We perceive attitudes as the driving force behind behavior and assume that the behavior a person chooses reflects his or her true attitudes. However, when people's attitudes are measured and their behavior observed, the consistency between the two is surprisingly low.[18] For example, students' attitudes toward cheating are not a good predictor of whether they actually *do* cheat; women's attitudes toward birth control are not a good predictor of their use of birth control pills; and people's attitudes about race are not a good predictor of their behavior in actual interracial situations.[19]

Why is the correspondence between attitudes and behavior low? One reason is that we do not have direct access to people's attitudes. We must rely on self-reports, and a person's attitude statement may not accurately reflect the underlying attitude. Why? Because people are not practiced at articulating their beliefs, and they may not give a clear statement of their true attitudes. In other instances, people are reluctant to espouse unpopular beliefs. Strong social pressures against racist or sexist attitudes, for example, discourage people from admitting such beliefs publicly. The more public the forum, the more pressure there is to portray oneself in socially desirable ways. Other jurors may shade their attitude statements to appear fair-minded and balanced in

---

[18] *See, e.g.,* Richard T. LaPiere, "Attitudes vs. Actions," 13 *Soc. Forces* 230 (1934); Allen W. Wicker, "Attitudes versus Actions: The Relationship of Verbal and Overt Behavioral Responses to Attitude Objects," 25 *J. Soc. Issues* 41 (Autumn 1969).

[19] Andrew R. Davidson & James J. Jaccard, "Variables that Moderate the Attitude-Behavior Relation: Results of a Longitudinal Survey," 37 *J. Personality and Soc. Psychol.* 1364 (1979).

their views, qualities that are clearly valued in jurors. Many people also wish to be cooperative and helpful when responding to questions about their beliefs. They may give the answer they believe the questioner wants to hear rather than an accurate appraisal of their attitudes. Judges and attorneys can decrease this tendency by asking balanced, open-ended questions that do not reveal the desired response and that encourage jurors to respond freely. Some judges and attorneys have found that posing questions in a factual context that differs from that of the case at bar is an effective method of encouraging jurors to reveal their true beliefs.

A second reason that attitude-behavior consistency is low is that behavior is influenced by a variety of forces, attitudes being only one. Situational pressures to behave in a certain way can overpower the influence of attitudes. For example, members of the House of Representatives voted overwhelmingly to give themselves a salary increase one year when the vote was anonymous. When a roll call was taken, the pay increase was overwhelmingly defeated. People's behavior is sensitive to the social norms and constraints of the situations they face. Jurors, too, can be subject to strong pressures to vote in a particular way, especially during group discussion, and they may endorse verdicts that are inconsistent with their general attitudes.

How, then, do we maximize the usefulness of jurors' attitude statements as predictors of behavior? First, questioning should be structured to encourage honesty and candor. Obstacles to truthful responding should be identified and removed whenever possible. For example, *in camera* voir dire may be appropriate in some cases to reduce social constraints on expressing unpopular attitudes. Questionnaires may also be a valuable substitute for face-to-face questioning about sensitive issues. It is easier to disclose one's true beliefs on an impersonal questionnaire than to look a judge or an attorney in the eye and say something he or she may dislike.

Second, questions about attitudes should be as specific and relevant as possible to the behavior being predicted, whether one is trying to predict how a potential juror will evaluate the evidence or what verdict that person will choose. The more relevant the attitude question, the better the predictive power of the response. For example, women's attitudes toward birth control in general are not a good predictor of their use of birth control pills in the succeeding two years. However, women's attitudes about using birth control pills in the next two years are a substantially better predictor of this behavior.[20] Thus, attitude questions should be as specific and relevant as possible to the behavior being predicted.

---

[20] *Id.*

Third, the stronger, more stable, and more salient an attitude, the better its predictive power.[21] Voir dire questioning should focus on these kinds of attitudes if the goal is to predict a juror's behavior.

JURORS AS INFORMATION PROCESSORS

The traditional legal model of jury trials conceptualizes jurors as passive observers and recorders of information who suspend judgment on the evidence and issues until they retire for deliberation.[22] The goal of delaying evaluation until the trial is concluded is appropriate given the protracted and adversarial nature of trials. If jurors render judgments on the early evidence, their decisions will be based on an incomplete and possibly one-sided view of the facts. It is, therefore, important that jurors remain open-minded throughout the proceedings.

Contrary to the traditional legal model, jurors do not simply record the evidence in memory for later use. They actively process incoming information, evaluating it and making judgments about it throughout the trial. This active approach to information processing is necessary because people have limited processing capacity. They cannot process and remember all the information that is presented, so they must decide what to commit to memory and what to dismiss as unimportant or irrelevant. As a result, they interpret, evaluate, and organize the evidence throughout the trial, as it becomes available.

Does this mean that jurors are not open-minded? Not necessarily. Several studies have investigated people's ongoing judgments in trial simulations.[23] After each segment of the trial, participants were asked to indicate their opinions about the likely guilt of the defendant. The results indicated that participants' judgments tracked the evidence in reasonable ways. Likelihood of guilt ratings increased after direct examination of prosecution witnesses and de-

---

[21] Carl A. Kallgren & Wendy Wood, "Access to Attitude-Relevant Information in Memory as a Determinant of Attitude-Behavior Consistency," 22 *J. Experimental Soc. Psychol.* 328 (1986); Mark Snyder & William B. Swann, Jr., "When Actions Reflect Attitudes: The Politics of Impression Management," 34 *J. Personality and Soc. Psychol.* 1034 (1976).

[22] B. Michael Dann, "'Learning Lessons' and 'Speaking Rights': Creating Educated and Democratic Juries," 68 *Ind. L. J.* 1229 (1993).

[23] *See, e.g.*, H. P. Weld & E. R. Danzig, "A Study of the Way in Which a Verdict is Reached by a Jury," 53 *Am. J. Psychol.* 518 (1940); Saul M. Kassin & Lawrence S. Wrightsman, *The American Jury on Trial: Psychological Perspectives* (1988).

creased after cross-examination. Similarly, likelihood of guilt ratings decreased after direct examination of defense witnesses and increased after cross-examination. Thus, although participants actively processed the incoming evidence and rendered mid-trial judgments on it, their judgments were not immutable. Participants were responsive to subsequent evidence, attending to it and incorporating it into their judgments. In that sense, then, these mock jurors remained open-minded.

Active information processing has at least two other potential advantages for jurors' performance. First, it may help jurors concentrate on the information being presented and keep their attention focused on the trial. The less time jurors' minds wander from the task, the more information they can potentially process. Second, involved audiences are more likely than uninvolved audiences to think about and evaluate a message's content.[24] Uninvolved audiences tend to rely on the expertise or attractiveness of the communicator as a means of evaluating persuasive messages. This suggests that jurors' evaluations of the evidence content can be enhanced by keeping them actively involved in the trial process. Allowing jurors to take notes during the trial and allowing jurors to ask questions of the witnesses are two trial innovations that capitalize on these processing effects. Both techniques encourage jurors to remain actively involved in the trial.

EVIDENCE REPRESENTATION

How do jurors make sense out of the evidence presented at trial? They must turn a collection of facts that vary in importance, credibility, and consistency into a verdict preference. How is this accomplished? Jurors process trial evidence by building a story about what happened.[25] People have extensive experience listening to, composing, and telling stories. A story is a familiar framework that allows people to process efficiently large amounts of information. It is understandable, then, that jurors would choose to build stories in the trial

---

[24] Richard E. Petty & John T. Cacioppo, "The Elaboration Likelihood Model of Persuasion," 19 *Advances in Experimental Soc. Psychol.* 124 (1986).

[25] Nancy Pennington & Reid Hastie, "Evidence Evaluation in Complex Decision Making," 51 *J. Personality & Soc. Psychol.* 242 (1986) (hereinafter Pennington & Hastie, "Evidence Evaluation"); Nancy Pennington & Reid Hastie, "Explanation-Based Decision Making: Effects of Memory Structure on Judgment," 14 *J. Experimental Psychol.: Learning, Memory and Cognition* 521 (1988) (hereinafter Pennington & Hastie, "Explanation-Based Decision Making").

context, where the goal is to determine what happened and make judgments about an incident.

Jurors' stories are based on the evidence presented at trial, with gaps in the stories filled by the juror's inferences about the evidence. These inferences are based on the juror's prior knowledge of the physical and social world. Once the story is complete, the juror can compare the story to the available verdict categories and choose the verdict that best fits the story constructed. Jurors' preference for the story framework has important implications for judges' and attorneys' presentation strategies. Jurors will try to build a story, and the easier this is to accomplish, the more credible the information will be perceived.

In one experiment, participants read an account of an actual murder trial, in which the evidence was presented in either story order or trial order.[26] Story order presented the evidence in chronological sequence; trial order preserved the evidence ordering used in the actual trial, which did not follow a chronological sequence. The evidence presented in both conditions was identical; the only difference was the order in which it was presented. The researchers hypothesized that evidence presented in story order would be easier to process and consequently more persuasive. Consistent with this reasoning, they found that 78 percent of participants found the defendant guilty when the prosecution evidence was presented in story order and the defense evidence was presented in trial order. However, only 31 percent of participants voted guilty when the prosecution evidence was presented in trial order and the defense evidence in story order. As predicted, information presented in a story format was more persuasive than information that violated a story structure.

The story model of jurors' information processing is an instance of a more general phenomenon known as "framing." People's decisions are influenced by the way information is presented, or framed. Many decision tasks can be framed in different ways without changing the objective characteristics; the underlying decision is the same, but the surface features vary. Logically, people's decisions should not be sensitive to changes in the surface features, or frame; the objective characteristics of the problem should govern the solution. However, people are influenced by framing.

In one experiment, participants were asked to choose one of two programs for combating a disease outbreak.[27] "Imagine that the U.S. is preparing for the outbreak of an unusual Asian disease, which is expected to kill 600 people.

---

[26] Nancy Pennington & Reid Hastie, "Explanation-Based Decision Making," *supra* note 25.

[27] Daniel Kahneman & Amos Tversky, "Choices, Values, and Frames," 39 *Am. Psychol.* 341 (1984).

Two alternative programs to combat the disease have been proposed. Assume that the exact scientific estimates of the consequences of the programs are as follows:

> If Program A is adopted, 200 people will be saved.

> If Program B is adopted, there is a one-third probability that 600 people will be saved and a two-thirds probability that no people will be saved.

When given a choice between Programs A and B, 72 percent of participants chose Program A. However, when these program descriptions were reframed to specify how many people will die rather than how many people will be saved, decision makers' preferences were dramatically different:

> If Program C is adopted, 400 people will die.

> If Program D is adopted, there is a one-third probability that nobody will die and a two-thirds probability that 600 people will die.

Program C is objectively identical to Program A—only the frame is different. The disease is expected to kill 600 people; if Program A saves 200 people, then 400 people will die, which is Program C's claim. Similarly, Program D is objectively identical to Program B. Therefore, Programs C and D offer exactly the same choice as Programs A and B. However, when given the choice between Programs C and D, only 22 percent of decision makers chose Program C.

Logically, the frame is irrelevant, but psychologically it has meaning and influence. This means that our decisions are not always based solely on a rational evaluation of the decision alternatives. The way those alternatives are framed can have a powerful impact on our decisions, which suggests that attention should be given not only to the objective content of information presented to the jury, but also to the way in which that content is presented. For example, as in the health policy decision described above, decision makers can be encouraged to accept more or less risk, depending on how the facts are framed.

Allowing attorneys to make interim commentary and summations has been proposed to assist jurors to process new information more effectively by placing it in context within the "frame" of the trial. Periodically during the trial, each attorney is given the opportunity to speak directly to the jury, to clarify or simply remind jurors of the evidence that has been presented. This procedure potentially has the advantage of refreshing jurors' memories about key evidence for both sides.

Application of the concept of framing to the instruction process suggests that instructions from the judge on the governing law should also help jurors frame the issues in legally appropriate ways, rather than basing their judgments on their naive understanding of the law. This reasoning assumes, of course, that the instructions are comprehensible to jurors.

Comprehending the Law

Because most jurors have no formal training in the law, the judge's instructions become the primary vehicle for educating jurors about the governing legal principles. This places considerable pressure on judge-jury communications to fulfill jurors' educational needs. Empirical research on pattern jury instructions across the country has revealed that people's comprehension of the instructions is quite poor.[28] On tests of comprehension, instructed participants often score no better than uninstructed participants. Linguistic barriers to comprehension include the use of legal jargon, unfamiliar vocabulary, complex grammar, and poor organization. Whenever possible, communications with the jury should be carefully worded to avoid these barriers. Significant improvements in mock jurors' comprehension of the law have been achieved when jury instructions are rewritten in simpler language.[29] Although delivery of pattern instructions is mandated by statute in many jurisdictions, judges do have the freedom to provide additional helpful information to the jury. In this spirit, judges might consider paraphrasing difficult sections of the pattern instructions to improve jurors' comprehension. In addition, judges can improve the comprehensibility of their other communications with the jury by being aware of these linguistic obstacles to understanding.

How should the judge's instructions be presented to maximize their educational value? Traditionally, the instructions are presented at the close of trial so that jurors have the law fresh in their minds when they retire for deliberation. Consequently, legally naive jurors listen to days or weeks of testimony with little or no guidance from the judge about how to interpret and evaluate the evidence. As we have seen, jurors actively process the information presented at trial, as it becomes available. In the absence of information about the legal rules, jurors must process the evidence and testimony through the filter of their own prior beliefs and chosen stories. In other words, incoming information will be interpreted in ways that are consistent with whatever knowl-

---

[28] Diamond & Levi, *supra* note 3; Elwork et al., *supra* note 10; Laurence J. Severance & Elizabeth F. Loftus, "Improving the Ability of Jurors to Comprehend and Apply Criminal Jury Instructions," 17 *Law & Soc. Rev.* 153 (1982).

[29] Diamond & Levi, *supra* note 3; Elwork et al., *supra* note 10; Severance & Loftus, *supra* note 28.

edge structure they have in place at the time that information is presented. To enhance jurors' abilities to process the evidence in legally appropriate ways, the judge should present the legal framework at the beginning of the trial, before the evidentiary stage of trial. In fact, empirical research has revealed that jurors instructed both before and after the evidence are better able to integrate facts and law than jurors instructed only after the evidence is presented.[30]

Providing a hard copy of the instructions, either written or taped, should also benefit jurors' comprehension. The instructions present a large volume of new and complex information that jurors must remember. However, memory space is limited and memories decay over time. As a result, jurors cannot retain all of the information contained in the instructions. Having access to a hard copy of the instructions can relieve some of the pressure on jurors to recall the law. In addition, the instructions are usually delivered orally by the judge while the jurors listen passively. They may understand some parts of the instructions and miss others. Written or taped instructions afford jurors the opportunity to fill the gaps in their understanding by rereading or replaying the appropriate segments.

Written instructions potentially have two additional advantages. Education research has revealed that students understand and remember more information when they read texts than when they listen to lectures.[31] Jurors' comprehension should improve by reading a written copy of instructions. In addition, material is better remembered when it is presented in several different forms than in a single form. Having the jurors both listen to and read the instructions should capitalize on this effect.

The effectiveness of procedural reforms of the instruction process depends on the presentation of comprehensible instructions. There is little value in preinstructing or providing a hard copy of instructions that are unintelligible to jurors. However, if the instructions are made accessible to lay people, these and other procedural changes can potentially enhance jurors' understanding and use of the law.

Jury simulation research has demonstrated that jurors spend about 20 to 25 percent of their deliberation time discussing the law.[32] Errors are frequent in these discussions; one study found that only 51 percent of jurors' statements

---

[30] Smith, *supra* note 10.

[31] Kassin & Wrightsman, *supra* note 23.

[32] Hastie, Penrod & Pennington, *supra* note 2; Elsworth, *supra* note 2.

about the law were accurate, and errors of law were corrected only 12 percent of the time.[33] In fact, it was just as likely that an accurate statement would be rejected in favor of an inaccurate one during discussion as it was that an inaccurate statement would be corrected. Clearly there is considerable room for improvement in jurors' comprehension, and some linguistic and procedural reforms may be helpful in achieving that goal.

JURIES AS DECISION MAKERS

When jurors retire to deliberate, they enter as individuals with independent opinions about the case and the appropriate outcome, and their goal is to combine those independent beliefs in a rational and meaningful way into a group judgment. How is consensus achieved? In group discussions, two types of social influence occur.[34] The first is informational influence, in which people are genuinely convinced by the persuasive arguments of their fellow discussants. Real opinion change occurs and the group decision reflects a genuine consensus among group members. The second is normative influence, in which people accede to the majority opinion in order to avoid social rejection. In this situation, individual group members may privately disagree with the group decision, making any consensus reported more apparent than real.

Ideally, jury deliberations should be dominated by informational influence, with normative pressures playing a minimal role in the consensus process. In reality, however, both types of influence occur in most groups, which suggests that the jury environment should be structured to encourage open information exchange and to minimize normative strong-arming. For example, when a jury deadlocks, a judge's efforts to break the stalemate should be geared toward encouraging or assisting the resolution of the jurors' informational conflicts and should avoid tipping the balance of normative pressures. One tool available to judges for helping juries break deadlocks is the *Allen* charge. However, empirical research indicates that the *Allen* charge does not have the desired effect of enhancing the jury's use of informational influence. Rather, it

---

[33] Elsworth, *supra* note 2.

[34] Morton Deutsch & Harold B. Gerard, "A Study of Normative and Informational Social Influence Upon Individual Judgment," 51 *J. Abnormal & Soc. Psychol.* 629 (1955).

operates by tipping the balance of normative pressures in favor of the majority, coercing the members of the minority faction into changing their votes.[35]

One proposed trial innovation is designed to break deadlocks specifically by assisting the jury's information exchange.[36] When a jury reports deadlock, the judge offers the assistance of court and counsel in resolving disputed factual or legal issues. This process may involve providing additional jury instructions, allowing further evidence to be presented on certain issues, or permitting counsel to present supplementary closing arguments. These procedures have at least two important advantages. First, they encourage jurors to keep their attention focused on resolving their informational disagreements, rather than simply intensifying normative pressure on the minority faction. Second, these interventions provide meaningful assistance in the resolution of disputed factual or legal issues. They are a means of filling gaps in the jurors' memories or clearing up misunderstandings that may stall the deliberation process.

THE JUDGE'S RESPONSE

Jurors face a difficult challenge making sense out of a large volume of evidence and testimony, learning a multitude of complex legal principles, integrating these two bodies of information, and achieving consensus on the appropriate verdict through group discussion. Because of the complex and multifaceted nature of the task, numerous obstacles to optimal decision making can arise. Careful attention to the knowledge and skills jurors bring to trial, the structure of the decision environment, and the content of communications with the jury can circumvent some of these problems and overcome others. The information-processing and decision-making strategies described in this chapter should provide a useful backdrop for evaluating the trial reforms proposed in this manual and identifying their potential costs and benefits for jurors' performance. With some creativity, judges can structure a trial environment that moves jurors closer to the goal of optimal decision making.

---

[35] Saul M. Kassin, Vicki L. Smith & William F. Tulloch, "The Dynamite Charge: Effects on the Perceptions and Deliberation Behavior of Mock Jurors," 14 *Law & Hum. Behav.* 537 (1990); Vicki L. Smith & Saul M. Kassin, "Effects of the Dynamite Charge on the Deliberations of Deadlocked Mock Juries," 17 *Law & Hum. Behav.* 625 (1993).

[36] Dann, *supra* note 22.

Chapter II

Jury Administration and Management

CONTRIBUTORS AND REVIEWERS

Janice Fernette, J.D.
National Center for State Courts
Williamsburg, Virginia

Paula L. Hannaford, J.D., M.P.P.
National Center for State Courts
Williamsburg, Virginia

Sam Harahan
Council for Court Excellence
Washington, D.C.

Hon. Howard McKibben
U.S. District Court, District of Nevada
Reno, Nevada

G. Thomas Munsterman
National Center for State Courts
Arlington, Virginia

§ II-1   CITIZEN EDUCATION CAMPAIGNS ABOUT JURY SERVICE

TECHNIQUE

Techniques consist of any one of a variety of public outreach strategies in which the community learns about the concept of trial by jury, including the importance of jury service. Examples include:

- press conferences with leaders of all branches of government pronouncing Jury Service Appreciation Week;

- public service advertising campaigns using newspapers, television, mass transit, public buildings, libraries, grocery stores, courthouses, and schools;

- targeted media outreach using informal radio and television interviews with trial judges, other court personnel, and attorneys;

- targeted educational outreach to high school government, speech, U.S. history, or civics classes through which judges explain the role of the jury in the judicial process; and

- the development of educational videos that put student audiences in the role of a simulated jury, hearing evidence and jury instructions and deciding cases.

ISSUES

- How do organizers of jury education campaigns encourage public relations experts to contribute their expertise and ideas for reaching the public effectively on a pro bono basis?

- How do organizers of jury education campaigns secure the positive support and participation of judicial leadership to encourage broad involvement by trial court judges in these activities?

- How do organizers of jury education campaigns raise sufficient financial resources to print poster campaign literature or produce and disseminate educational videos?

- How do organizers of jury education campaigns secure the active involvement and follow-through of the "partnering" bar or civic groups that coordinate jury education programs with the court?

- How do organizers of jury education campaigns develop new twists, themes, or dimensions for the jury education campaign to keep them interesting for the public year after year?

Procedures

The endorsement and support of court leadership is the key to formulating a broad-based committee to plan and execute proposed citizen education campaigns about jury service. The planning committee also should include noncourt representation.

A legislative resolution that proclaims the month of October (for example) as "Jury Appreciation Month" is one easy and useful vehicle around which to build an annual citizen education campaign. A public relations program organized around a "Jury Service Week" or other period of limited duration has many advantages. It provides the judiciary with a forum in which to educate citizens about the justice system generally and jury service in particular. It provides a method to correct misinformation or distortions about jurors' responsibilities that special interest groups (e.g., the Fully Informed Jury Association) may be actively promulgating. It fosters more effective court relations with the community. Finally, it operates as a form of self-education, offering judges and court staff the opportunity to assess the level of public education and understanding about the jury system.

If public service advertising is to be used, it is frequently necessary to request mass transit advertising space six to 12 months in advance. While public service advertising through posters and other media is not prohibitively costly, it can cost $2,500 to $7,500 to design, print, and disseminate 1,000 to 2,000 jury education campaign posters. Donated corporate sponsorship of a poster campaign is one avenue for financing this activity.

One example of a successful campaign occurred in Pittsburgh, Pennsylvania. The theme "Jury Service: Your Role in the Justice System" was selected. During the week, a giant electronic billboard that overlooks the city broadcast the theme and thanks to those who serve on jury duty. A booth in the lobby of the City-County Building had staff in Jury T-shirts who passed out literature on jury service, demonstrated the new automation system ("see, it is random"), gave out a "juror quiz" that asked everyday jury questions ("Who was the 12th Angry Man?"), and even gave out bumper stickers. A video terminal showed juror orientation videos throughout the day. Citizens serving on jury duty that week were given special lapel buttons. Local TV news covered the event with coverage focused on the booth.

In Duluth, Minnesota, a longer-term effort had many facets including advertising and posters around the city and in the newspapers that carried the catchy slogan "It Isn't Fair, If You're Not There." The initiative was successful because of the involvement of a number of different organizations and individuals. The Lake Superior Ad Club provided technical expertise in creating the multimedia approach. They produced several audio and video public service announcements using the theme. The League of Women Voters was instrumental in tying the responsibility for jury service with voter registration drives conducted districtwide throughout the year. A free bus pass program was developed with the transit authority for jurors. Placards were placed in the buses as well. Mailers were specially targeted for distribution in low-income and minority areas of the district. The cost to the court for all of these brochures, audio and video tapes, posters, and the outside help was under $4,000.

The use of educational videos that explain the jury system can open up a whole new avenue of court/school system interchange. The Council for Court Excellence, a civic group based in Washington, D.C., has "You Decide," an educational package with a companion teachers' guide that is now in use in school systems in more than 20 states. A personal appearance by a trial court judge during school classes or at civic group meetings also makes a significant impression. To encourage this type of interaction, the chief judge can send a personal letter to each secondary school principal or to each civic association president, encouraging him or her to invite judges to speak about trial by jury.

ADVANTAGES

1.   Jury education campaigns provide an opportunity for the judicial branch to teach important values of citizenship such as trial by jury.

2.   Jury education campaigns provide a vehicle for fostering effective court relations with the community.

3.   Jury education campaigns educate the judiciary about the extent of public knowledge and understanding of jury service.

DISADVANTAGES

1.   An effective jury education campaign takes considerable work to plan and execute. Support and interest by the judicial leadership are a critical foundation.

2. Many judges are uncomfortable communicating with the media.

3. Evaluating the effect of a public education campaign is very difficult.

REFERENCES

The Council for Court Excellence has numerous publications and educational materials available for conducting public education campaigns about jury service. For additional information, contact:

Council for Court Excellence
Suite 750 South
1800 M Street, NW
Washington, DC 20036
(202) 785-5917

§ II-2   One-Day/One-Trial Terms of Jury Service

Technique

A person's term of jury service is limited to the completion of one trial. If not selected for a jury on the first day, he or she fulfills the jury service term by having been available on that day. Persons may be on call for several days, but once they report, their service is completed by serving one day or one trial.

Issues

- How severely does a one-day/one-trial system affect the administrative costs associated with jury management?

- What effect does the loss of "seasoned" jurors have on jury verdicts?

- By what amount should jury managers adjust the number of persons called for service to compensate for the shorter duration of jury service and to ensure an adequate number of prospective jurors?

Procedures

The court calls prospective jurors to serve for a period of only one day. If selected as a juror on that day, the person serves until the case is completed. If not selected, the prospective juror is considered to have fulfilled the obligation of service until called again—generally many years later.

Some courts require prospective jurors to be available—that is, to call in and see whether they must report for jury service—for several days or weeks. Once the person has been summoned for jury service, however, his or her obligation ends at the completion of one day or one trial. Some courts consider persons who are available, but are not asked to report, to have completed their obligation.

The practice was first used in Houston (Harris County), Texas in 1972. Today, approximately 40 percent of all U.S. citizens live in jurisdictions that use one-day/one-trial systems, both in small and in large courts. The practice is statewide in Massachusetts, Connecticut, Florida, and Colorado, and is used in most courts in New York, Arizona, North Carolina, and Texas.

Advantages

1. Jury service that is limited to the longer of one day or one trial reduces the hardship associated with service, thus reducing the need for exemptions or excuses from jury service.

2. The reduced number of persons excused with one-day/one-trial jury service terms increases the representativeness and inclusiveness of the jury pool.

3. One-day/one-trial jury service terms encourage courts to make more efficient use of juror time (since they have only one day to use the prospective juror's services), thus increasing juror satisfaction with jury service.

4. Because one-day/one-trial jury service terms require courts to summon greater numbers of prospective jurors, more persons have the educational experience of serving on a jury, which is generally a positive experience.

Disadvantages

1. Compared with courts that have longer terms for jury service, courts that use a one-day/one-trial system have to summon greater numbers of persons for jury service.

2. Compared with longer jury service terms, one-day/one-trial systems have increased administrative costs for postage, forms, and court staff.

3. One-day/one-trial systems necessarily preclude the development of "seasoned jurors" or the ability to track juror performance on prior trials.

4. One-day/one-trial systems require courts to conduct juror orientation more frequently.

5. Inefficient use of juror time by courts using one-day/one-trial systems can result in a wasted day and a poor jury experience for the person summoned for jury service.

Authority

Mass. Ann. Laws ch. 234A § 39 (1996) (defining the "reasonable" term of jury service as three days and prohibiting trial courts from releasing persons called for jury service unless the three-day term would impose an extreme hardship).

REFERENCES

American Bar Association, Committee on Jury Standards, *Standards Relating to Juror Use and Management* 42-48 (1993) (Standard 5 describes recommended terms of and availability for jury service).

G. Thomas Munsterman, *Jury System Management* (National Center for State Courts, 1996).

G. Thomas Munsterman, *Reduced Terms of Jury Service in the Federal Courts* (National Center for State Courts, 1986).

Janice T. Munsterman, G. Thomas Munsterman, Brian Lynch & Steven D. Penrod, *The Relationship of Juror Fees and Terms of Service to Jury System Performance* (National Center for State Courts, 1991).

§ II-3   A More Sensible Way of Paying Jurors

Technique

The financial hardship of serving on a jury is related to the fees paid to jurors as well as the length of jury service and the employment status of the juror. In recognition of this relationship, jurors in many one-day/one-trial courts are not paid for the first day, but are paid if they are selected for a trial that requires them to return for a second day (or more days). Other courts pay a nominal fee to jurors for their first day of service and a higher rate for successive days. Unemployed persons, including those retired or those at home, are reimbursed for actual expenses including child care if applicable. These techniques differ from the traditional method of paying jurors, which is by flat rates ranging from $5 to $40 per day, plus mileage in many jurisdictions.

Issues

- If most persons serve only one day under one-day/one-trial systems, should they be paid for the first day of jury service?

- How willing are legislatures to mandate private employers to subsidize the jury system by requiring them to continue to compensate employees who are summoned for jury service? For how many days is it reasonable to require employers to continue compensation for employees summoned for jury service?

- What is the projected cost to state and county governments of increasing juror fees for the second and subsequent days of jury service?

- Should federal, state, and county employees be paid juror fees?

- How do courts determine a "reasonable daily rate" for jury fees?

- Should parking, mileage, and child care be included with juror fees? If so, how should these costs be indexed?

Procedures

The state adopts a fee structure that bases the amount paid to jurors on their length of jury service, employer, and employment status. State law may require employers to continue to compensate employees called for jury service for a certain number of days.

In seven states, employers are required by statute to pay employees who are summoned for jury service. In some states, this requirement is subject to the size of the employer (e.g., number of employees) or number of days of jury service. In addition, some states require the employer to make up the difference between the jury fee and the employee's regular salary or wages. Other courts, such as the Dallas County (Texas) District Court, have established systems that permit jurors to donate their juror fees to charity. See Appendix 1, "Sample Jury Summons Form."

ADVANTAGES

1. More equitable systems of juror compensation decrease the need to grant exemptions or excuses based on financial hardship, thus improving the representativeness of the panels from which juries are selected.

2. More equitable systems for juror compensation recognize the value of jurors' service, thus increasing juror satisfaction.

3. The increased costs associated with implementing more equitable juror compensation systems encourage courts to use jury pools more efficiently.

DISADVANTAGES

1. More equitable juror compensation systems are more costly to state and county governments.

2. State statutes that require employers to continue to compensate employees who are summoned for jury service shift the cost of jury service to private employers.

AUTHORITY

Dean v. Gadsten Times, 412 U.S. 343 (1973) (holding that a state statute requiring employers to continue to compensate employees called for jury service is not unconstitutional).

Colo. Rev. Stat. § 13-71-126 (Supp. 1995) (requiring employers to pay employees regular wages up to $50 per day for the first three days of jury service).

Conn. Gen. Stat. § 51-247 (Supp. 1996) (requiring employers to pay employees regular wages for the first five days of jury service).

Mass. Gen. Laws Ann. ch. 234A § 48 (West 1986) (requiring employers to pay employees regular wages for the first three days of jury service).

REFERENCES

American Bar Association, Committee on Jury Standards, *Standards Relating to Juror Use and Management* 133 (1993) (Standard 15 addresses juror compensation).

Brookings Institution, *Charting a Future for the Civil Jury System: A Report from an American Bar Association/Brookings Symposium* 29-30 (1992) (recommending increases in jury fees and employer-paid leave of absence for jury duty).

STUDY

Janice T. Munsterman, G. Thomas Munsterman, Brian Lynch & Steven D. Penrod, *The Relationship of Juror Fees and Terms of Service to Jury System Performance* (National Center for State Courts, 1991).

RELATED APPENDIX

Appendix 1: Sample Jury Summons Form

§ II-4   Additional Source Lists

Technique

The court supplements its primary juror source lists (usually voter registration lists) with additional source lists to enhance the inclusiveness and representativeness of the jury pool. See also § II-5 "Stratified Jury Selection."

Issues

- How difficult is it to eliminate duplication among the various source lists?

- What types of source lists are appropriate supplements to voter registration lists?

- What costs does the court incur to obtain additional source lists?

- How often should supplemental source lists be updated?

Procedures

Voter registration lists vary with respect to their inclusiveness and representativeness of the population. Voter registration lists typically include only 60 to 70 percent of the population over age 18 and overrepresent older, upper-income, well-educated, and nonminority persons in the jurisdiction. To enhance the representativeness of the jury pool and to expand the coverage of those persons who may be called, the court may combine and supplement its voter registration lists with additional source lists. The most commonly used supplement is the list of licensed drivers and holders of identification cards provided by the state Department of Motor Vehicles. Among other lists considered are residents (according to state census), utility and telephone customers, newly naturalized citizens, property owners, motor vehicle owners, and state tax payers, including welfare and unemployment recipients. The utility of adding additional lists is determined by the unique names that the supplemental list provides over the list(s) already used. For instance, if the voters plus drivers list combination covers close to 100 percent of the population, which typically occurs, additional lists will add only the names of those persons who do not drive or are not registered to vote. Some jurisdictions permit residents to add their names to the master jury list if they are not already included on existing source lists, which simply adds their name to the source list but does not give them any priority over other persons.

After the juror source lists have been combined, the names can be sorted by social security number or some other matching criteria to identify duplicates. Removing duplicates is necessary to provide each person with an equal probability of selection. As of August 1996, 12 states use only voter registration lists, six states use only lists of licensed drivers, two states use state-unique lists, and 25 use a combined voters and drivers list. Five states add some additional lists to the voters and drivers lists.

ADVANTAGES

1. Additional source lists increase inclusiveness, thereby bringing more people into the jury process and distributing the educational value and burden more equitably across the population.

2. Representativeness of the jury pool is improved.

DISADVANTAGES

1. Combining multiple lists creates duplication of names. If duplicates are not removed, some persons have an increased probability of selection.

2. Lists may contain the names of persons unqualified for jury service (e.g., noncitizens, minors), which reduces the yield of the number of persons summoned.

3. Lists may be costly and difficult to combine.

AUTHORITY

People v. Wheeler, 503 P.2d 748, 759 (Cal. 1978) ("Obviously if [the source] list is not representative of a cross-section of the community, the process is constitutionally defective *ab initio*.")

People v. Harris, 679 P.2d 433 (Cal. 1984) (concluding that the state's use of a voter registration list, which did not represent a fair cross-section of the community, as the sole source list for impaneling juries deprived the defendant of his right to a jury trial).

REFERENCES

American Bar Association, Committee on Jury Standards, *Standards Relating to Juror Use and Management* 10 (1993) (Standard 2 addresses jury source lists).

Stephanie Domitrovich, "Jury Source Lists and the Community's Need to Achieve Racial Balance on the Jury," 33 *Duq. L. Rev.* 39 (1994).

G. Thomas Munsterman, *Jury System Management* (National Center for State Courts, 1996).

G. Thomas Munsterman & Janice T. Munsterman, "The Search for Jury Representativeness," 11 *Just. Sys. J.* 1 (1986).

§ II-5   STRATIFIED JURY SELECTION

TECHNIQUE

The court uses weighted sampling techniques based on location within the jurisdiction or on the racial or ethnic characteristics of the prospective jurors. This technique improves the likelihood that the panels from which juries are selected fairly represent the demographics of the court's jurisdiction. It can compensate for jury source lists that do not fairly represent the population or for disproportionate response and qualification rates by persons called for jury service. Stratified selection is also known as structured or clustered sampling.

ISSUES

- Are stratified juries constitutional based on contemporary Equal Protection and Due Process jurisprudence?

- Do stratified juries meet the requirements of the federal Jury Selection and Service Act or corresponding state statutes?

PROCEDURES

The court evaluates the response and qualification rates of potential jurors according to a given set of demographic characteristics, such as geographic locality, race, or ethnicity. Using that information, the court calls for jury service a disproportionately higher number of persons from those geographic jurisdictions or racial or ethnic minorities that have comparatively lower response rates. This system is more likely to produce jury panels that reflect the racial and ethnic demographic composition of the court's jurisdiction.

Stratified jury selection may supplement other strategies that have not produced the desired cross-section of the community. Strategies include additional source lists, updated addresses, follow-up procedures for persons who fail to respond to jury summonses, increases in juror compensation and services, and decreased terms of jury service.

Examples of courts that use stratified juries include the United States District Court for the District of Connecticut, which mails additional juror questionnaires to "municipalities . . . whose Hispanic Population is equal to or greater than ten percent of its total population." The United States District Court for the Eastern District of Michigan uses a "post-qualification" system in which the court randomly strikes from the list of qualified jurors the precise number of "white and other" potential jurors needed to obtain a qualification list reflective of population. In Georgia, county jury commissioners adjust the numbers of qualified jurors to correspond to the county's racial and ethnic composition.

ADVANTAGES

1. Stratified selection corrects for underrepresentation in jury pools.

2. Conducting the research necessary to implement stratified selection helps the court identify specific causes of underrepresentation.

3. Stratified selection may protect jury selection systems from legal challenge based on intentional discrimination or Sixth Amendment claims.

DISADVANTAGE

Stratified jury selection may be subject to legal challenge based on the Equal Protection Clause or the Due Process Clause of the U.S. Constitution or the federal Jury Selection and Service Act (and corresponding state statutes).

AUTHORITY

Jury Selection and Service Act, 28 U.S.C. §§ 1861, 1863 (1989 and Supp. 1996).

REFERENCES

Albert W. Alschuler, "Racial Quotas and the Jury," 44 *Duke L. J.* 704 (1995) (comparing a proposal to abolish all-white grand juries in Hennepin County, Minnesota, to other methods of ensuring racially representative juries).

Nancy J. King, "Racial Jurymandering: Cancer or Cure? A Contemporary Review of Affirmative Action in Jury Selection," 68 *N.Y.U. L. Rev.* 707 (1993) (arguing that the practice of stratified jury selection should survive strict scrutiny under the Equal Protection Clause of the U.S. Constitution).

Nancy J. King & G. Thomas Munsterman, "Stratified Juror Selection: Cross-Section by Design," 79 *Judicature* 273 (1996) (describing potential legal challenges to stratified juror selection).

RELATED APPENDIX

Appendix 2: [U.S. Dist. Ct., Dist. of Conn.] Modification to the Second Restated
Plan for Random Selection of Grand and Petite Jurors Pursuant to Jury
Selection and Service Act of 1968 (as Amended)

§ II-6   ADA Compliance

Technique

Title II of the Americans with Disabilities Act prohibits public entities, including state court programs and services, from excluding from participation, denying benefits to, or otherwise discriminating against individuals with disabilities. The act requires state courts to make reasonable modifications in policies, practices, and procedures, ensure effective communication with disabled persons, and make physical facilities accessible to disabled persons.

Issues

- Is the juror source list likely to include persons with disabilities?

- Does state law exempt or excuse individuals from jury service based on disability?

- What "reasonable accommodations" are necessary to permit disabled individuals to serve as jurors (e.g., sign language interpreters, computer-aided transcriptions or assisted-listening devices for persons with visual impairments)?

- What modifications should be made to make the courthouse physically accessible to disabled persons?

Procedures

The court conducts a thorough review of its juror source lists to determine the extent to which persons with disabilities are excluded. In some instances, persons with disabilities may be excluded as a result of state statutes or court rules pertaining to juror qualifications, exemptions, or excuses. Such statutes and court rules are repealed or overruled.

To make courts accessible to persons with disabilities, courts may need to make physical modifications to their facilities. Modifications include securing access to jury rooms by installing ramps or elevators in multilevel facilities, wide-frame doors, handicapped-accessible bathrooms, and large-print signs. Juror orientation and educational materials should be available in a handicapped-accessible form (e.g., plain English, large print, Braille, video captions, and audio tapes).

During trials, assistance services such as sign language interpreters, computer-aided transcriptions, and assisted-listening devices should be provided as needed. Trial judges should instruct lawyers, litigants, and witnesses about accommodations for jurors with disabilities. Jury instructions should be provided verbally and in writing and should include any special instructions concerning deliberations with disabled jurors.

Advantage

Compliance with the ADA expands the pool of potential jurors and increases the overall representativeness of juries.

Disadvantage

Education for court personnel, facility modifications, and assistance services for disabled persons may require additional expenditures of court funds.

Authority

Americans with Disabilities Act, 42 U.S.C. §§ 12131-134 (Supp. 1996).

Galloway v. Superior Court, 816 F. Supp. 12 (D.C. 1993) (enjoining court from categorically excluding blind persons from jury selection).

References

American Bar Association, Commission on Mental and Physical Disability Law and Commission on Legal Problems of the Elderly, *Into the Jury Box: A Disability Accommodation Guide for State Courts* (1994).

American Bar Association, Commission on Mental and Physical Disability Law and Commission on Legal Problems of the Elderly, *Opening the Courthouse Door: An ADA Access Guide for State Courts* (1992).

"Courtroom of the Future," 1 *Ct. Manager* 20 (Summer 1986) (describing a computer-aided transcription system that translates stenographic notes directly into English on a computer screen).

Shirley T. Herald, "Provision of Services to Hearing-Impaired Persons," 3 *Ct. Manager* 6 (Spring 1988) (describing judicial approaches for ensuring court interpreters for hearing-impaired persons).

D. Nolan Kaiser, "Juries, Blindness and the Juror Function," 60 *Chi.-Kent L. Rev.* 191 (1984) (challenging the assertion that eyesight is a critical qualification for jury service).

D. Nolan Kaiser, "Just Justice: A Reply to Mr. McConnell," 60 *Chi.-Kent L. Rev.* 215 (1984) (presenting arguments in favor of permitting blind persons to serve as jurors).

Harold C. Manson, Note, "Jury Selection: The Courts, the Constitution, and the Deaf," 11 *Pac. L. J.* 967 (1980) (arguing that the Sixth Amendment prohibits a blanket exclusion of deaf persons for jury service).

Marshall, *Removing Communication Barriers for Blind or Visually Impaired Participants in the Court & Penal Systems* (American Foundation for the Blind, 1993).

James G. McConnell, "Blind Justice or Just Blindness?" 60 *Chi.-Kent L. Rev.* 209 (1984) (arguing that only litigants have standing to object to the exclusion of a class of persons from jury service).

§ II-7   Limited Releases from Jury Service

Technique

The court adopts standards or rules for excusing individuals from jury service that ensure that such releases will be granted only under very limited circumstances.

Issues

- What policies and procedures should the court adopt to govern the grant or denial of releases from jury service?

- Should particular classes of persons be excused from jury service automatically?

- How will limiting the grounds for being excused from jury service affect the number of persons who fail to report at all?

- If a person defers jury service until a later date, how much time should be permitted to elapse before the court requires a person to fulfill his or her obligation for jury service?

Procedures

Jury service is an important aspect of citizenship, and all appropriate means may be used to ensure that qualified citizens serve. Exemptions and excuses from jury service generally are limited to the following qualifications:

- that persons be 18 years of age or older;

- that persons be citizens of the United States;

- that persons be residents of the jurisdiction in which they have been summoned to serve as jurors;

- that persons be able to understand and communicate effectively in English; and

- that persons convicted of felonies have had their civil rights restored.

Other classes of persons are not automatically released from service, and releases are based on true hardship rather than inconvenience. The court requires persons requesting to be released from jury service to swear by affidavit or otherwise that their excuse is legitimate. A deferral—preferably of short duration—should be the preferred alternative to an outright and permanent release from jury service.

The court designates one or more judges to serve as the jury judge and confers on him or her the authority to grant or deny requests to be released from jury service. Factors the judge may wish to consider in granting a release on hardship grounds include the following:

- the prospective juror would suffer extreme financial hardship;

- the prospective juror has a physical or mental disability or impairment that does not affect the person's competence to act as a juror, but would put him or her at risk of mental or physical harm;

- the prospective juror's services are required immediately for the protection of the public health and safety and other reasonable arrangements cannot be made to relieve that individual of those responsibilities during the period of jury service; or

- the prospective juror has personal obligations to provide for the care of another.

ADVANTAGES

1. Having established criteria for granting releases from jury service reduces the incidence of discriminatory, inconsistent, or arbitrary standards.

2. Limiting releases from jury service broadens the base of prospective jurors.

DISADVANTAGE

The court's failure to release persons from jury service on the grounds of inconvenience may result in some dissatisfaction.

REFERENCE

American Bar Association, Committee on Jury Standards, *Standards Relating to Juror Use and Management* 34-42 (1993) (Standard 4 discusses eligibility for jury service).

§ II-8   JURY ORIENTATION VIA CABLE TELEVISION

TECHNIQUE

The court arranges to broadcast juror orientation via the local public cable television access channel. This form of juror orientation, which supplements in-court orientation, provides information about reporting procedures (such as call-in systems), jury schedules, parking and eating facilities, juror pay, and security concerns.

ISSUES

- How does the court provide juror orientation for persons who do not own televisions, do not have cable access, or whose work schedules prevent viewing during broadcast days and times?

- What should the court do in jurisdictions that are served by multiple cable carriers?

- Does juror orientation via cable television substitute for in-court orientation?

PROCEDURES

The court arranges with the local cable television access channel to broadcast juror orientation. In more populated, urban areas, the court may have to coordinate with multiple cable carriers. The juror summons then lists the orientation viewing times, broadcast channel(s), and requests prospective jurors to watch the cable orientation before reporting for jury duty. Cable television orientation can be broadcast at several different times and days of the week to accommodate prospective jurors' schedules.

The Circuit Court for Fairfax County (Virginia) originated this technique. Many jurisdictions now use it.

ADVANTAGES

1. Televised juror orientation provides information about reporting procedures including court location, parking, and other matters to prospective jurors in the comfort of their own homes before reporting for jury service.

2. Televised juror orientation provides public education about jury service for interested viewers.

DISADVANTAGES

1. Televised juror orientation requires coordination with cable television personnel.

2. The court must provide alternative methods of presenting juror orientation for individuals who do not own televisions or lack access to cable television systems.

REFERENCES

American Bar Association, Committee on Jury Standards, *Standards Relating to Juror Use and Management* 140-147 (1993) (Standards 16(a) and (b) discuss information to be included in juror orientation).

G. Thomas Munsterman, "Jury News," 9 *Ct. Manager* 6, 20 (Fall 1994) (describing cable television juror orientation program established in Fairfax, Virginia).

APPENDIX

Copies of video orientations for jurors can be borrowed from the NCSC library. For information, contact:

Peggy Rogers
Librarian
National Center for State Courts
300 Newport Avenue
Williamsburg, VA 23185
(757) 253-2000

§ II-9   How to Relieve Juror Boredom

Technique

To minimize the boredom associated with juror "downtime" during pretrial and trial proceedings, the court equips the jury waiting area with an environment conducive to private work and supplies appropriate entertainment or diversion. This technique may supplement other strategies, such as call-in systems, designed to use jurors' time effectively and efficiently. During lengthy breaks during court proceedings, the court also may permit jurors to leave the courthouse with instructions to return at a certain time. This technique may also be helpful during especially lengthy or sequestered trials or deliberations.

Issues

- What types of entertainment or diversions are appropriate for the jury room (e.g., videotapes, newspaper clippings, group outings)?

- Who is responsible for organizing activities and preparing materials?

Procedures

The court equips jury facilities with quiet work areas and telephones and computer modem access to permit jurors to conduct personal business during court recesses and proceedings that do not require their attendance. These facilities can reduce any hardship imposed on jurors who are absent from work. Other helpful facilities include a snackbar, a newsstand, and isolated areas in which jurors can watch television or videos.

The juror summons or juror information handbook should instruct jurors to bring materials with them to keep them occupied during court recesses. Some courts have made arrangements to provide appropriate diversions for jurors. Examples include:

- establishing a lending branch of the local public library;

- obtaining undeliverable magazines and newspapers from the U.S. Postal Service for juror use;

- encouraging jurors to donate books for a juror library; and

- scheduling speakers on local public activities and functions.

At all times, the court should keep jurors informed of the progress in the disposition of the docket or calendar. During lengthy breaks from court proceedings, the court may permit jurors to leave the courthouse with instructions to return at a certain time or provide them with beepers to call them back as needed. Jurors may take the time to visit area shops or enjoy walking tours near the courthouse. If the courthouse is located near local museums or area attractions, the court may provide jurors with free or discounted passes for these activities.

ADVANTAGES

1. Providing appropriate diversions and accommodations reduces juror stress and aggravation, which tends to increase juror attention during court proceedings and deliberations.

2. Decreased juror boredom increases satisfaction with jury service.

DISADVANTAGE

The court incurs the incidental costs of providing diversions and accommodations, such as the costs of the activities themselves and the administration and monitoring of juror activities.

REFERENCE

Shari S. Diamond, "What Jurors Think: Expectations and Reactions of Citizens Who Serve as Jurors," in Robert E. Litan ed., *Verdict: Assessing the Civil Jury System* 282, 286-87 (1993).

Chapter III

Voir Dire
(Or, In Plain English, Jury Selection)

CONTRIBUTORS AND REVIEWERS

Hon. Marvin Aspin
U.S. District Court, N.D., Illinois
Chicago, Illinois

Julie Campanini
FTI Corporation
Chicago, Illinois

David Graeven
Trial Behavior Consulting, Inc.
San Francisco, California

Paula L. Hannaford, J.D., M.P.P.
National Center for State Courts
Williamsburg, Virginia

Prof. Nancy King
Vanderbilt University School of Law
Nashville, Tennessee

Prof. Stephen Landsman
DePaul University College of Law
Chicago, Illinois

Prof. Nancy S. Marder
University of Southern California
Law School
Los Angeles, California

Cathy Miller
Trial Behavior Consulting, Inc.
San Francisco, California

Peter Pappas, Esq.
Adams, Kleemeir, Hagan, Hannah
& Fouts, L.L.P.
Greensboro, North Carolina

Philip Pfaffly, Esq.
Robins, Kaplan, Miller & Ciresi
Minneapolis, Minnesota

Hon. Lawrence Waddington (ret.)
Los Angeles County Superior Court
Santa Monica, California

Daniel Wolfe, J.D., Ph.D.
FTI Corporation
Chicago, Illinois

§ III-1   Lawyer-Conducted Voir Dire

Technique

The court permits the trial attorneys to question the jury panel directly, rather than submitting all voir dire questions through the judge. See also § III-2, "Opening Statements to the Entire Jury Panel," and § III-3, "Questionnaires to Assist Jury Selection."

Issues

- Are voir dire questions posed by lawyers more likely to reveal juror bias than questions posed by the judge?

- Does the difference in status between the judge and the members of the jury panel intimidate potential jurors, preventing them from answering voir dire questions candidly or completely?

- What effect does permitting lawyers to conduct voir dire have on the length of those proceedings?

- What restrictions should the judge place on lawyers conducting voir dire?

Procedures

Voir dire is a formal process of inquiry conducted to ensure that individuals selected as jurors will consider the evidence fairly and impartially. As a practical matter, however, voir dire also offers the trial attorneys their first opportunity to give the jury a favorable impression about their respective clients. Because of the inherent tension between these two objectives—uncovering juror bias and engaging in advocacy—the majority of federal judges and a substantial portion of state judges have, over time, assumed a dominant role in examining potential jurors in voir dire. The judicial role during voir dire ranges across a continuum from judges who deny lawyers an active role in the examination of potential jurors to those who are not even present during voir dire, leaving the lawyers to select a mutually acceptable jury among themselves.

Proponents of lawyer-conducted voir dire offer several arguments to support their position. Relying on several empirical studies, they claim that lawyers tend to uncover juror bias more effectively than judges. Specifically, lawyers are more familiar with the facts of the case and consequently are more attuned to the nuances in juror values or beliefs that are likely to influence juror decision making. Jurors also tend to be less intimidated by lawyers than by judges and thus more likely to respond candidly and completely to questions posed during voir dire. Recognizing these considerations, more judges are permitting the trial lawyers to conduct all or part of voir dire.

Opponents of lawyer-conducted voir dire stress that this practice permits lawyers to abuse the voir dire process, converting it into an opportunity to establish a rapport, to elicit promises from jurors, to engage in indoctrination of the jury, and to intimidate or embarrass jurors. Moreover, permitting lawyers to question potential jurors directly converts jury selection into a part of the adversary process, rather than a routine function of court management and administration. They argue that lawyers have other methods available for eliciting information about jurors (e.g., juror questionnaires) that do not pose as great a risk for abuse.

Judges who regularly grant lawyers a substantial role in voir dire examinations report that setting clear guidelines about appropriate voir dire examination during the pretrial conference helps curb excessive or inappropriate advocacy by the lawyers. For example, firm time restrictions on voir dire examination, required pretrial disclosure of the lawyers' expected lines of inquiry, and judicial review of juror questionnaires provide the judge with effective tools for exercising appropriate control over the voir dire process. See also § IV-1, "Pretrial Limits on Each Party's Time at Trial," § III-3, "Questionnaires to Assist Jury Selection," and § III-4, "Privacy Considerations in Voir Dire."

Statistics indicate that about 30 percent of federal courts and a large percentage of state courts allow or require attorney participation in voir dire.

ADVANTAGES

1. Lawyers have intimate knowledge of the facts and issues of the case. As a result, they are likely to recognize problems of juror bias that often are not immediately apparent to the judge.

2. As advocates in an adversarial proceeding, trial lawyers tend to be highly motivated to search out bias in potential jurors, enabling them to make intelligent challenges, both for cause and peremptories.

3. Some studies suggest that jurors are less intimidated, and thus respond to voir dire questions more candidly, when lawyers conduct voir dire than when judges conduct voir dire.

4. Permitting lawyers to conduct voir dire impresses on the jury panel the importance of the participation of all parties from the very start of the trial proceedings.

5. Direct participation of counsel in voir dire heightens litigants' perceptions that the trial proceedings are fair and enhances their confidence in the justice system.

DISADVANTAGES

1. Direct participation of counsel in voir dire tends to lengthen the trial proceedings.

2. Without adequate supervision by the trial judge, counsel may use voir dire inappropriately to engage in pretrial argument.

3. Without adequate supervision by the trial judge, lawyers may pose voir dire questions that inappropriately infringe on juror privacy.

AUTHORITY

Fed. R. Civ. Proc. Rule 47(a) (1996) (authorizing the court to permit the trial attorneys to question prospective jurors directly).

REFERENCES

John Guinther, *The Jury in America* 49-58 (1988) (summarizing the policy, history, and empirical literature about lawyer- and judge-conducted voir dire).

Valerie Hans & Neil Vidmar, *Judging the Jury* 71-72 (1986) (discussing the arguments and evidence favoring and opposing lawyer-conducted voir dire).

David Suggs & Bruce D. Sales, "Juror Self-Disclosure in the Voir Dire: A Social Science Analysis," 56 *Ind. L. J.* 245, 250-58 (1981) (examining the social science literature relevant to attorney- versus judge-conducted voir dire).

STUDIES

Gordon Bermant & John Shapard, "The Voir Dire Examination, Juror Challenges, and Adversarial Advocacy," in Bruce D. Sales ed., *The Trial Pro-*

cess 69, 75-92 (1981) (discussing the conflicting interests of the bench and bar in conducting voir dire and describing differences in practice according to regional and jurisdictional characteristics).

Susan E. Jones, "Judge- Versus Attorney-Conducted Voir Dire," 11 *Law & Hum. Behav.* 131 (1987) (study findings support the hypothesis that attorneys are more effective than judges in eliciting candid self-disclosure from potential jurors).

§ III-2   OPENING STATEMENTS TO THE ENTIRE JURY PANEL

TECHNIQUE

The trial attorneys make brief, nonargumentative statements to the entire jury panel before examination of the prospective jurors by the judge or counsel. By setting the stage for the voir dire questions that follow, these statements provide the jury panel with some indication of the relevance of particular questions and the need for candid responses by the panel members.

ISSUES

- Do mini-openings by counsel impart more case-related information than the traditional brief synopsis usually read to the jury panel by the judge?

- Does this technique provide a better frame of reference about the case and the questioning process, enabling panel members to respond more appropriately?

- Do opening statements to the entire panel unduly protract the jury selection process?

- What time limitations, if any, should the judge set for opening statements to the panel?

- Will counsel be able and willing to resist the temptation to become argumentative and long-winded, requiring the judge to intervene?

- In what types of cases or litigation issues are opening statements to the panel appropriate?

- What other techniques, if any, should the trial judge employ in conjunction with opening statements to the jury panel?

PROCEDURES

Prior to trial (e.g., at the pretrial conference), the judge and attorneys discuss and decide whether opening statements to the entire jury panel will facilitate jury selection. This technique may be more helpful for cases involving complex or particularly difficult factual issues than for shorter, more routine cases. The trial judge instructs the attorneys that the statements are not an opportunity to engage in pretrial argument. Rather, the statements should inform prospective jurors about the case, especially the issues that are likely to arise in voir dire. Time limits on the length of opening statements prevent these statements from prolonging jury selection excessively.

The trial judge may also require that counsel prepare preliminary jury instructions for distribution to the jury panel in conjunction with the opening statements. See § V-9, "Preinstructing the Jury." Using the combination of written preliminary instructions and verbal opening statements to highlight important trial issues serves a dual purpose. First, the jury panel is more likely to understand the basis for, and respond candidly to, voir dire questions. Second, the jurors who are ultimately selected will be more attentive to trial testimony and evidence pertaining to those issues.

Before permitting counsel to begin, the judge informs the panel of the statements to be made by counsel, their purpose, and their anticipated length. Counsel then present short, informative statements that are designed to help the panel members understand the relevancy of the voir dire questions that follow and the need for candid responses to these questions. The judge may supplement the statements of the attorneys with any additional information about the jury selection process before beginning examination of the jury panel.

Little information is available regarding the history and frequency of use of opening statements to the entire jury panel. Arizona is the only state known to have institutionalized the practice by court rule; however, judges in a number of jurisdictions have experimented with them or use them on a regular basis. Generally, they report that the disadvantages commonly attributed to this technique are not borne out in practice. Some judges note, however, that some attorneys have difficulty, at least initially, fashioning and delivering a brief, nonargumentative, and properly informative statement intended solely to set the stage for jury selection.

ADVANTAGES

1. By providing the jury panel with information about the case, opening statements help prospective jurors understand why particular questions are being asked and why candid responses will help the judge and attorneys identify jurors likely to be impartial.

2. Opening statements to the jury panel may reduce, and possibly eliminate, the need to preface jury selection questions with a description or reference to anticipated evidence—a technique that often provokes an objection and intervention by the judge.

3. The procedure affords the attorneys an early opportunity to introduce themselves, their clients, and their cases. As a result, the transition from

judge-conducted voir dire to attorney-conducted voir dire, if the latter is allowed, tends to be smoother and shorter.

DISADVANTAGES

1. If time limits for opening statements are not imposed and enforced, the jury selection process may take appreciably longer than it otherwise would.

2. Lawyers often are tempted to give their complete opening arguments rather than brief, nonargumentative statements designed to alert the panel members to issues likely to arise during voir dire.

3. Judges often have their hands full keeping voir dire within appropriate bounds without adding opportunities for counsel to engage one another in pretrial confrontations.

4. Little or no social science research has been conducted to demonstrate that opening statements significantly improve the voir dire process either for the judges or attorneys conducting voir dire or for the prospective jurors.

5. The jurors who are ultimately selected will hear some of the same information twice, once during opening statements to the jury panel and again during opening arguments by counsel.

AUTHORITY

Arizona Rules of Civil Procedure, Rule 47(b)(2) (authorizing the parties to present brief opening statements to the entire jury panel prior to voir dire).

REFERENCE

Arizona Supreme Court Committee on More Effective Use of Juries, *Jurors: The Power of 12: Report of the Arizona Supreme Court Committee on More Effective Use of Juries* 59-61 (1994).

§ III-3   QUESTIONNAIRES TO ASSIST JURY SELECTION

TECHNIQUE

The attorneys prepare juror questionnaires to be distributed to and completed by the jury panel prior to the commencement of the oral jury selection process. The attorneys review the questionnaire responses to focus their questioning during jury selection and better identify potential juror bias. Courts may also use juror questionnaires to prescreen the jury panel for qualification criteria (e.g., citizenship, residency).

ISSUES

- Who is responsible for preparing, copying, distributing, and compiling the responses of the juror questionnaires?

- How long or comprehensive should the questionnaire be?

- What level of oversight should the trial judge exercise over the preparation and administration of juror questionnaires?

- What consequences do jurors face for failure to answer the questionnaire completely?

- How should the attorneys use juror questionnaire responses in the oral jury selection process?

- How much time should the court grant the trial attorneys to review and analyze the questionnaire responses?

PROCEDURES

Pretrial or supplemental juror questionnaires are tools available to the trial attorneys to identify potential juror bias prior to commencing the traditional voir dire process. This technique permits the trial attorneys to make the most efficient use of the voir dire process to select a fair and impartial jury.

In most jurisdictions, the attorneys for either party can move the court to permit juror questionnaires. The motion should include a copy of the proposed questionnaire. If the motion is granted, the court's order should note any modifications to the questionnaire and should include any procedural or administrative requirements for the questionnaires, such as the amount of time counsel will have to compile and analyze the responses. The moving party typically prepares the questionnaires and coordinates their administration. After the jury panel completes the questionnaires, the moving party also provides copies of the responses to the court and opposing counsel.

Distribution and administration of the juror questionnaires can be handled in a number of ways. To accommodate the amount of time required to compile and analyze longer, more comprehensive questionnaires, the court can mail the questionnaire to the jury panel with a stamped, self-addressed return envelop. Mailed questionnaires should include instructions about how to complete the questionnaire and the deadline for returning it. Mailed questionnaires also should include a written oath to be signed by the prospective juror that he or she has personally completed the questionnaire and that the questionnaire responses are true and accurate to the best of his or her knowledge.

For questionnaires that do not require as much time for analysis, the jury panel may be instructed to bring the completed questionnaire with them when they report for jury service. Alternatively, the court clerk or jury manager can distribute the questionnaires at the time the jury panel reports for service. In the latter case, the written oath may be included in the questionnaire or the court clerk can administer the oath verbally.

The questionnaire should include an introduction that informs the jury panel about the purpose of the questionnaire. The introduction should not make false assurances about the confidentiality of jury panel responses. See § III-4, "Privacy Considerations in Voir Dire." The introduction often provides a brief explanation of the case. Questions included in the questionnaires should be clear, concise, stated in plain English, and easily understood by the jury panel. See also § V-11, "Plain English at Trial," and § VI-2, "Plain English Jury Instructions." Juror questionnaires typically ask jury panel members to answer questions about five basic areas of inquiry:

- biographical and demographic information;

- knowledge of the parties in the case, including the attorneys representing the parties and witnesses testifying for the parties;

- awareness of the case, including first-hand knowledge or knowledge gained from pretrial publicity;

- opinions about the case, including preexisting attitudes and beliefs about relevant case information; and

- preexisting attitudes, beliefs, values, and experiences, including prior jury service or prior experience with the justice system as a victim, party, or witness.

The attorneys for the parties should develop an effective system for quickly identifying and evaluating questionnaire responses. Overly broad or open-ended questions tend to yield extraneous and often irrelevant information that is difficult and time-consuming to compile and analyze. Using supplemental data sheets to condense important information to one page for quick reference and constructing an electronic database to sort through large quantities of data are two common evaluation methods.

ADVANTAGES

1. Juror questionnaires can prevent contamination of the jury panel by hostile jurors. Members of the jury panel who have specific information or strong opinions about the case reveal this information in their responses to the questionnaire rather than through verbal statements before the entire jury panel.

2. Juror questionnaires maximize the efficient use of time allotted for voir dire by providing the judge and attorneys with routine biographical information and by identifying panel members with prior knowledge or strong preexisting opinions about the parties or the case. Based on this information, some members of the jury panel may be excused altogether while the trial judge and attorneys begin voir dire with case-relevant and follow-up questions to the remaining panel members.

3. Jury panel responses to questionnaires may be more expansive and more candid than responses to verbal voir dire questions. Sensitive or personal information concerning prospective jurors can be revealed in their written responses, relieving jury panel members of concerns about disclosing sensitive or embarrassing information publicly. Additionally, the use of pretrial questionnaires prevents jury panel members from conforming their responses to the perceived "correct" or majority response of the panel. See also § III-5, "Individualized Voir Dire."

4. Questionnaires can be combined with the summons for jury service, providing a vehicle for jury panel members to inform the court of severe hardships or other reasons for disqualification from jury service. But see § II-7, "Limited Releases from Jury Service."

DISADVANTAGES

1. Constructing and designing juror questionnaires can be difficult and cumbersome, particularly when the specific details of the case require inquiry into a broad range of juror characteristics.

2. Answering juror questionnaires may be difficult or impossible for jury panel members who have poor written communication skills because of disability, lack of education, or limited familiarity with written English. See also § II-4, "Additional Source Lists," and § II-6, "ADA Compliance."

3. The administrative costs associated with distributing questionnaires to the jury panel and copying the responses for the court and opposing counsel can outweigh the benefits of this technique, especially with large jury panels.

4. Written responses to questionnaires deprive the trial judge and attorneys of the ability to observe prospective jurors' nonverbal communication during voir dire—an element of questioning on which many judges and attorneys claim to rely to determine the honesty and reliability of the individual's response.

5. A requirement that jury panel members sign a written oath that they have personally answered the questionnaire does not guarantee that the panel member has, in fact, done so. Sometimes a spouse or significant other will complete the questionnaire and fail to reveal important information, especially about juror attitudes and beliefs.

6. The use of pretrial juror questionnaires shifts control of the voir dire process from the trial judge to the attorneys—a result that some trial judges find objectionable, particularly if the technique appears to benefit one party to the detriment of the other or otherwise jeopardizes the appearance of a fair trial.

REFERENCES

American Bar Association, Committee on Jury Standards, *Standards Relating to Juror Use and Management* 101, 106 (1993) (Standard 11(c) and commentary describe the use of juror questionnaires to determine qualification for jury service).

Lisa Blue, Ted A. Donner & Jane N. Saginaw, *Jury Selection: Strategies and Science* § 8:11-12 (1986) (provides sample jury questionnaires).

Floyd J. Fowler, *Survey Research Methods* (rev. ed. 1988) (a technical manual for questionnaire design and administration).

Jeffrey T. Frederick, *Mastering Voir Dire and Jury Selection* 122-48 (1995) (practitioner's manual for preparing juror questionnaires).

Richard B. Klein, "Low-Tech Automated Jury Instructions," 35 *Judges' J.* 36 (Summer 1996) (describing videotaped instructions for the completion of general civil and criminal voir dire questionnaires).

Elissa Krauss & Beth Bonora, eds., *Jurywork: Systematic Techniques* § 2.10[1][c][iii] (vol. 1, 2d ed. 1995) (describing preparation procedures for voir dire questionnaires).

Timothy R. Murphy, Genevra Kay Loveland & G. Thomas Munsterman, *A Manual for Managing Notorious Cases* 171-87 (National Center for State Courts, 1992) (Appendix 8 describes the use of juror questionnaires in *United States v. Marion S. Barry, Jr.*).

V. Hales Starr & Mark McCormick, *Jury Selection: An Attorney's Guide to Jury Law and Methods* 46-47, 132-33 (2d ed. 1993).

STUDY

Dennis Bilecki, "Efficient Method of Jury Selection for Lengthy Trials," 73 *Judicature* 43 (June-July 1989) (study of the effect of pre-voir dire questionnaires on the costs associated with jury selection in complex trials).

§ III-4   PRIVACY CONSIDERATIONS IN VOIR DIRE

TECHNIQUE

Voir dire often solicits very personal or potentially embarrassing or harmful information about prospective jurors. To protect juror privacy, the court offers jury panel members the option of responding to voir dire questions *in camera*. The offer for *in camera* voir dire also is extended to the panel prior to completing case-specific qualification questionnaires that solicit personal, embarrassing, or harmful information. The use of this technique must be consistent with the requirements of *Press Enterprises v. Superior Court (I)*, 104 S. Ct. 819 (1984).

ISSUES

- Does *in camera* voir dire place unwarranted restrictions on public or media access to judicial proceedings?

- How should the court inform the jury panel of the availability of *in camera* voir dire?

- How should the court determine whether information solicited during voir dire is sufficiently sensitive to warrant *in camera* proceedings?

- Following the disclosure of a juror's private information during *in camera* voir dire, what criteria should the court consider in determining whether there exists a compelling justification for withholding or redacting the information from the record?

PROCEDURES

In camera voir dire is conducted on the record with counsel for both parties present. This technique relieves the jury panel member from revealing personal information in open court and in the presence of the entire panel and other individuals, such as court staff or spectators, who may be present in the courtroom.

In camera voir dire is subject to the legal standards set forth in *Press Enterprises v. Superior Court*, 104 S. Ct. 819 (1984). Prior to conducting closed proceedings, the court must explore alternatives to closed proceedings (such as securing the juror's consent to in-court disclosure) and determine whether the juror has a compelling privacy interest that outweighs the presumption favoring public access to judicial proceedings. Compelling privacy interests of jurors include protection from physical harm or the threat of physical harm.

The judge has several alternative methods of protecting juror privacy if he or she finds that a juror has a significant privacy interest. The court may excuse the juror from jury service. He or she may conduct voir dire *in camera*, but release all or part of the transcript, depending on the nature of the information deemed to be private. For example, the full transcript may be released; the name of the juror may be withheld, with the remainder of the transcript released; or selected parts of the record may be sealed to protect the juror's privacy.

ADVANTAGES

1. *In camera* voir dire protects jurors from the embarrassment or harm that might result from revealing private information in open court.

2. *In camera* voir dire increases jurors' willingness to respond candidly to voir dire questions, thus enhancing the likelihood of selecting an impartial jury.

DISADVANTAGES

1. *In camera* voir dire infringes on public and media access to judicial proceedings under the First Amendment.

2. *In camera* voir dire may not result in more honest responses to voir dire questions, insofar that the juror understands that all or part of the *in camera* transcript will be released following the closed proceeding.

AUTHORITY

Press Enterprises v. Superior Court, 104 S. Ct. 819 (1984) (holding that, absent a compelling justification, the First Amendment guarantees of open criminal proceedings apply to voir dire proceedings).

Pantos v. City and County of San Francisco, 198 Cal. Rptr. 489 (1984) (holding that the master list of qualified jurors, including subsidiary summons lists, are public records subject to public inspection).

Copley Press, Inc. v. San Diego County Superior Court, 278 Cal. Rptr. 443 (1991) (requiring courts to inform venire members that responses to voir dire questionnaires are public records and cannot be held confidential).

People v. Simms, 29 Cal. Rptr. 2d 436 (2d Dist. 1994) (holding that a criminal defendant does not require prior court authorization to obtain the name, address, and telephone number of a juror).

REFERENCES

American Bar Association, Committee on Jury Standards, *Standards Relating to Juror Use and Management* 58, 66 (recommending that voir dire practices protect juror privacy and do not exceed the purpose of the voir dire process).

Jennifer S. Buckley, Note, *"Press Enterprise Co. v. Superior Court:* A Juror's Right to Privacy," 1985 *Det. C. L. Rev.* 449 (1985) (describing the difficulty courts face in protecting juror privacy following the court's decision in *Press Enterprise*).

Susan L. Greenberg, Note, "Spotlight on the Jury: Trial Publicity and Juror Privacy," 6 *Comm./Ent. L. J.* 369 (1984) (proposing that courts institute policies to secure a juror's consent to be identified before the media may release that information to the public).

Timothy R. Murphy, Genevra K. Loveland & G. Thomas Munsterman, *A Manual for Managing Notorious Cases* 97-120 (National Center for State Courts, 1992) (Appendix 1 is a primer on media access rights to judicial proceedings including voir dire).

Nancy A. Novak, Note, "Jury on Trial: Juror's Constitutional Right to Privacy Falls Under Scrutiny of the Courts," 3 *San Diego Just. J.* 215 (1995) (examining whether jurors have a constitutional right to privacy).

§ III-5   Individualized Voir Dire

Technique

Members of the jury panel are sequestered from one another and questioned individually by the judge and/or attorneys. Sequestering the panel members during voir dire encourages greater self-disclosure and enhances the likelihood of revealing juror bias without the potential risk of "tainting" the jury panel with the panel member's responses (e.g., concerning the panel member's knowledge of the case through pretrial publicity). Individualized voir dire also protects juror privacy. See also § III-4, "Privacy Considerations in Voir Dire." This technique is especially helpful in high-profile trials.

Issues

- Under what circumstances is individualized voir dire appropriate?

- What is the effect of individualized voir dire on the length of the trial procedures?

Procedures

Voir dire typically takes place in a group setting in which the panel members respond to questions posed by the trial judge or attorneys in the presence of other panel members. Studies about group conformity have demonstrated that to avoid calling attention to themselves, panel members subjected to collective questioning do not willingly volunteer information about themselves or reveal opinions that deviate from those of the other panel members. Sequestered and individualized voir dire prevents panel members from looking to one another for the "correct answers," thus encouraging more truthful self-disclosure by panel members.

Collective questioning during voir dire is an appropriate technique for posing preliminary questions to the jury panel (e.g., "Does any member of this jury panel know the parties or their attorneys?" "Does any member of this jury panel have personal knowledge of the case?"). Follow-up questions that inquire of the opinions of the panel members concerning issues relevant to the case are posed to panel members individually and out of the presence of one another. Conducting individualized voir dire in a setting less formal than the courtroom (e.g., the jury room or the chambers of the trial judge) also enhances the panel members' willingness to disclose personal information. See

§ III-4, "Privacy Considerations in Voir Dire." The use of supplemental juror questionnaires also can facilitate this process by permitting individualized panel responses that are shielded from other panel members. See § III-3 "Questionnaires to Assist Jury Selection." A modified version of this method is to pose follow-up voir dire questions to smaller groups of panel members who responded in a similar manner to preliminary questions.

ADVANTAGES

1. Individualized voir dire typically takes place in a less formal setting and requires a less formal conversational tone by the judge and attorneys. The relative lack of formality tends to place panel members more at ease, encouraging them to respond to questions more candidly than they might otherwise respond.

2. Individualized voir dire takes place out of the presence of other panel members, relieving panel members' discomfort about revealing personal information in front of each other. This technique also prevents individuals from overhearing the responses of other panel members and conforming their answers to those perceived to be "correct" or held by the majority of the panel.

DISADVANTAGE

Individualized voir dire can substantially lengthen voir dire, particularly when alternative techniques, such as supplemental juror questionnaires, can accomplish the same objectives with less effort.

REFERENCES

American Bar Association, Project on Standards for Criminal Justice, *Standards Relating to Fair Trial and Free Press* 130-36 (1983) (Standard 3.4(a) recommends individualized voir dire for cases involving a high risk that members of the jury panel may have been exposed to prejudicial pretrial media reports).

Elissa Krauss & Beth Bonora, eds., *Jurywork: Systematic Techniques* § 2.10[1][c][i] (vol. 1, 2d ed. 1995) (describing the technique).

David Suggs & Bruce D. Sales, "Juror Self-Disclosure in the Voir Dire: A Social Science Analysis," 56 *Ind. L. J.* 245, 258-61 (1981) (examining the social science literature relevant to group conformity and its significance during voir dire).

STUDY

Michael T. Nietzel & Ronald C. Dillehay, "The Effects of Variation in Voir Dire Procedures in Capital Murder Trials," 6 *Law & Hum. Behav.* 1 (1982) (study results showed that bias in potential jurors is best revealed when members of the jury panel are sequestered and examined individually).

RELATED APPENDIX

Appendix 3: *United States v. Soghanalian*, 777 F. Supp. 17 (1991) (Defendants' Motion Requesting Permission to Question Jurors Individually and Out of the Presence and Hearing of Other Jurors)

§ III-6   *Batson* Enforcement

Technique

In accordance with the three-step inquiry outlined in *Batson v. Kentucky*, the judge gives the opponent of a peremptory strike an opportunity to establish a prima facie case that the peremptory is being exercised in a discriminatory fashion based on race or gender. If the attorney challenging the peremptory meets this burden, the judge permits the proponent of the peremptory to offer a nondiscriminatory justification for the strike. The judge then determines whether the justification offered is nondiscriminatory or pretextual. In making this determination, the judge may require that the attorney offering the justification fully explain his or her reasons for exercising the peremptory. This inquiry takes place on the record, but out of the presence of the jury. When ruling on the peremptory challenge, the judge clearly states the reasons supporting his or her finding that the peremptory is either neutral or pretextual.

Issues

- How closely should the judge inquire into "implausible or fantastic" or "silly or superstitious" justifications that are offered to show that the peremptory is made in a nondiscriminatory fashion?

- Have lawyers moved from offering race- and gender-based reasons for peremptory strikes to reasons that sound facially neutral but, in fact, mask underlying discrimination based on race or gender?

- What should judges do about peremptory strikes exercised on the basis of discrimination toward other groups, such as those based on religion, age, or sexual orientation, that are not currently recognized as a protected class under *Batson* jurisprudence?

- Insofar that judges will differ in determining whether a justification offered to support a peremptory strike is neutral or pretextual, can judges avoid inconsistency or the appearance of capriciousness in applying *Batson*?

- If, after applying the *Batson* test, the trial judge overrules a peremptory challenge, should he or she replace the struck juror with a prospective juror of the same race or gender of the previously struck juror?

Procedures

Batson v. Kentucky established a three-step inquiry for evaluating whether a peremptory strike is racially discriminatory and thus impermissible under the Equal Protection Clause of the Fourteenth Amendment. First, the party objecting to the peremptory is required to establish a prima facie case of purposeful discrimination. The burden then shifts to the proponent of the peremptory to offer a nondiscriminatory reason for exercising the peremptory. The judge must then determine whether the reason so offered is nondiscriminatory or pretextual. Legal scholars and commentators disagree about the ultimate impact that the U.S. Supreme Court's recent decision in *Purkett v. Elem* will have as a deterrent against racially discriminatory use of peremptories, but generally agree that the decision vests substantial discretion in the trial judge to determine the credibility of proffered justifications for peremptory strikes.

To apply *Batson,* the judge provides an opportunity to the proponent of the peremptory to offer a race- or gender-neutral justification before ruling on the peremptory challenge. Some judges require the attorneys to submit peremptory challenges in writing to proponents of the peremptory before presenting them to the judge. Other judges inquire whether there are any objections to peremptory strikes, or pause to allow objections, prior to reading the names of stricken jurors. Any objections and discussion concerning the objections should be made on the record and outside the presence of the jurors.

The judge may inquire further into the justification offered by the proponent of the peremptory to determine whether the justification is pretextual. At each step of the *Batson* inquiry, the judge should state the facts on which he or she relied in making his or her findings (e.g., that the attorney challenging the peremptory strike has established a prima facie case of purposeful discrimination, that the proponent of the peremptory has offered a race- or gender-neutral, or a pretextual, justification for exercising the peremptory).

Advantages

1.   Ensuring that all discussion concerning peremptory challenges, including the factual basis for the judge's ruling, takes place on the record permits appellate courts to review the decision without having to second-guess the actions of the trial judge.

2.   Further inquiry by the judge into the justifications offered by the proponent of peremptory strikes discourages the practice of obscuring discriminatory peremptory strikes with facially neutral justifications, thus enhancing the representativeness of the jury.

3. Ensuring that jury selection is untainted by discrimination enhances
    the perception of the parties and the public that the court is a fair tribu-
    nal.

DISADVANTAGES

1. Conducting each step of the *Batson* inquiry into the basis for exercising
    peremptory strikes may delay the voir dire proceedings.

2. Insofar that a peremptory strike is one that requires no explanation,
    inquiring into the basis for a peremptory strike is an inherent contradic-
    tion. It also intrudes on the judgment of the proponent of the peremp-
    tory and compromises the role of the judge as a neutral arbiter.

3. By requiring a nondiscriminatory justification for exercising peremp-
    tory strikes, the trial judge potentially forces the trial attorney to dis-
    close his or her trial strategy or other information protected by work
    product privilege.

AUTHORITY

Batson v. Kentucky, 476 U.S. 79 (1986) (prohibiting the state from using its
    peremptory strikes in a criminal jury trial to purposely exclude potential
    jurors on grounds of race).

Powers v. Ohio, 499 U.S. 400 (1991) (holding that purposeful racial discrimi-
    nation in the exercise of peremptory strike violates equal protection re-
    gardless of whether the defendant is of the same race as the stricken ju-
    rors).

Edmonson v. Leesville Concrete Co., 500 U.S. 614 (1991) (extending *Batson* to
    civil trials).

Georgia v. McCollum, 112 S. Ct. 2348 (1992) (extending the *Batson* prohibition
    of the state's exercise of peremptory strikes for a racially discriminatory
    purpose to the defendant's exercise of peremptory strikes).

United States v. Pichay, 986 F.2d 1259, 1260 (9th Cir. 1993) (*per curiam*) ("Nei-
    ther the Supreme Court nor any circuit has held that the Equal Protection
    Clause prohibits the government from striking venire persons on account
    of youth").

State v. Davis, 504 N.W.2d 767, 768 (Minn. 1993) (allowing peremptory challenges on the basis of religion and holding that Batson does not extend to such strikes), *cert. denied*, 114 S. Ct. 2120 (1994).

Casarez v. State, No. 1114-93, 1994 WL 695868, at *22 (Tex. Crim. App. Dec. 14, 1994) (holding that peremptory strikes may not be exercised on the basis of religion).

J.E.B. v. Alabama ex rel. T.B., 114 S. Ct. 1419 (1994) (extending *Batson* to prohibit exercise of peremptory strikes for a discriminatory purpose based on gender).

Purkett v. Elem, 115 S. Ct. 1969 (1995) (*per curiam*) (explaining that the burden of persuasion regarding racial motivation rests within, and never shifts from, the opponent of the strike).

Woodson v. Porter Brown Limestone Co., No. 01S01-9411-CV-00149 (Tenn. S. Ct. Feb. 14, 1996); 64 USLW 2569 (Mar. 19, 1996) (describing *Batson* procedures).

Minetos v. City University of New York, 925 F. Supp. 177 (1996) (barring the use of peremptory challenges on the grounds that they are used in an inherently discriminatory fashion and thus violate equal protection).

REFERENCES

Albert W. Alschuler, "The Supreme Court and the Jury: Voir Dire, Peremptory Challenges, and the Review of Jury Verdicts," 56 *U. Chi. L. Rev.* 153, 163-211 (1989) (examines *Batson* and concludes that the Equal Protection Clause and peremptory challenges are incompatible).

Jeffrey S. Brand, "The Supreme Court, Equal Protection and Jury Selection: Denying That Race Still Matters," 1994 *Wis. L. Rev.* 514 (demonstrating that the procedures instituted in *Batson* have failed to reveal racially motivated peremptory strikes).

Nancy S. Marder, "Beyond Gender: Peremptory Challenges and the Roles of the Jury," 73 *Tex. L. Rev.* 1041 (1995) (proposing the elimination of peremptory strikes as inconsistent with the role of the jury as a reflection of community values and beliefs).

STUDY

Kenneth J. Melilli, "*Batson* in Practice: What We Have Learned About *Batson* and Peremptory Challenges," 71 *Notre Dame L. Rev.* 447 (1996) (comprehensive study analyzing the reasons proffered after a *Batson* challenge for use of peremptory challenges and concluding that the majority of peremptory strikes could be sustained as a strike for cause).

§ III-7   REDUCING OR ELIMINATING PEREMPTORY CHALLENGES

TECHNIQUE

By statute, court rule, or case law, the jurisdiction either reduces the number of peremptory challenges available to each party during voir dire or eliminates the use of peremptory challenges altogether.

ISSUES

- How will the reduction or elimination of peremptory challenges affect the standard for granting challenges for cause? Will judges feel compelled to grant challenges for cause for only the appearance of bias?

- What effect will reducing or eliminating peremptory challenges have on the scope of inquiry during voir dire?

- Will reducing or eliminating peremptory challenges increase or decrease the likelihood of impaneling an impartial jury?

- Will reducing or eliminating peremptory challenges increase the number of appeals based on juror bias discovered after the verdict has been returned?

- How will reducing or eliminating peremptory challenges affect jury administration?

- What effect will reducing or eliminating peremptory challenges have on public confidence in the justice system?

- Will reducing or eliminating peremptory challenges improve the quality of jury deliberations?

PROCEDURES

The peremptory challenge, a procedure used to remove people suspected of bias from the jury, is deeply rooted in the American justice system. Historically, the peremptory challenge was established by statute as a protective mechanism for criminal defendants. For both civil and criminal trials, peremptory challenges operated as a check against nonrandom selection, a common characteristic of "keyman" jury selection systems in use through the middle of the twentieth century. In addition, the availability of peremptory challenges may reduce the risk of hung juries, thus relieving pressure on policy makers to eliminate unanimity requirements.

Typically both parties are permitted to exercise a certain number of peremptory challenges when selecting the jury, although many jurisdictions allot a greater number of peremptories to defendants. Although ABA Standards recommend five peremptory challenges per side in felony trials (three per side in misdemeanor trials and in civil litigation), the number of peremptory challenges varies greatly among jurisdictions—up to 20 for criminal defendants in noncapital felony trials (ten in misdemeanor trials) and up to eight per side in civil litigation.

Recently, some jurisdictions have begun to question whether the traditional justifications for peremptory challenges continue to exist given the changes in the jury selection process. Only one court has issued an outright prohibition on peremptory challenges thus far. However, a number of jurisdictions have proposed reducing the number of peremptories, especially in capital criminal cases for which the number of peremptories varies widely. Maryland, for example, reduced the number of peremptory challenges to reduce expenditures for juror fees and costs of jury administration. Other jurisdictions have adjusted the number of peremptories in an effort to ensure parity between the parties (e.g., prosecution/defendant, plaintiff/defendant).

The debate over the use of the peremptory challenge has existed for a substantial period of time. However, recent developments have contributed to new interest in proposals to reduce or eliminate peremptory challenges. Proponents of these ideas cite logistical and philosophical advantages. For example, some proponents favor reducing or eliminating peremptories on the ground that attorneys almost never have sufficient information about potential jurors to make intelligent or effective use of peremptory challenges. Moreover, the use of jury consultants in selecting the jury tends to perpetuate the belief that wealthier litigants have an unfair advantage at trial, thus undermining public confidence in the justice system.

Other proponents argue that peremptory challenges are inherently discriminatory, notwithstanding *Batson* procedures for countering these abuses. See also § III-6, "*Batson* Enforcement." They cite the proliferation of appeals seeking to extend *Batson* beyond discrimination based on race or gender—for example, to ethnic background, religious belief, disability, and other characteristics—as evidence that peremptory challenges are used only to exclude jurors based on group characteristics perceived as unsympathetic to the challenging party. They view peremptory challenges as fundamentally inconsistent with the goal of seating juries representative of the communities in which they are impaneled. It makes little sense, they argue, to ensure that the jury panel reflects the demographic characteristics of the jurisdiction while permitting the parties to hand-pick a jury that does not reflect these characteristics. Finally, some proponents argue that reducing or eliminating peremptories will reduce the number of individuals summoned for jury duty, thus making more effective use of jurors' time and court resources.

Opponents of these proposals also raise compelling philosophical and practical reasons to support their position. They maintain that the traditional justification for peremptory challenges—ensuring an unbiased jury—continues to be valid. As a result, the opportunity to participate in the selection of the jury increases public confidence in the legitimacy of the verdict and the likelihood that the parties will be satisfied that they have had their day in court. Opponents also question many of the benefits and legal grounds claimed by proponents of proposals to reduce or eliminate peremptories. They argue, for example, that any efficiencies gained by reducing the number of individuals summoned for jury duty would be lost because of increases in the length and complexity of the jury selection process. Trial attorneys would need to engage in more intensive questioning of potential jurors to determine whether a challenge for cause is warranted. Opponents also claim that skilled attorneys use peremptory challenges very effectively to eliminate juror bias. Reducing or eliminating peremptories, therefore, interferes with attorneys' legitimate trial strategies.

Finally, opponents have expressed three legally based concerns about reducing or eliminating peremptories. Although they acknowledge the legal basis for representative jury panels, they point out that neither federal nor state law (constitutional or statutory) mandates that the juries from these panels be representative of the communities from which they are drawn. Moreover, they caution that this proposal would prompt judges to lower the standard for granting a challenge for cause, muddling the distinction between challenges for cause and peremptory strikes. They also warn that post-verdict investigations of jurors—and corresponding appeals based on post-verdict discovery of juror bias—are likely to increase.

ADVANTAGES

1. Reducing or eliminating peremptory challenges limits the opportunities for trial attorneys to exercise discriminatory peremptory challenges in an impermissible fashion.

2. Reducing or eliminating peremptory challenges enhances the representativeness of the jury.

3. Reducing or eliminating peremptory challenges makes more efficient use of the individuals summoned for jury service, increasing juror satisfaction and reducing the administrative costs associated with calling extra people.

4. Reducing or eliminating peremptory challenges may reduce the use of jury consultants by some litigants, thus reducing the appearance that wealthy litigants have an unfair advantage.

DISADVANTAGES

1. Reducing or eliminating peremptory challenges limits attorneys' ability to remove jurors suspected of bias from the jury panel.

2. Reducing or eliminating peremptory challenges would lengthen the voir dire process by prompting attorneys to engage in more intensive questioning of jurors to determine if they should challenge for cause.

3. Reducing or eliminating peremptory challenges would prompt judges to lower the threshold for granting motions to strike for cause, creating uncertainty and disparities among jurisdictions as to what constitutes grounds to support a strike for cause.

4. Reducing or eliminating peremptory challenges prevents the parties from participating fully in jury selection, undermining the appearance of a fair trial and public confidence in the verdict.

AUTHORITY

Minetos v. City University of New York, 925 F. Supp. 177 (1996) (ruling that peremptory challenges are inherently discriminatory and unconstitutional under the Equal Protection Clause).

Batson v. Kentucky, 476 U.S. 79, 108 (1986) (Marshall, J., in concurrence, argued for the elimination of peremptory challenges from the criminal justice system).

Ross v. Oklahoma, 487 U.S. 81 (1988) (reaffirming in dicta that peremptory challenges are not constitutionally mandated, but serve only as a means to select an impartial jury).

REFERENCES

Albert W. Alschuler, "The Supreme Court and the Jury: Voir Dire, Peremptory Challenges, and the Review of Jury Verdicts," 56 *U. Chi. L. Rev.* 153, 163-211 (1989) (examines *Batson* and concludes that the Equal Protection Clause and peremptory challenges are incompatible).

American Bar Association, Committee on Jury Standards, *Standards Relating to Juror Use and Management* (1993) (Standard 9 proposes a maximum number of peremptory strikes per side for civil, misdemeanor, felony [noncapital], and capital cases).

Nancy S. Marder, "Beyond Gender: Peremptory Challenges and the Roles of the Jury," 73 *Tex. L. Rev.* 1041 (1995) (proposing the elimination of peremptory strikes as inconsistent with the role of the jury as a reflection of community values and beliefs).

STUDIES

Shari S. Diamond & Hans Zeisel, "A Courtroom Experiment on Jury Selection and Decision-Making," 1 *Personality and Soc. Psychol. Bull.* 276 (1974) (study finding a difference in the acquittal rates of actual juries as compared to rates of mock juries composed of peremptorily challenged jurors).

Kenneth J. Melilli, "*Batson* in Practice: What We Have Learned About *Batson* and Peremptory Challenges," 71 *Notre Dame L. Rev.* 447 (1996) (comprehensive study analyzing the reasons proffered after a *Batson* challenge for use of peremptory challenges and concluding that the majority of peremptory strikes could be sustained as a strike for cause).

Hans Zeisel & Shari S. Diamond, "Effect of Peremptory Challenges on Jury and Verdict," 30 *Stan. L. Rev.* 491 (1978) (examining the effectiveness of voir dire in actually achieving an unbiased jury).

RELATED APPENDIX

Appendix 4: Number of Peremptory Challenges by State and Case Type

§ III-8   ROUTINE USE OF ANONYMOUS JURIES

TECHNIQUE

As a matter of routine practice, the court withholds the names, addresses, and other identifying information about jurors and their families from the parties, their counsel, the public, and the media. This technique can be used for either civil or criminal trials.

ISSUES

- Does anonymity affect jurors' honesty during voir dire?

- Does anonymity affect jurors' commitment to personal beliefs?

- What effect does anonymity have on juror deliberations and verdicts?

- Do anonymous juries feel less responsible for their verdicts or take their duties less seriously?

- Do anonymous juries deprive criminal defendants of the presumption of innocence?

- Do anonymous juries deprive criminal defendants of the right to an impartial jury?

- Do anonymous juries unconstitutionally interfere with public and media access to judicial proceedings under the First Amendment?

PROCEDURES

Many courts have used anonymous juries for cases in which disclosure of the jurors' identities places them at risk of physical harm or intimidation. However, this selective use of anonymous juries has a potential prejudicial effect, especially in criminal trials, insofar that jurors may perceive the defendant to be an unusually dangerous individual. Routine use of anonymous juries, in contrast, does not carry this stigma.

To impanel an anonymous jury, the court assigns a number to all persons called for jury service. This number functions as the juror's identification number for the entire term of jury service. The summons for jury service instructs each member of the jury panel to report to court and to identify him or herself using the assigned number. Alternatively, the court assigns the juror identification number when the jury panel member first reports for jury service. All references to the juror (e.g., in jury questionnaires, voir dire, and trial proceedings) that are accessible to the parties, their counsel, or the public or media are made according to this identification number.

When used on a routine basis, this technique relieves jurors' suspicions that criminal defendants are particularly dangerous, thus eliminating any potential prejudice that might otherwise exist. The judge explains to the members of the jury panel that this technique is a routine practice of the court adopted to protect their privacy from intrusions by *anyone* with an interest in the case, including parties, counsel, or the media. The judge instructs the prospective jurors that following their release from jury service, they are free to disclose their identities, but for the duration of any court proceedings they should refrain from doing so. See also § VII-1, "Advice Regarding Post-Verdict Conversations."

The court discloses a juror's name to the parties or their counsel only on a showing that the juror's identity is likely to lead to evidence sufficient to impeach the verdict or sustain a challenge for cause. The parties or their counsel must also demonstrate that disclosure of the juror's name is needed to provide the court with adequate information to rule on a motion for a new trial or a motion to excuse the juror. The standards established in federal cases for granting post-trial interviews or hearings (e.g., requiring a preliminary showing of juror misconduct) might serve as a basis for developing standards for disclosing a juror's name. For cases in which the media request post-verdict access to jurors, the court discloses a juror's name only if the juror consents to the disclosure.

ADVANTAGES

1.   Anonymous juries increase jurors' willingness to respond honestly to voir dire questions, thus enhancing the likelihood of selecting an impartial jury.

2.   Anonymous juries relieve jurors' fears of retaliation for potentially unpopular verdicts, thus improving the quality of jury deliberations and the fairness of verdicts.

3.   Anonymous juries safeguard jurors from intimidation during trials.

4.   Anonymous juries may reduce the need to sequester juries.

DISADVANTAGES

1. Anonymous juries increase jurors' suspicions that particular parties, especially criminal defendants, are dangerous.

2. Anonymous juries may feel less responsible for their verdicts.

3. Anonymous jury systems complicate jury administration.

4. Excessive post-verdict restrictions on access to jurors' names prevents trial counsel and independent researchers from engaging in legitimate self-education and jury research.

AUTHORITY

18 U.S.C. § 3432 (Supp. 1996) (authorizing the use of anonymous juries in capital cases to protect the life or safety of the jurors and their families).

Hamer v. United States, 259 F.2d 274 (9th Cir. 1958) (holding that use of an anonymous jury did not deprive the defendant of his Sixth Amendment rights since voir dire was sufficient to ensure the selection of an impartial jury).

REFERENCES

J. Clark Kelso, "Report of the Blue Ribbon Commission on Jury System Improvement," 33-36 (Judicial Council of California, 1996) (recommending that the California legislature proscribe anonymous juries in all cases).

Nancy J. King, "Nameless Justice: The Case for the Routine Use of Anonymous Juries in Criminal Trials," 49 *Vand. L. Rev.* 123 (1996) (arguing that routine withholding of jurors' names and other identifying information does not violate First or Sixth Amendment requirements).

RELATED APPENDIX

Appendix 5: Suggested Procedures for the Management of Anonymous Juries

§ III-9 Nondesignation of Alternates and Jurors

Technique

Both jurors and alternates selected from the jury panel sit in the jury box and hear the entire trial. Jurors and alternates are not informed of their status until all parties have presented their evidence and closing arguments and the judge has given final instructions. The jurors are then identified and begin deliberations while the alternates are released from jury service.

An alternative method is to select a "jury," the size of which is equal to the total number of jurors and alternates that would ordinarily be selected, without making any distinctions between jurors and alternates. Jurors and alternates are selected randomly and only after both parties have presented their evidence and closing arguments and the judge has given final instructions.

In either case, the persons serving on the jury do not know until the end of the trial who will be selected to deliberate, resulting in greater attentiveness to the trial proceedings by all of them.

Issues

- Should alternates know from the beginning of the trial that they are so designated?

- Is it deceptive to designate jurors and alternates without informing them of their status?

- Does this technique cause resentment by alternates that might affect their willingness to serve as jurors in subsequent trials?

- Are alternates more attentive during trial proceedings if they are not informed that they will not be included in deliberations?

Procedures

There are two separate methods associated with this technique. Under the first method, the jurors and alternates are designated by the trial attorneys during voir dire. For example, a common practice in Wisconsin for designating the alternate is to use the last picked juror who survives peremptory challenges. Their status as either jurors or alternates is not revealed until the jury is ready to deliberate, however. In that method, the attorneys can plan their trial strategy around their knowledge of the juror and alternate composition.

Immediately before deliberations, the judge dismisses the alternates and the remaining jurors retire to deliberate.

Under the second method, the trial judge and attorneys make no distinction between jurors and alternates until the end of the trial. The number of "jurors" hearing the evidence is equal to the total number of jurors and alternates that would normally be selected for the trial. After both parties have rested, the deliberating jurors are selected in one of two ways. Alternates can be selected "by lot"—that is, jurors in excess of the maximum number permitted to deliberate are excused randomly by drawing their names or jury identification numbers. Alternatively, the court permits the trial attorneys to exercise a limited number of additional peremptory challenges immediately prior to final instructions.

The trial judge and attorneys should consider how jurors are likely to interpret the choice of selection procedures for designating jurors and alternates as well as how the trial judge explains and justifies this process.

ADVANTAGES

1. Jurors take jury service more seriously and are more attentive to the trial proceedings when they believe that they will be required to deliberate after both parties present their case.

2. Alternates do not perceive themselves as second-class citizens as a result of their status.

3. When the designation of jurors and alternates is made by random drawing after both parties have rested, all jurors are given an equal opportunity to serve.

4. When the designation of jurors and alternates is made by the exercise of additional peremptory strikes, the attorneys have the opportunity to dismiss a juror who has not paid attention during the trial or who has shown some other type of bias that may affect his or her ability to deliberate fairly.

DISADVANTAGES

1. Jurors may feel dissatisfaction, frustration, or resentment for being dismissed prior to deliberations after having paid close attention during the course of the trial proceedings.

2. Keeping the designation of jurors and alternates a secret may cause them to feel betrayed, possibly affecting how the jurors who ultimately deliberate view the trial judge and attorneys.

3. When the designation of jurors and alternates is made by the exercise of additional peremptory strikes, jurors may feel apprehensive or self-conscious throughout the trial knowing that they may be excused before deliberations. Alternates are more likely to take the strike personally than they would had it occurred at the beginning of the trial. Other jurors, hoping to be excused from deliberations, may intentionally fail to pay attention or purposefully demonstrate bias during the trial proceedings.

4. The opportunity to strike alternates using additional peremptory challenges may prompt the trial attorneys to continue to investigate jurors after the trial has commenced, creating an additional source of tension throughout the trial. This opportunity also could affect the timing of objections to the selection process.

REFERENCE

Stephen A. Saltzburg, "Improving the Quality of Jury Decisionmaking," in Robert E. Litan ed., *Verdict: Assessing the Civil Jury System* 341, 354-55 (1993) (describing techniques involving alternate jurors and jury sizes).

§ III-10 Variable Jury Size/No Alternate Jurors

Technique

A jury is selected that is larger than a given minimum jury size. If a juror is excused during the trial, the jury size is reduced. All remaining jurors deliberate. A minimum jury size is set by law, below which the jury is no longer considered viable. This technique is recommended only for civil trials.

Issue

- Does variable jury size affect the verdict or degree of proof required by the parties?

Procedures

Rather than selecting a given number of jurors plus a number of alternates, the court impanels a jury that is equal in size to the jurors plus alternates. All are sworn as trial jurors. If a juror must be excused during the trial, the trial proceeds with the smaller jury. A minimum jury size is established by statute or court rule to ensure that the jury does not fall below the constitutionally proscribed number of jurors.

Theoretically, an increase in the jury size would increase the difficulty in obtaining convictions in criminal cases because of the comparatively higher standard of proof. Consequently, this technique is recommended only for civil trials.

Advantages

1. All persons selected are active jurors. The jury is a unit from the beginning of the trial.

2. The same level of scrutiny is applied to the selection of all the jurors.

Disadvantage

In criminal trials, the difficulty in obtaining convictions increases as the number of jurors increases because of the higher standard of proof.

AUTHORITY

Fed. R. Civ. Proc. Rule 48 (1996) (providing for juries consisting of six to 12 jurors and no alternates).

Ballew v. Georgia, 435 U.S. 223 (1978) (holding that a criminal conviction rendered by a jury consisting of fewer than six persons constitutes a denial of due process).

Chapter IV

Pretrial Management

CONTRIBUTORS AND REVIEWERS

Joe Cecil, Ph.D., J.D.
Federal Judicial Center
Washington, D.C.

Hon. B. Michael Dann
Superior Court of Arizona
Phoenix, Arizona

Paula L. Hannaford, J.D., M.P.P.
National Center for State Courts
Williamsburg, Virginia

Gregory P. Joseph, Esq.
Fried, Frank, Harris,
Shriver & Jacobson
New York, New York

Prof. Janeen Kerper
California Western School of Law
San Diego, California

Doug Laird, Esq.
Polsinelli, White,
Vardeman & Shalton
Kansas City, Missouri

Jeff Mitchell
DePaul University
Downers Grove, Illinois

G. Thomas Munsterman
National Center for State Courts
Arlington, Virginia

Curtis E. von Kann, Esq.
Ross, Dixon & Masback, L.L.P.
Washington, D.C.

§ IV-1   Pretrial Limits on Each Party's Time at Trial

Technique

The parties agree on overall time limits to be allocated for direct and cross-examination, reading depositions, showing exhibits, and presenting computer simulations or other evidentiary demonstrations as each party sees fit.

Issues

- At what point should time limits be established? Before discovery? After discovery, but before trial?

- What activities by the trial attorneys should be subject to time limits?

- Do time limitations put pro se parties or parties whose counsel have little trial experience at a comparative disadvantage?

- Can the court determine, in advance of trial, a fair and reasonable amount of time required to present a case?

- Who monitors the amount of time each party expends at trial?

Procedures

At the pretrial conference, the trial attorneys agree on overall time limits for presenting their case at trial. Each side may distribute its allocated time to voir dire, opening or closing arguments, direct or cross-examination, reading depositions, showing exhibits, and presenting computer simulations or other evidentiary demonstrations as each party sees fit.

If the attorneys are unable to agree on time limitations, the trial court imposes reasonable overall time limits based on the number and complexity of issues, the respective evidentiary burdens of the parties, the nature of proof to be offered, and the feasibility of shortening the trial through stipulations, preadmission of exhibits, and other techniques. Judicial time limits on trial proceedings generally are reviewed under an abuse of discretion standard.

The court clerk monitors the amount of time expended by the parties and periodically advises the trial attorneys of the amount of time each has remaining. Activities subject to time limitations may include opening and closing arguments, direct and cross-examination of witnesses, and trial objections. The judge firmly enforces the time limits at trial, but may extend them for good cause shown.

Judges who have used overall time limits (as opposed to specific time limits on witness testimony or other aspects of trial proceedings) report that they encourage better preparation by the trial attorneys. As a result, the trial attorneys conduct opening and closing arguments in a more direct fashion, use greater selectivity in their choice of witnesses, and present less cumulative and peripheral evidence at trial. Juror comprehension and interest increase from these improved, more focused presentations.

On motion by either party, the judge may advise the jury of the time limits to prevent jurors from making unwarranted inferences from a party's failure to call all possible witnesses.

ADVANTAGES

1. Time limits force counsel to assess their available evidence in advance of trial and determine the most effective and efficient method of presenting it.

2. Better prepared evidentiary presentations improve jurors' comprehension of the evidence and interest in the trial proceedings.

3. Compared to specific limits on the number of, or time for, direct and cross-examination of lay witnesses and expert witnesses, overall time limits avoid micromanagement by the judge and thus reserves discretion to the trial attorneys, who have much greater familiarity with the evidence, about how best to utilize the time allotted.

4. Overall time limits reduce the opportunity for abuse or manipulation by opposing counsel associated with less comprehensive time limits or rules. For example, a "cross can't exceed direct" rule operates to the disadvantage of the lawyer cross-examining an important witness whose direct testimony was brief and conclusory. Similarly, a rule stating that "plaintiff's case is limited to X hours or days" may invite cross-examiners to eat up the plaintiff's time or vice versa for a defendant's limit.

5. Time limits allocate courtroom time—a scarce public resource—among all litigants waiting to have their cases tried.

DISADVANTAGES

1. Setting pretrial time limits requires knowledge about the amount of time necessary to present certain types of evidence.

2. Pro se litigants and attorneys with less litigation experience are at a comparative disadvantage and may jeopardize their clients' interests by failing to utilize their allotted time effectively.

3. Setting pretrial time limits also requires reasonable familiarity with the issues and evidence of the particular case. Judges with little time to become acquainted with their cases before trial may find it difficult to set such limits.

AUTHORITY

MCI Communications Corp. v. American Telephone and Telegraph Co., 708 F.2d 1081 (7th Cir. 1983) (upholding a 26-day time limit for each party to present its case in chief, despite original estimates by the defendant that the time would take eight to nine months).

Johnson v. Ashby, 808 F.2d 676, 678 (8th Cir. 1987) (affirming the discretion of the trial court to set reasonable time limits).

United States v. Reaves, 636 F. Supp. 1575 (E.D. Ky. 1986) (admonishing the trial court to tailor mandatory time limits to each specific case to avoid arbitrary limits).

SCM Corp. v. Xerox Corp., 77 F.R.D. 10 (D. Conn. 1977) (recommending aggregate limits to permit counsel the greatest possible flexibility and discretion in presenting the case).

Fed. R. Civ. Proc. Rule 16(c)(15) (authorizing time limits on evidentiary presentations).

Fed. R. Evid. Rule 403 (authorizing the exclusion of otherwise relevant evidence in the interest of efficient trial management).

Fed. R. Evid. Rule 611(a) (mandating judicial oversight and control of evidentiary presentations for the purpose of trial economy).

Ariz. Civ. Proc. Rule 16(h) (authorizing time limits on trial proceedings).

REFERENCES

Federal Judicial Center, *Manual for Complex Litigation, Third* §§ 21.643 and 22.35 (1995).

Patrick E. Longan, "Civil Trial Reform and the Appearance of Fairness," 79 *Marq. L. Rev.* 295, 326-327 (1995) (recommending time limits as an appropriate method of balancing judicial interests in efficiency and fairness).

William W Schwarzer, "Reforming Jury Trials," 132 F.R.D. 575, 578 (1991) ("Jurors do not have an unlimited attention span. Their capacity to absorb, retain, and effectively use information (especially on unfamiliar subjects) is finite").

Studies

Administrative Office of the U.S. Courts, *Civil Justice Expense and Delay Reduction Plans, Pilot Courts and Early Implementation Districts,* Appendix II (1992) (reporting on early results from reform initiatives).

Patrick E. Longan, "The Shot Clock Comes to Trial: Time Limits for Federal Civil Trials," 35 *Ariz. L. Rev.* 663 (1993) (examining the economic justifications for imposing time limits on parties).

§ IV-2   Pretrial Admission of Exhibits and Deposition Testimony

Technique

During the pretrial conference, the trial attorneys apprise the court of all exhibits and deposition testimony to be introduced. After the judge rules on any objections to the evidence, exhibits and depositions admitted at pretrial are deemed admitted from the time the trial commences. The trial attorneys may make reference to this evidence at any point in the trial, including during opening statements.

Issues

- Does pretrial admission of exhibits and deposition testimony, and the corresponding reduction in evidentiary objections, result in a faster, more efficient trial?

- What is the most convenient fashion of memorializing the court's pretrial rulings (e.g., handwritten on the face of each document, an appendix to the pretrial order, dictated onto a tape for later transcription by a law clerk or secretary)?

Procedures

In preparing for the pretrial conference, the trial attorneys exchange lists of the exhibits and deposition testimony they intend to introduce at trial. At the pretrial conference, the attorneys come prepared either to stipulate to the admissibility of the exhibit or deposition testimony offered by other parties or to state their objections to its admissibility. To the extent possible given the nature of the evidence, the judge rules on the objections at the pretrial conference. The judge may use his or her authority to sanction parties that make frivolous or vexatious objections.

Exhibits and depositions admitted at pretrial are deemed admitted from the time that trial commences. The trial attorneys may make reference to this evidence at any point in the trial, including during opening statements. This technique avoids the risk of confusing or boring jurors with lengthy presentations of foundational evidence and reduces the amount of juror "downtime" while the judge considers evidentiary objections.

ADVANTAGES

1. Pretrial admission of exhibit and deposition evidence eliminates the need to respond to technical evidentiary objections, thus conserving valuable court and juror time.

2. Pretrial admission of evidence avoids the risk of confusing or boring jurors with lengthy evidentiary presentations offered solely to establish a foundation for admissibility.

3. Pretrial rulings on the admissibility of exhibit and deposition testimony narrow the issues and enable the trial counsel to plan more effectively for trial.

4. Pretrial rulings also provide the trial attorneys with the opportunity to overcome some evidentiary objections by eliminating inadmissible evidence, obtaining alternative sources of proof, or presenting necessary foundation evidence.

DISADVANTAGE

This technique requires a great deal of pretrial time by the court and counsel to consider and rule on technical evidentiary objections. The benefits of pretrial admission may be wasted if trial developments cause the evidence, or objections thereto, to be mooted or withdrawn.

AUTHORITY

Fed. R. Civ. Proc. Rule 16(c)(3) (1996) (encouraging pretrial stipulations in the interest of trial economy).

Local Civ. Rules (U.S. E.D. N.C.) Rule 24.03 (1996) (setting forth procedures for evidentiary stipulations and their effects on subsequent trial matters).

Local Rules U.S. Bankr. Ct. (E.D. Va.) Rule 111(B) (1996) (setting forth procedures for admission of prestipulated evidence).

REFERENCES

Federal Judicial Center, *Manual for Complex Litigation, Third* §§ 21.642 (1995).

Gus J. Solomon, "Techniques for Shortening Trials," 65 F.R.D. 485, 491 (1975) (Address delivered before the Ninth Judicial District Conference in Reno, Nevada, Aug. 2, 1974, describing several procedural matters including pretrial admission that can be disposed of during the pretrial conference).

§ IV-3   Reordering the Sequence of Expert Testimony

Technique

In cases heavily dependent on expert testimony, the judge and attorneys reorder the sequence of proof so that opposing experts offer their testimony consecutively rather than at sporadic stages throughout the trial. Alternatively, opposing experts can offer joint testimony at trial or at an experts' conference during which the experts engage in a structured conversation before the jury in an effort to identify points on which they agree or disagree and the basis for their conclusions. This technique permits the jury to determine the extent of real difference between opposing experts and to compare and evaluate these differences side by side. This technique can be used in conjunction with others, such as conducting juror tutorials or permitting the jury to submit questions to the expert witnesses. See also § IV-5, "Jury Tutorials," and § V-7, "Jurors' Questions to Witnesses."

Issue

- Does reordering the sequence of expert testimony place the defense at a comparative disadvantage (e.g., by structuring the order of proof around the plaintiff's or prosecutor's theory of the case)?

Procedures

Opposing expert witnesses typically appear at sporadic stages of the trial to present their own conclusions and reasoning without truly joining issue with the reasoning and explanation offered by other experts. Jurors thus find it difficult to determine the extent of real difference between the experts and the degree to which each could persuasively defend his or her own conclusions in a dialogue with the other. Reordering the sequence in which opposing experts offer their testimony provides the jury with an opportunity to evaluate how expert opinions hold up in a true exchange with opposing experts.

To implement this technique, the judge and attorneys conduct a pretrial conference with the expert witnesses to identify the disputed issues and limit the trial testimony to those issues. For undisputed issues that will require some explanation to ensure that jurors fully comprehend the expert presentations, the judge and attorneys may use the pretrial conference to plan a "juror tutorial." See § IV-5, "Jury Tutorials." During the pretrial conference, the judge and attorneys determine the sequence of proof to be followed at trial as well as any special arrangements for the presentation of expert testimony (e.g., consecutive or joint testimony) or the procedures for permitting jurors to submit questions to the experts. See § V-7, "Jurors' Questions to Witnesses." The pretrial order records the agreement of the parties on these points.

ADVANTAGES

1. Jurors receive a clearer understanding of the nature and extent of differences between experts and the soundness of their views.

2. By gaining increased understanding of the expert testimony, jurors feel more confident of their ability to deal with technical issues rather than abdicating their decisional authority to the party's experts.

DISADVANTAGES

1. Such procedures place additional managerial burdens on judges.

2. Some increase in cost of experts to parties is likely to result.

3. Reordering the sequence of expert testimony may disrupt the trial strategy of counsel, especially defense counsel.

AUTHORITY

Fed. R. Evid. Rule 611(a) (1996) (mandating judicial oversight and control of evidentiary presentations for the purpose of trial economy).

Fed. R. Evid. Rule 614 (1996) (authorizing the court to call and examine witnesses on its own motion).

Fed. R. Evid. Rule 702 (1996) (authorizing expert testimony).

Fed. R. Evid. Rule 706(a) (1996) (authorizing the court to appoint its own expert witnesses).

Daubert v. Merrell Dow Pharmaceuticals, 113 Sup. Ct. Rptr. 2786, 2795 (1993) (holding that Rule 702 contemplates some degree of regulation of the subject and theories about which experts may testify).

United States v. Daccarett, 6 F.3d 37, 58 (2nd Cir. 1993) (noting that in *Daubert,* the Supreme Court sanctioned more active supervision of expert testimony by the trial court).

Deimer v. Cincinnati Sub-Zero Products, Inc., 58 F.3d 341, 344 (7th Cir. 1995) (holding that the trial court did not abuse its discretion by excluding the testimony of plaintiff's expert who did not conduct studies or analysis to substantiate his opinion).

Hibiscus Assoc. v. Bd. of Trustees, 50 F.3d 908, 917 (11th Cir. 1995) (affirming the decision of the trial court to exclude expert testimony that was not needed to clarify facts and issues that jurors were able to comprehend for themselves).

REFERENCES

"Confronting the New Challenges of Scientific Evidence," 108 *Harv. L. Rev.* 1481, 1589-93 (1995) (discussing methods of addressing problems associated with complex, scientific evidence).

Curtis E. von Kann, "Reinventing the Jury Trial," *Legal Times*, Jan. 2, 1995, at 20 (describing a hypothetical medical malpractice case using innovations to present expert testimony).

Jack B. Weinstein, "Rule 702 of the Federal Rules of Evidence is Sound: It Should Not be Amended," 138 F.R.D. 631, 640 (1992) (Speech delivered to the U.S. Eighth Circuit Judicial Conference, Colorado Springs, Colorado, July 10, 1991, proposing improvements in procedures relating to expert testimony rather than amending Rule 702).

§ IV-4   APPOINTING COURT EXPERTS

TECHNIQUE

According to federal rules of procedure and most corresponding state rules, the judge has the authority to appoint experts to offer testimony or serve in a variety of trial and pretrial functions.

ISSUES

- Under what circumstances should the court appoint an expert?

- What tasks should the court ask the expert to perform?

- How should the judge identify qualified experts? What criteria should the judge use to evaluate and select an expert?

- How are court-appointed experts compensated?

- Does discovery by the parties differ in any significant respect for court-appointed experts versus party-retained experts? Are there any differences in trial procedures for court-appointed witnesses (e.g., regarding examination of the witness)?

- Is the court's sponsorship of the appointed expert revealed to the jury?

PROCEDURES

Courts may consider appointing an expert in extraordinary circumstances in which the traditional adversarial system and parties' experts have not provided a basis for a reasoned and principled disposition. Such cases often involve evidence that is particularly difficult to comprehend or testimony by credible experts who find little basis for agreement. Cases in which there is a compelling public interest in the accurate resolution of a factual issue may also involve an absence of testimony on one side of an issue. Experts also may be appointed to offer testimony on behalf of an indigent criminal defendant.

An appointed expert may perform a variety of functions beyond offering testimony on the issues in dispute. For example, appointed experts also may address a narrow inquiry in a pretrial hearing or educate the judge and jury about underlying issues on which the parties' experts testify. See also § IV-5,

"Jury Tutorials." The appointed expert should be assigned specific duties on the record, in the presence of the parties or in a written order.

In cases presenting especially difficult issues, the court may appoint more than one expert and have the appointed experts work together as a panel. Among the duties assigned to such a panel may be the identification and evaluation of claims, defenses, and scientific issues that arise in the litigation. In some instances, the work of a panel has been supervised by a special master.

The expert should be appointed well in advance of trial to enable him or her to offer effective service without delaying the trial. This typically requires early identification of disputed issues of expert testimony. Parties, through their attorneys, should be involved in the selection and instruction of appointed experts. Parties should be encouraged to nominate candidates for appointment and to agree on a suitable candidate (although often such encouragement will be unavailing). The judge also may recruit candidates for appointment by contacting colleges, universities, and professional organizations. In cases involving unsettled scientific or technical questions, however, judges may consider limiting the role of a court-appointed expert to providing the judge and jury with a neutral, objective assessment of the respective strengths and weaknesses of the parties' evidence.

The court should make clear its anticipated form of communication with the expert. Ex parte communication on issues other than ministerial matters should be undertaken only with the permission of the parties or on the record. Depositions of the appointed expert should be conducted under an order setting forth proper areas of inquiry and preferably in the presence of a judicial official. Typically, the appointed expert will present findings in a written report. Parties should be given an opportunity to review and respond to the report. The appointed expert may also present findings by testimony at trial or in a pretrial hearing.

When the appointed expert testifies before a jury, the court must determine whether to disclose to the jury that the expert was appointed by the court. If the court decides to disguise the court appointment, the court may direct the party who is favored by the expert's findings to call the expert without indicating the court's sponsorship of the appointed experts. Each party should have an opportunity to question the appointed expert concerning his or her findings.

Typically parties should pay the cost of the appointed expert. The judge should require the parties to pay a designated amount into a court account at the outset, and the court then makes arrangements to compensate the expert from these funds.

Few federal judges oppose appointment of experts in principle, and more than four out of five judges indicate that court-appointed experts are likely to be helpful in at least some circumstances. But only one in five has ever appointed an expert in a civil case. Appointments are made in extraordinary circumstances in which the dispute turns on evidence that is not readily comprehensible and the traditional adversary process has failed to produce information needed for resolving a highly technical dispute. There is little empirical information about state court utilization of court-appointed experts.

ADVANTAGES

1. Appointed experts provide the courts with a source of information and expertise that is independent of the parties' control and interests.

2. Appointed experts may respond to issues that are specifically tailored to address the concerns of the court.

3. Appointment of an expert (and perhaps the threat of such an appointment) may improve the quality of the testimony offered by the parties' experts.

DISADVANTAGES

1. Appointment of an expert diminishes the parties' control over presentation of information.

2. Appointment of an expert is likely to increase cost and may delay the proceedings.

3. Appointed experts may venture beyond their proper duties and address ultimate issues that are within the domain of the judge or jury.

4. Jurors and judges may disregard competent testimony by parties' experts and consider testimony only by the appointed expert.

5. Some scientific and technical questions have not been studied sufficiently for an expert to make any reliable conclusions about disputed facts. A court-appointed expert will have no greater or more objective insight than the disputing parties' experts.

AUTHORITY

Fed. R. Evid. Rule 706 (1996) (describing procedures for the appointment of court experts).

18 U.S.C. § 3006A(e) (1993) (authorizing the court to retain expert witnesses for indigent defendants when necessary to ensure adequate representation).

Reilly v. United States, 863 F.2d 149, 154-61 (1st Cir. 1988) (describing the appropriate role of a court-retained "technical advisor" in federal court).

REFERENCES

Joe S. Cecil & Thomas E. Willging, "Accepting Daubert's Invitation: Defining a Role for Court-Appointed Experts in Assessing Scientific Validity," 43 *Emory L. J.* 995 (1994) (reports on a study of federal district court judges' experiences with appointment of experts under Rule 706 of the Federal Rules of Evidence).

Samuel R. Gross, "Expert Evidence," 1991 *Wis. L. Rev.* 1113, 1211 (survey of problems with expert testimony and recommendation for greater use of court-appointed experts).

Jack B. Weinstein & Margaret A. Berger, *Weinstein's Evidence: Commentary on Rules of Evidence for the United States Courts and State Courts* § B6 706[01] (1993) (cases and commentary relevant to appointment of experts).

STUDIES

Nancy J. Brekke, Peter J. Enko, Gail Clavet & Eric Seelan, "Of Juries and Court-Appointed Experts: The Impact of Nonadversarial versus Adversarial Expert Testimony," 15 *Law & Hum. Behav.* 451 (1991) (study finding that juries did not accord more weight to nonadversarial expert testimony, nor did nonadversarial expert testimony negatively affect evaluations of trial fairness or judge competence).

B. L. Cutler, H. R. Dexter & Steven D. Penrod, "Nonadversarial Methods for Sensitizing Jurors to Eyewitness Evidence," 20 *J. Applied Soc. Psychol.* 1197 (1990).

§ IV-5   Jury Tutorials

Technique

For cases involving highly technical or complicated issues that require understanding of unfamiliar terminology or concepts or that depend heavily on expert testimony, the trial attorneys or opposing experts conduct a "tutorial" to help the jurors better understand the evidence. The tutorial presentation is considered a portion of the opening statement to the jury.

Issues

- Are trial attorneys capable of presenting a neutral, nonadversarial tutorial for the jury?

- Should the tutorial be conducted by a court-appointed expert rather than the trial attorneys or opposing experts?

- Should the tutorial experts be the same experts who will testify at trial?

Procedures

Jurors presented with unfamiliar terminology or complex concepts for the first time often find it difficult to digest this new information and apply it simultaneously to their evaluation of expert testimony. Juror tutorials introduce new information and new concepts to the jurors, providing them with a sufficient understanding of basic materials to evaluate the import of expert testimony at trial. The tutorial is conducted jointly by the parties as part of the opening statement.

To implement this technique, the judge and attorneys agree on an appropriate format for the juror tutorial. The tutorial should provide a basic explanation of unfamiliar terms and concepts. In addition, the judge and attorneys can make a joint presentation of undisputed issues that would otherwise be offered as expert testimony by both parties.

The juror tutorial should be relatively informal, with material presented as in a classroom lecture. Although the tutorial is made a part of the trial record, the judge should instruct the jury that the material presented in the tutorial is merely background information, not evidence. If expert witnesses conduct the tutorial, they need not be sworn. The format for the tutorial should provide an opportunity for the jurors to ask clarifying questions about the material presented.

One of the earliest known uses of this technique was by federal appellate judge Pamela Ann Rymer (9th Cir.), when she was a U.S. District Court judge. In a 1984 computer software patent case, she found herself unfamiliar with the terms and references of the software's application to the computer. She asked the parties to convene a tutorial for herself, the deputy clerk, the court reporter, and the law clerk. The one-day tutorial, conducted on a Saturday, was informal and off the record with ample opportunities for questions. She found it so useful that she asked that it be repeated in the opening statements to the jury. The experts agreed on which topics each would cover. The presentation stopped short of the claims in the case but did end with an explanation of how the computer program, which was the subject of the case, operated.

ADVANTAGES

1.   An early explanation of basic terms and concepts enables jurors to better understand the evidence when it is presented at trial.

2.   All expert witnesses can present their testimony in a more direct and focused fashion, without having to explain basic terms and concepts as part of their testimony.

3.   Background information is presented to the jury only once, at the beginning of the trial, rather than several times over the course of the trial.

4.   The tutorial presentation is less formal and adversarial than in-court testimony, which enhances juror comprehension.

DISADVANTAGES

1.   Juror tutorials require additional time and effort by the judge to preview the presentation and limit it to uncontested matters.

2.   Preparation of a juror tutorial can require a significant time commitment by the judge and trial attorneys.

3.   Tutorial presenters may find it difficult to constrain themselves to the agreed-upon material, prompting interruptions and objections that destroy the advantage of a nonadversarial presentation.

REFERENCE AND STUDY

Interview with Hon. Pamela Ann Rymer (U.S.C.A. 9th Cir.) (notes on file with the National Center for State Courts, Williamsburg, Virginia).

§ IV-6   MODIFYING DAILY SCHEDULES

TECHNIQUE

In longer trials, the judge schedules trial testimony for certain hours of the day or days of the week and requires juror attendance at the courthouse only during those times.

ISSUES

- What effect does this modification have on the length of the trial proceedings?

- What effect does this modification have on the ability of the judge to respond to trial scheduling matters in a spontaneous or flexible manner?

PROCEDURES

During the pretrial conference, the judge sets out the daily trial schedule with established periods during which the jury need not be present. The schedule includes specific periods during the day, either before jurors report for service or after they are excused for the day, in which the court hears trial motions. To enable the court to respond to trial motions without disruption to the daily schedule, the court may require the trial attorneys to file all trial motions in writing. The court then rules on motions the following day or the day following receipt of the respondent's written reply.

ADVANTAGES

1. A modified daily trial schedule reduces the amount of jury "downtime" during regular trial periods.

2. An established trial schedule provides jurors with advance notice about the days and times they will have available for conducting personal affairs (e.g., doctors appointments).

3. This technique increases the efficiency of trial procedures by requiring the judge and attorneys to anticipate and correctly estimate time needed to conduct matters that do not involve the jury.

4. This technique also provides opportunities for the judge and attorneys to attend to personal and business matters that do not involve the case at trial.

DISADVANTAGES

1. Modified trial schedules may lengthen the number of days for some trials.

2. This technique reduces (somewhat) the flexibility of the judge to respond immediately to trial motions.

3. The schedules of the judge and attorneys may become out of sync with those of their colleagues.

§ IV-7   Juror Notebooks

Technique

In lengthy trials and trials of complex cases, jurors are supplied with three-ring notebooks for keeping documents and other information about the case.

Issues

- In which types of cases are juror notebooks appropriate?

- Will the jurors' use of the notebooks distract them during the trial?

- What kinds of information should the notebooks contain?

- Who prepares the notebooks? Who pays for the costs associated with juror notebooks?

- What kind of supervision should the judge provide over the preparation and use of the notebooks?

- What exhibits should be copied for inclusion in the notebooks? Should only the relevant portion of an exhibit be used? Should it be highlighted?

- When important exhibits are admitted during the trial, should copies be added to those the jurors already have?

Procedures

At a pretrial conference in a complex case or in a case in which a protracted trial is anticipated, the judge and trial attorneys jointly decide whether juror notebooks would assist the jurors. If notebooks are favored, the judge and attorneys identify the categories of documents and information to be included and assign responsibility for preparing the notebooks. Regardless of who assembles the notebooks, the judge closely supervises their preparation to ensure that they help jurors without overloading them with excessive quantities of material. Before the notebooks are copied, the attorneys stipulate to the contents of the final version or, absent such a stipulation, the judge approves the notebooks.

Suggestions for notebook contents include:

- paper for taking notes (see § V-6, "Juror Notetaking");

- preliminary jury instructions (see § V-9, "Preinstructing the Jury");

- a short statement of parties' claims and defenses;

- a list of witnesses by name, including identifying information and phonetic spellings when helpful;

- photographs of key witnesses;

- copies of key exhibits;

- a glossary of technical terms;

- a seating chart for the courtroom that identifies all trial participants (see § IV-11, "Place Cards or Seating Charts"); and

- final jury instructions (see § VI-5, "Written or Recorded Instructions for Jurors").

Additional documents that are distributed to the jurors during the trial should be notebook-ready. Jurors should be given an opportunity to insert them in their notebooks at the time they are distributed to avoid noise and distraction. Preliminary jury instructions should be removed, discarded, and replaced by the final jury instructions before the latter are read to the jury by the court.

During overnight recesses in the trial, a court employee secures the notebooks and returns them to jurors when they reconvene. Jurors are permitted to take their notebooks with them to the jury room during recesses and for deliberations.

ADVANTAGES

1. Juror notebooks assist jurors to organize, understand, and recall large amounts of information during lengthy and complex trials.

2. Multipurpose juror notebooks reduce juror stress in lengthy trials.

DISADVANTAGE

Preparation of juror notebooks requires additional time, effort, and expense.

AUTHORITY

Ariz. R. Civ. Proc. Rule 47(g) (1996) (authorizing the use of juror notebooks and describing their contents).

REFERENCES

American Bar Association, Special Committee on Jury Comprehension, *Jury Comprehension in Complex Cases* 34-37 (1989).

John V. Singleton, "Jury Trial: History and Preservation," 32 *Trial Law. Guide* 273, 279 (1988).

§ IV-8   BIFURCATION, TRIFURCATION, OR POLYFURCATION OF TRIAL PROCEDURES

TECHNIQUE

Trials are bifurcated, trifurcated, or polyfurcated to permit jurors to decide issues from a single cause of action in logical segments (e.g., liability, compensatory damages, punitive damages) without becoming distracted or confused by issues relevant to other segments.

ISSUES

- What is the difference between bifurcation and severance?

- What kinds of issues lend themselves to bifurcation?

- Does bifurcation favor defendants and disadvantage plaintiffs or vice versa?

- Does bifurcation violate due process rights or the Seventh Amendment right to trial by jury?

- How should alternate jurors be utilized in bifurcation trials?

PROCEDURES

Bifurcation under Federal Rules of Civil Procedure Rule 42(b) and corresponding state rules differs from severance of an action under FRCP Rule 21. Bifurcation results in separate proceedings on different issues within one cause of action. Severance, on the other hand, divides claims into more than one cause of action, such as the severance of an unrelated counterclaim from the original lawsuit.

The distinction has a number of practical consequences relating to appealability of a result in the first proceeding. The judgment in the first segment of a bifurcated trial or proceeding generally is not appealable unless it resolves the cause of action as a whole (e.g., a finding of no liability in a liability/damages bifurcation). At the conclusion of the case, the trial court's decisions relating to bifurcation are appealable, but will be set aside only upon a clear showing of abuse of discretion. In cases involving severance, however, the results of each trial are separate because each constitutes its own cause of action.

Similar differences exist with respect to the jurisdiction of the court and the court's ability to transfer all or part of an action. The trial court retains its jurisdiction over all segments of the bifurcated trial. When the court severs a single cause of action into separate actions, however, the trial court must have an independent jurisdictional basis for each of the severed actions. In a bifurcated action, one of the bifurcated parts cannot be transferred to another court without transferring the whole cause of action. In contrast, severed causes of action may be transferred to other courts.

One common method of bifurcating trials is to separate distinct elements of the cause of action. In a negligence action, for example, counsel first present evidence of liability and the jury renders its verdict on that element alone. If liability is found, counsel then present their evidence regarding damages and the jury renders a verdict on that element. If the same jury is used for both segments of the trial, alternate jurors should be permitted to observe, but not participate in, the deliberations of the first segment. See § VI-7, "Permitting Alternates to Observe Deliberations."

Because a determination of damages is often the more complicated and contentious segment of the trial, many courts have experimented with "reverse bifurcation," especially in mass tort cases. Conducting the damages segment of the trial first often provides opportunities for settlement on liability issues. Another common method of bifurcation is to separate the presentation of evidence, holding two or more trials on different issues. This procedure is most commonly employed when issues are factually distinct and/or dispositive of the balance of the case (e.g., bifurcation of the affirmative defense of statute of limitations or lack of insurance coverage).

The trial court also has the discretion to conduct each of the bifurcated trials before a different jury, although its ability to do so is limited by the Seventh Amendment's guarantee of a right to a jury trial. Although some overlap in evidence is permitted, a trial court cannot bifurcate an action in such a way that two juries consider essentially the same factual issues. The legal and factual issues can also be bifurcated to conduct separate bench trials on the nonjury issues, unless by doing so the court infringes on the jury's ability to determine the factual issues of the case. Examples of bifurcated bench trials include interpretations of an insurance contract, equitable recession, and defenses based upon statute of limitation.

Although motions for bifurcation usually are brought prior to the pretrial conference, they can be brought at any time prior to trial. However, an untimely motion for bifurcation may result in the party waiving its right to seek bifurcation. If the objective is to save possible expensive or intrusive discovery, the motion should be brought as early as possible. The movant must show that there is little significant overlap in the issues or risk of denial of bifurcation either on Seventh Amendment grounds or for failure to promote judicial economy. The movant also must demonstrate that bifurcation will result in a fair and impartial trial. Many courts require a "compelling" justification for bifurcation.

ADVANTAGES

1. Bifurcation may prevent jury confusion of issues, particularly when allegations of "bad faith" have been joined to insurance coverage claims. For example, bifurcation can avoid prejudice from the admission of evidence of settlement offers by the insurer or settlement demands by the plaintiff that may be construed as admissions of liability or concessions or caps on damages.

2. Bifurcation may permit both parties to postpone and possibly avoid costly or intrusive discovery.

3. Bifurcation may avoid the time and expense of litigating certain issues altogether. At least one empirical study has shown that separating the liability and damages segments of trials decreases the length of the trial proceedings by 20 percent.

4. The time required for jury service may be shortened substantially, thereby reducing the adverse effects of jury service. In some instances, jurors may find bifurcated service less onerous, because their time away from their personal and occupational obligations is broken into segments.

DISADVANTAGES

1. Issues that initially appear separate and distinct may ultimately prove so factually interrelated that bifurcation results in loss of time, retrial of many of the same issues tried in the first proceeding, and a risk of inconsistent verdicts.

2. Bifurcation may require counsel and their witnesses to gear up for trial twice, thereby increasing costs.

3. Lay and expert witnesses may be substantially inconvenienced by having to appear on two or more separate occasions in two or more proceedings.

4. Inconvenience to jurors may increase by having them return to hear successive segments of the proceeding. Depending on the length of de-

lay between trial segments and the complexity of the case, it may be necessary to refresh the jurors' recollections about some aspects of the earlier segments.

5. The evidence presented in different segments of bifurcated trials can dramatically favor one side or the other—in some cases predetermining the ultimate outcome of the trial in ways that would not occur if all the elements of the action were tried in the same proceeding.

AUTHORITY

Federal Rule of Civil Procedure 42(b) (1996) (authorizing severance of claims in jury trials).

In re Benedictin Litigation, Hoffman v. Merrel Dow Pharmaceuticals, Inc., 857 F.2d 290 (6th Cir. 1988), *cert. denied* 488 U.S. 1006 (holding that trifurcation was neither an abuse of discretion nor a violation of due process or Seventh Amendment rights to a jury trial).

REFERENCES

Albert P. Bedecarré, "Rule 42(b) Bifurcation at an Extreme: Polyfurcation of Liability Issues in Environmental Tort Cases," 17 *B. C. Envtl. Aff. L. Rev.* 123 (1989) (arguing that excessive separation of issues within claims risks undue prejudice to parties without substantial savings in court efficiency).

Susan E. Bitanta, Comment, "Bifurcation of Liability and Damages in Rule 23(b)(3) Class Actions: History, Policy, Problems, and a Solution," 36 *Sw. L. J.* 743 (1982) (favoring bifurcation procedures as a practical tool for evaluating class certification status for class action suits).

Douglas L. Colbert, "The Bifurcation of Civil Rights Defendants: Undermining Monell in Police Brutality Cases," 44 *Hastings L. J.* 499 (1993) (arguing that bifurcation is prejudicial in Section 1983 cases insofar that it does not afford the plaintiffs an opportunity to overcome the jury's pro-police bias).

Commercial and Federal Litigation Section of the New York State Bar Association, "The Mini-Trial: Bifurcation as an Efficient Device to Promote the Resolution of Civil Cases," 53 *Alb. L. Rev.* 19 (1988) (examining bifurcation as an intermediate device for resolving disputes for which summary judgment is inappropriate).

Philip Corboy, "Will Split Trial Solve Court Delay? A Negative Response," 52 *Ill. B. J.* 1004 (1964) (an early article arguing against bifurcated trials).

Federal Judicial Center, *Manual on Complex Litigation, Third* 119-20 § 21.632 (1995) (discussing the advantages and disadvantages of severance in complex litigation).

Jennifer M. Granholm & William J. Richards, "Bifurcated Justice: How Trial-Splitting Devices Defeat the Jury's Role," 26 *U. Tol. L. Rev.* 505 (1995) (arguing that bifurcation withholds from jurors evidence necessary to render a fair verdict, denigrating the role of the jury and the decision-making abilities of jurors).

Verla S. Neslund, Comment, "The Bifurcated Trial: Is it Used More Than it is Useful?" 31 *Emory L. J.* 441 (1982) (examining mandatory bifurcation for criminal trials in which an insanity defense is raised).

Judith W. Pendell, "Enhancing Juror Effectiveness: An Insurer's Perspective," 52 *Law & Contemp. Probs.* 311, 315-17 (1989) (examining empirical support for claims that jurors in unitary trials are more likely to interpret causation evidence in favor of plaintiffs than jurors in bifurcated trials).

Charles A. Wright & Arthur R. Miller, *Federal Practice and Procedure* §§ 2388-2390 (West 1995 and Supp. 1996) (describing the application of FRCP Rule 42(b) in federal courts).

STUDY

Hans Zeisel & Thomas Callahan, "Split Trials and Time Savings: A Statistical Analysis," 76 *Harv. L. Rev.* 1606 (1963) (concluding that bifurcation of personal injury cases into separable liability and damages issues saves approximately 20 percent of trial time).

§ IV-9   COMPUTER SIMULATIONS

TECHNIQUE

Counsel present evidence to the jury in the form of a computer-generated simulation (sometimes called "animations" or "reconstructions") for illustrative or substantive purposes.

ISSUES

- Does the simulation fairly depict that which it purports to depict?

- If it portrays a scientific theory, is that theory admissible under governing law? Has it been accurately incorporated into a reliable mathematical model (and thus into reliable simulation)?

- How complete are the underlying data that are incorporated into the simulation?

- How much of the simulation is based on assumptions of fact? Are they reasonable? Is the formula valid? Has it been applied accurately?

- Is the simulation based on hearsay? If so, is the hearsay admissible? Or may an expert rely upon it in any event (e.g., Fed. R. Evid. 703)?

- Were the data input accurately? How simple or complex is the mathematical manipulation of data?

- Were the data collected routinely or for litigation? Are they fairly presented?

- Have they been unfairly "massaged"?

- Was the data processing done routinely or for litigation? Is the program sold commercially? If any programming was done, is it error-free?

- Is the simulation independently verifiable?

- Is the computer simulation unfairly prejudicial under the circumstances?

- Should the simulation go back to the jury room? Can it be furnished in a format that the jurors can use and not alter?

PROCEDURES

When the trial attorneys plan to introduce a computer simulation as evidence, they disclose this plan to opposing parties prior to trial to permit adequate review without delaying the trial. Computer simulations must be disclosed under Federal Rule of Civil Procedure 26(a)(2)(B) and many corresponding state rules when offered in conjunction with an expert. They are an appropriate subject for discovery and for pretrial orders of the court. A simulation should not, in any event, be played for the jury before the opposing party has had an opportunity to review it.

A monitor or monitors of sufficient size should be provided to permit the jury, court, and counsel to see the simulation simultaneously when played at trial. At the court's discretion, a simulation may be used in opening or closing arguments.

Issues of admissibility of computer simulations should be addressed either prior to trial or in a manner that does not unduly delay the proceedings before the jury. If the court rules that any part, but not all, of the simulation is admissible, the proponent has the responsibility of editing it to excise the inadmissible matter. If the excludable matter is audio, the volume may simply be turned off at the appropriate time.

The simulation can be stopped on a single image at any point during the presentation to facilitate viewing or explanatory testimony. In addition, the court may require testimony from the stand either before, during, or after the simulation is shown. Concerns about the potential of a simulation to confuse or mislead can be addressed in a limiting instruction identifying the purpose for which the evidence is being offered (e.g., to illustrate a litigation theory); the principal underlying assumptions (e.g., that it is based on one party's version of events); and any salient differences between the exhibit and the facts in issue (e.g., the portrayal is not to scale or omits certain variables).

ADVANTAGES

1. Simulations encapsulate information efficiently, effectively, and understandably.

2. Simulations replace or supplement lengthy verbal descriptions with something a lay person can easily comprehend.

3. Simulations save trial time and help eliminate confusion about concepts that are difficult to observe or understand.

DISADVANTAGE

Simulations simplify reality—mathematical models cannot take account of everything—creating a risk of unfair distortion.

AUTHORITY

The admissibility of computer-generated simulations is generally a function of applicable evidence law.

REFERENCES

American Bar Association & Engineering Animation, Inc., "Computer Animation in the Courtroom: A Primer," (1996) (CD-ROM tutorial developed by the Lawyers Conference of the Judicial Administrative Division).

Federal Judicial Center, *Manual for Complex Litigation, Third* 397-98 (1995) (describing computer animation, its uses in complex litigation, and its advantages and disadvantages).

Jordan S. Gruber, *Electronic Evidence* (1995) (treatise on the use of electronic evidence).

Gregory P. Joseph, *Modern Visual Evidence* (1984 and Supp. 1996) (comprehensive treatise on the preparation and presentation of demonstrative evidence in trial proceedings).

§ IV-10 Deposition Summaries

Technique

The trial judge encourages or requires the parties to prepare summaries of pretrial depositions that are read to the jury as a narrative rather than in the question-and-answer format.

Issues

- Should deposition summaries be mandatory for depositions over three hours (or 150 pages) or some other arbitrary limit?

- Do deposition summaries shift work from the court to the parties?

- Do deposition summaries save time or do they create more work for the parties with little chance for a more efficient and effective presentation to the jury?

- Is anything more boring for a juror than to listen to a lawyer and his legal assistant read an unedited 400-page deposition?

- Is it possible for jurors to assimilate information that is presented in the least lively manner?

- Should the civil justice system be more interested in the rights of the parties to try the case in the manner they select or should jury comprehension be the overriding goal?

Procedures

Trial counsel jointly prepare the deposition summary in a manner similar to the regular designation of deposition testimony. The party proffering the testimony first prepares the summary and the opposing party then adds a narrative to the summary based upon that party's perspective of the deposition. If either side believes a summary is wrong or misleading, objections are resolved by the judge. Copies are provided to the jurors before the summaries are read. The copies are retrieved immediately after the summary is read.

Proposed, but not yet adopted, Arizona rules recommend that no summary proposed by a side be more than four pages in length and no addition to the summary be more than four pages in length. Other courts require summaries but do not specify page limits.

The practice of requiring litigants to prepare deposition summaries is not widely accepted by U.S. courts. Procedural rules in several jurisdictions make note of discretionary use of deposition summaries, although this practice still represents a small minority position.

ADVANTAGES

1. Deposition summaries save the jury and the court time both during trial proceedings and motions hearings.

2. Deposition summaries aid juror comprehension of "witness" testimony.

3. The use of deposition summaries avoids the tedium associated with reading full depositions at trial—a practice that can drive the most committed jurors to distraction.

4. Significant trial time can be saved by limiting the deposition summaries to a precise page limit.

DISADVANTAGES

1. Parties can abuse deposition summaries, especially those of particularly knowledgeable witnesses, by using them as mini-opening statements or even closing arguments.

2. This practice shifts work from the courts to litigants by requiring them to spend substantial time summarizing depositions.

3. Disputes over the contents of deposition summaries are sometimes more time-consuming and difficult to resolve than ruling on the admissibility of deposition questions and answers.

AUTHORITY

Fed. R. Evid. 1006 (1996) (authorizing the use of deposition summaries).

Rules 29th Jud. Dist. Ct. (St. Charles, La.) Rule VII(B) (1996) (requiring the parties to prepare summaries of all depositions for submission before the pretrial conference).

Rules U.S. Dist. Ct. (E.D. Va.) Local Rule 21(G) (1996) (authorizing deposition summaries in bench trials).

Rules U.S. Bankr. Ct. (E.D. Va.) Local Rule 406(F) (1996) (authorizing deposition summaries in bench trials).

REFERENCES

Arizona Supreme Court Committee on More Effective Use of Juries, *Jurors: The Power of 12: Report of the Arizona Supreme Court Committee on More Effective Use of Juries* 88-90 (1994) (recommending an amendment to the Arizona Rules of Civil Procedure authorizing use of deposition summaries at trial).

William W Schwarzer, Nancy E. Weiss & Alan Hirsch, "Judicial Federalism in Action: Coordination of Litigation in State and Federal Courts," 78 *Va. L. Rev.* 1689, 1730 n.177 (1992).

STUDY

American Bar Association, Special Committee on Jury Comprehension, *Jury Comprehension in Complex Cases* 37-38 (1989) (reporting unanimous negative juror responses to depositions being read at trial).

§ IV-11 PLACE CARDS OR SEATING CHARTS

TECHNIQUE

In short cases or cases with multiple attorneys or parties, the court distributes place cards or name tags to assist jurors in identifying pertinent individuals. Seating charts, identifying the parties, the trial attorneys, and other relevant individuals, are given to jurors prior to trial.

ISSUES

- Who is responsible for making place cards and seating charts?

- For what types of cases are these devices advisable?

PROCEDURES

In short trials or trials in which there are multiple attorneys, parties, and witnesses, place cards or name tags help jurors identify and distinguish the various individuals appearing in the courtroom. Before trial, counsel furnish the court with the names of all parties, witnesses, and attorneys who will participate in the trial. This technique should not be used for criminal trials in which the identification of the defendant is a disputed issue. A seating chart may be placed in the juror notebooks prior to trial. See § IV-7, "Juror Notebooks."

Court staff prepare the place cards or name tags. Existing computer software for this purpose is available for easy printing on heavy bond or light cardboard paper. When using such software, however, court staff should use caution with the size and style of lettering. Some software packages tailor the font size and style to the length of the name. Thus, long names appear very small and short names very large.

ADVANTAGE

Place cards or name tags help jurors recognize and distinguish parties, lawyers, and witnesses.

DISADVANTAGE

Place cards or name tags will prejudice criminal defendants for cases in which identification is a contested issue at trial.

Chapter V

Trial Procedures

CONTRIBUTORS AND REVIEWERS

Hon. James R. Carrigan
U.S. District Court
Denver, Colorado

Cynthia R. Cohen, Ph.D.
Verdict Success
Manhattan Beach, California

Hon. B. Michael Dann
Superior Court of Arizona
Phoenix, Arizona

Prof. Shari Diamond
American Bar Foundation
Chicago, Illinois

Janice Fernette, J.D.
National Center for State Courts
Williamsburg, Virginia

Nathanial Fick, Esq.
Fick & Petty
Towson, Maryland

David B. Graeven
Trial Behavior Consulting, Inc.
San Francisco, California

Paula L. Hannaford, J.D., M.P.P.
National Center for State Courts
Williamsburg, Virginia

Amy B. Jackson, Esq.
Venable, Baetjer, Howard & Civiletti
Washington, D.C.

Robert E. Kehoe, Jr., Esq.
Law Offices of Robert E. Kehoe, Jr.
Chicago, Illinois

Prof. Joe Kimble
Thomas M. Cooley Law School
Lansing, Michigan

John McShane, Esq.
Bowman & Brooke
Minneapolis, Minnesota

Steven O. Rosen, Esq.
Miller, Nash, Wiener,
Hager & Carlson
Portland, Oregon

Vicki R. Slater, Esq.
Allred & Donaldson
Jackson, Mississippi

§ V-1   Videotaped Trials for Absent Jurors

Technique

During lengthy trials in which there is high risk of losing jurors because of illness or emergencies, the trial proceedings are videotaped and the judge requires jurors who are absent to view the segments of the trial that they missed.

Issues

- Does juror viewing of the videotape take place on an honor system? Or should court staff act as proctors?

- At what point should jurors view the trial proceedings that they missed? As soon as they return? At the end of trial?

- Can jurors keep copies of tapes?

- What is the effect of viewing testimony or evidence out of the sequence in which it was presented at trial?

- What is the effect of viewing video testimony versus live testimony?

Procedures

Lengthy trials (e.g., those anticipated to last several weeks or more) often require the court to impanel several alternates on the jury to replace jurors that may be excused because of illness or personal emergencies. Rather than dismissing jurors who will be absent only temporarily, the court can require jurors to view a videotape of the trial proceedings. This system eliminates the need for multiple alternates and conserves court resources.

The court purchases or rents video equipment and hires or trains personnel to operate the equipment during trial. Jurisdictions that prohibit cameras in the courtroom may need to obtain consent to implement this technique. During the trial, the judge sets aside a specific time each week for jurors to watch the trial proceedings that they missed. These time periods can include those times established for motion arguments and other trial matters for which jurors would not otherwise be present. See also § IV-6, "Modifying Daily Schedules."

To ensure that jurors actually watch the videotape, the judge assigns court personnel to monitor the jurors during the viewing. Court personnel also have responsibility for editing out or fast-forwarding through sidebar conferences, references to inadmissible evidence, and other aspects of the trial proceedings that the jury was not intended to see or consider.

ADVANTAGES

1. Videotaping the trial proceedings eliminates the need for the court to suspend trial proceedings to accommodate juror absences due to temporary illness or emergencies.

2. Videotaping the trial proceedings reduces the need for large numbers of alternates in the jury pool.

DISADVANTAGES

1. The costs of purchasing or renting video equipment and hiring or training personnel to operate the equipment may exceed the costs of keeping extra alternates on the jury panel.

2. Ensuring that jurors actually watch the videotapes requires active monitoring by court personnel.

§ V-2   JURORS VIEW VIDEOTAPED TRIAL RATHER THAN LIVE TESTIMONY

TECHNIQUE

The entire trial is videotaped outside of the jury's presence. The court then edits the videotape to eliminate sidebar conferences, references to inadmissible evidence, and trial motions. An impaneled jury then views the edited videotape and renders its verdict.

ISSUES

- Who is responsible for setting up video equipment and taping trial proceedings? Can these costs be passed directly to the parties?

- What is the effect of viewing video testimony versus live testimony?

- What effect does placing jurors in a completely passive role (as viewers) have on verdicts? on juror satisfaction with jury service?

- Does the production quality of the videotape affect jurors' perception of the trial?

PROCEDURES

At the pretrial conference, the judge assigns a "taping deadline," rather than a trial date, for the case. The trial attorneys videotape the witness testimony in a deposition format, raising objections to questions during direct or cross-examination as if at trial. After an attorney makes an objection, the witness answers the question.

The judge later rules on the objection and edits the videotape accordingly. Therefore, if the judge sustains an objection, the judge deletes the examining counsel's question, the opposing counsel's objection, and the witness's answer. If the judge overrules the objection, the judge deletes only the objection.

The trial attorneys provide two copies of the videotape to the court—one reserved as a master videotape and one to be edited for viewing by the jury. They are permitted to file written briefs to support or oppose specific evidentiary objections.

The court establishes a "dual docket" system, one for live and one for videotaped trials. After the videotape editing is complete, the jury is impaneled using conventional selection methods. The jury views the edited videotape trial and renders its verdict accordingly.

This technique was first used in Ohio and Pennsylvania in the early 1970s. Although it was evaluated favorably at that time, few courts implemented this technique. Both jurisdictions appear to have abandoned the technique over time, perhaps because of increased emphasis on "active" jury techniques.

ADVANTAGES

1. The dual docket system reduces the need to preassign trial dates.

2. Prerecorded video trials reduce the likelihood of last-minute trial postponements or delays because witnesses are tardy or unavailable. They also alleviate scheduling problems, especially for expert witnesses.

3. Removing the uncertainty inherent with live witness testimony makes the parties better able to evaluate their cases for settlement purposes.

4. Inadmissible evidence and testimony are more easily and more thoroughly excluded from the videotape than from the live trial, thus eliminating the need for admonitions to the jury to disregard inadmissible evidence and the corresponding risk that the jury will not follow the judge's limiting instructions.

5. Audio and visual controls on the video monitor can be adjusted to ensure that all jurors can hear and see evidence and testimony clearly.

DISADVANTAGES

1. Taping and editing videotaped trials may be excessively expensive for parties, particularly to achieve the level of production quality needed to hold jurors' attention. For example, many jurors may be accustomed to high-quality video technology through cable and commercial television.

2. Videotaped trials also envision a very passive (viewer-only) role for jurors that may increase juror dissatisfaction and prevent opportunities for juror education.

3. Opportunities for more interactive jury innovations will be difficult to use (e.g., juror questions to witnesses).

AUTHORITY

Ohio R. Civ. Proc. Rule 40 (1996) (authorizing videotaped trials).

Ohio R. Superintendence for Ct. of Com. Pls. Rule 10(E) (1996) (describing the citation format to be used when referencing videotaped trials).

Ohio R. Superintendence for Ct. of Com. Pls. Rule 12(B) (1996) (authorizing videotaped trials and establishing procedures for conducting such trials).

REFERENCES

Marshall J. Hartman, "Second Thoughts on Videotaped Trials," 61 *Judicature* 256 (1978) (examining potential problems arising from the use of videotaped trials).

James L. McCrystal, "Videotaped Trials: A Primer," 61 *Judicature* 250 (1978) (describing the Ohio system).

Thomas J. Murray, Jr., "Videotaped Depositions: The Ohio Experience," 61 *Judicature* 258 (1978) (describing modifications to the Ohio rules of superintendence to permit videotaped trials).

Fredric N. Tulsky, "Pa. Courts May Tell Jurors: 'Let's Go to the Videotape,'" *Nat'l L. J.* 36 (March 16, 1987) (reporting on the Pennsylvania implementation of videotaped trials).

STUDY

James L. McCrystal & Ann B. Maschari, "In Video Veritas: The Jury No Longer Need Disregard the Prerecorded Taped Trial," 22 *Judges' J.* 40 (Summer 1983) (empirical study of the cost savings associated with videotaped trials).

§ V-3   Projection of Real Time Transcription

Technique

The use of computer-aided transcription permits hearing-impaired jurors, attorneys, and parties to view witness testimony and statements of counsel and the court displayed in real time on video monitors.

Issues

- Is the "computer-integrated courtroom" or "total access courtroom" required under the Americans with Disabilities Act (ADA)? See also § II-6, "ADA Compliance."

- Should judges, attorneys, and all jurors be supplied with monitors?

- Will the system include real time video projection of the witness with a captioned translation or only lines of printed testimony?

- Can parties object to the transcriptions they consider to be incorrect?

- Would jurors have access to the computer transcript in deliberations? Would computer-aided memory be given equal weight in deliberations? What instructions would then be required?

- Will the captioning be available for videotaped depositions or other videotaped evidence?

Procedures

To implement this technique, the court must have access to the proper technology and be staffed with court reporters who are trained and certified on real time transcription. Existing technology makes its possible to provide jurors either with "closed-caption" images of witness, counsel, and court statements or with printed lines of text only.   The technology operates by translating shorthand symbols that are typed by the court reporter. Consequently, a single symbol may be interpreted as several different words. If the technology does not recognize a symbol, it will not translate it at all but will print an unreadable series of letters.

Providing video monitors for the judge and attorneys gives them the opportunity to correct or insert the proper terms during the course of the trial. Prior to the trial, the attorneys can also provide the court reporter with any terminology specific to the case, such as names, dates, medical or specialized terminology, or unusual terms. These terms are then pre-entered in the computer's internal dictionary to enhance the accuracy of the transcription.

The real time transcription equipment simultaneously projects the testimony on video screens and creates a hard-copy, written transcript as the official trial record, subject to correction for misinterpreted transcription symbols. If jurors are given access to the transcript during deliberations, only the corrected transcript is made available to them.

ADVANTAGES

1. Computer-aided transcription permits hearing-impaired individuals to follow court proceedings, thus moving the court closer to the accessible justice system mandated by the ADA.

2. Real time transcription simultaneously creates the written transcript, permitting the judge and trial attorneys to refer to prior testimony when handling objections or motions, preparing for cross-examination or closing arguments, and confronting witnesses with earlier testimony or prior inconsistent statements.

3. Real time transcription may facilitate media coverage of a trial in jurisdictions where cameras are prohibited.

DISADVANTAGES

1. Monitors distract the jury's attention from the witness stand.

2. The purchase and installation costs associated with this technology can be prohibitively expensive.

3. Real time transcription requires a higher degree of precision by court reporters.

4. There is a four- to five-word delay from speech to the computer screen.

5. Jurors who rely exclusively on the real time transcription (e.g., hearing-impaired jurors) may not fully understand the translated statements because of misinterpreted transcription symbols.

6. When only printed-text transcriptions are available, jurors reading testimony on computer monitors will miss the opportunity to study the witness's demeanor.

REFERENCES

American Bar Association and National Judicial College, *Court Related Needs of the Elderly and Persons with Disabilities* 56-57 (1991).

Kristi Bleyer, Kathryn S. McCarty & Erica Wood, *Into the Jury Box: A Disability Accommodation Guide for State Courts* 33 (1994).

§ V-4 Dual Juries

Technique

The court impanels two (or more) juries for cases involving multiple parties, defendants, or claims arising out of the same cause of action. This technique reduces the number and complexity of issues that any one jury must decide while promoting judicial economy by presenting otherwise duplicative evidence in a single trial.

Issues

- What is the threshold number of defendants or criminal counts in a single case that would warrant dual juries?

- What kind of resources and facilities (e.g., jury deliberation rooms, courtroom space, etc.) must the court have available to accommodate multiple juries?

- What impact does excusing one jury and retaining another—for example, to hear evidence relevant to only one defendant or criminal count—have on the decision making of the excused jury?

- What happens if the juries render inconsistent verdicts?

- What kind of jury instructions, if any, correct for references by counsel to inadmissible evidence?

Procedures

For cases involving multiple defendants or multiple criminal counts, dual juries permit the presentation of otherwise duplicative testimony and evidence and reduce the complexity of questions to be asked of any one jury. In addition, using dual juries in multiple defendant criminal cases reduces the risk that a single jury will incorrectly consider evidence that is admissible against one defendant but inadmissible against another. The use of dual juries involves a number of logistical considerations. In particular, court facilities (e.g., separate jury deliberation rooms, courtroom jurybox) should be sufficiently large to accommodate the needs of two or more juries.

In practice, multiple juries are generally impaneled separately. Opening and closing statements are presented to the juries separately. Jury instructions for each jury are developed separately and do not make reference to facts or law presented only to the other jury. Juries deliberate separately and deliver separate verdicts.

In cases involving antagonistic defenses by multiple defendants, both juries hear the prosecution's case but hear the defendants' respective cases separately. When the dual jury is used in cases involving out-of-court statements by co-defendants, each jury is removed during introduction of the co-defendant's out-of-court statement against that co-defendant.

The major problem associated with these trials is a variation on the *Bruton* error problem—namely, preventing evidence that is admissible against one party, but inadmissible against another, from being presented accidentally to the wrong jury during the course of a joint trial. A secondary problem is an increased risk of inconsistent verdicts, although this risk is no greater in dual jury trials than in completely separate trials.

This technique is used only infrequently in criminal trials. There are no known cases in which it was used in a civil trial.

ADVANTAGES

1. Dual juries promote economy by reducing duplication of testimony and evidence.

2. Dual juries reduce the number and complexity of issues that any one jury is asked to decide.

3. Dual juries reduce the risk that a jury will incorrectly consider evidence or testimony introduced for another purpose (e.g., against a different defendant, relevant to a different criminal count, etc.).

4. Dual juries reduce the emotional burden for victims of crime who would have had to testify twice.

DISADVANTAGES

1. Dual juries require larger court facilities to accommodate the greater numbers of jurors.

2. Dual juries present multiple logistical problems, including ensuring that a jury hears only admissible evidence relevant to the claims or issues it is asked to decide.

AUTHORITY

United States v. Sidman, 470 F.2d 1158 (9th Cir. 1972) (holding that the impaneling of two juries in a two-defendant criminal case did not violate the defendants' constitutional, statutory, or procedural rights).

REFERENCES

James G. Apple, Paula L. Hannaford & G. Thomas Munsterman, *A Manual for Cooperation Between State and Federal Courts* (Federal Judicial Center, 1996) (discussing the logistical obstacles to joint state-federal trials in mass tort cases).

Alex A. Gaynes, "Two Juries/One Trial: Panacea of Judicial Economy or Personification of Murphy's Law," 5 *Am. J. Trial Advoc.* 283 (1981) (examining the problems that arise during the use of a dual jury in *U.S. v. Patrick and Thomas Hanigan*, CR-79-206-TUC-RMB [U.S. District Court, Phoenix, Ariz.]).

§ V-5   Juror Discussions of Evidence During the Trial

Technique

Jurors are instructed at the outset of the trial that they may discuss the evidence among themselves during the trial, but only in the jury room and only when all of them are present. They are cautioned that discussion is appropriate only as long as they keep open minds on all issues until they have heard all of the evidence, all instructions on the law, and all arguments of counsel.

Issues

- Will juror discussions contribute materially to juror comprehension or recall and improve the quality of deliberations and verdict?

- Will discussions of the evidence before hearing all of the evidence, legal instructions, and arguments encourage the jury to make premature judgments about specific aspects of the case?

- Should specific noncourtroom time be set aside to accommodate juror discussion?

Procedures

As part of the preliminary jury instructions, the judge instructs the jurors that they may discuss the evidence among themselves in the jury room during breaks in the trial. Jurors are cautioned, however, that they may not discuss the case with any other person until after the verdict and should avoid forming opinions about the outcome of the case until they have heard everything. The judge reminds the jurors from time to time, as necessary, of the importance of keeping an open mind on ultimate issues until jury deliberations begin.

If violations of the court's admonitions and conditions occur, the judge, with the aid of counsel, takes immediate corrective action regarding individual jurors or the jury as a whole.

Since December 1995, jurors in trials of civil cases in Arizona have been instructed that, subject to certain limitations, they may discuss the evidence in the jury room as the trial proceeds. Some other states are considering adopting this technique. With the exception of a handful of judges across the country using the procedure on an experimental basis, judges generally continue to instruct in accordance with the traditional admonition.

The State Justice Institute has awarded a research grant to the National Center for State Courts to examine the effectiveness of this technique. The results of that study are expected to be available in mid-1998.

ADVANTAGES

1. Juror discussions about the evidence can improve juror comprehension by permitting jurors to sift through and mentally organize the evidence into a coherent picture over the course of the trial.

2. Juror discussions about the evidence may improve juror recollection of evidence and testimony by emphasizing and clarifying important points during the course of the trial.

3. Juror discussions about the evidence may increase juror satisfaction by permitting an outlet for jurors to express their impressions of the case before retiring for deliberations.

4. Juror discussions about the evidence may promote greater cohesion among the jurors, reducing the amount of time needed for deliberations.

5. Jurors find it difficult to adhere to admonitions about not discussing evidence. Permission to engage in such discussions bridges the gap between the court's admonitions and jurors' activities.

DISADVANTAGES

1. Juror discussions of the evidence facilitate or encourage the formation or expression of premature judgments about an evidentiary issue or the result of the case.

2. An aggressive, overpowering juror might dominate discussions and have undue influence on the views of others.

3. Allowing juror discussions prior to deliberations may detract from the ideal of the juror as a neutral decision maker.

4. The quality of deliberations may decline as jurors become more familiar with each other's views.

5. Sanctioned and structured discussions might produce a narrower and more confined set of final deliberations.

6. Juror stress might increase because of the conflicts produced by prior discussions.

AUTHORITY

Ariz. Rule of Civil Procedure 39(f) (1996).

Winebrenner v. United States, 147 F.2d 322 (8th Cir. 1945) (holding that instructions permitting jurors to discuss evidence during trial constitute reversible error), *cert. denied*, 325 U.S. 863 (1945).

United States v. Klee, 494 F.2d 394 (9th Cir. 1974) (holding that an instruction permitting jurors to discuss evidence was not *per se* reversible error, but should be evaluated under the harmless error rule).

Meggs v. Fair, 621 F.2d 460 (1st Cir. 1980) (holding that there is no constitutional requirement that the jury be instructed not to discuss the evidence prior to final submission).

REFERENCES AND STUDIES

B. Michael Dann, "'Learning Lessons' and 'Speaking Rights': Creating Educated and Democratic Juries," 68 *Ind. L. J.* 1229, 1261-68 (1993) (discussing the legal support for this technique and proposing jury instructions).

Elizabeth F. Loftus & Douglas Leber, "Do Jurors Talk?" 22 *Trial* 59 (January 1986) (estimating that over 10 percent of jurors discuss the facts of the case with family, friends, or other jurors before the close of the case).

William W Schwarzer, "Reforming the Jury Trial," 1990 132 F.R.D. 575, 593-94 (1991) (discussing the practical and theoretical problems associated with a blanket prohibition on juror discussions about the evidence in complex litigation).

RELATED APPENDIX

Appendix 6: Arizona Rules of Civil Procedure Rule 39 (1996)

§ V-6 Juror Notetaking

Technique

Jurors are permitted to take notes for use during the trial and during deliberations.

Issues

- Should notetaking be limited to longer and more complex trials?

- Are juror notes destroyed after the trial? May jurors keep their notes?

- Are jurors permitted to take their notes home with them during the trial? If so, do the notes need to be kept secured to avoid theft or loss?

- How much time do jurors need to organize and review their notes during the trial?

- Who is responsible for providing jurors with writing materials?

Procedures

Notes serve as a useful memory aid for the evidence presented during trial as well as making it easier for jurors to follow and comprehend the issues and arguments in complex litigation. Studies of this widespread technique indicate that the jury is better informed about the evidence and the proper application of law during its deliberations. In most jurisdictions, the trial judge has discretion to permit jurors to take notes. However, if the jurisdiction does not, by statute or court rule, expressly permit jurors to take notes, all parties should consent to juror notetaking prior to trial.

If juror notetaking is permitted, the court furnishes notepads and writing utensils. The judge instructs the jury about court policy about whether jurors may retain their notes when court is in recess and whether jurors may discuss their notes during the trial. See § V-5 "Juror Discussions About Evidence During the Trial." The trial judge also instructs the jury about the purpose of juror notetaking. Such instructions can include the following:

- Juror notetaking is permitted, but not required;

- Notetaking should not distract the jury's attention from the trial proceedings;

- Jurors' notes are confidential;

- Notes are for the private use of jurors and will not become an official document or part of the trial record;

- Jurors should use their notes to refresh their memory of evidence presented at trial but notes should not be relied upon as definitive fact;

- Notes have no greater weight than memory;

- In deliberations, note-aided and nonaided memory are of equal significance; and

- Jurors should not be influenced by another juror's notes.

ADVANTAGES

1. Empirical research demonstrates that notetaking aids memory for both factual and conceptual items.

2. Notetaking encourages more active participation in jury deliberations, leading to a more thorough discussion by the jurors of the issues confronting them.

3. Juror notes help the jury reconstruct the presented evidence more efficiently during deliberations, which decreases deliberation time.

4. The process of notetaking keeps jurors alert and interested in the trial, increasing juror satisfaction with jury service.

5. Notetaking increases jurors' confidence that their deliberations correctly apply the jury instructions.

DISADVANTAGE

Jurors who take notes may participate more effectively in jury deliberations than those who do not.

AUTHORITY

Ariz. Rules of Civil Procedure Rule 39 (1996).

Ariz. Rules of Criminal Procedure Rule 18.6(d) (authorizing juror notetaking and describing relevant procedures and policies).

Reference

Larry Heuer & Steven Penrod, "Increasing Juror Participation in Trials Through Notetaking and Question Asking," 79 *Judicature* 256 (1996) (discussing prior research on notetaking, including limitations in methodology).

Studies

American Judicature Society, *Toward More Active Juries: Taking Notes and Asking Questions* (1991) (empirical study finding no evidence of prejudice to either party as a result of notetaking by jurors).

Larry Heuer & Steven Penrod, "Juror Notetaking and Question Asking During Trials," 18 *Law & Hum. Behav.* 121 (1994) (study results disproving many disadvantages associated with juror notetaking, but failing to verify its advantages).

David L. Rosehan, Sara L. Eisner & Robert J. Robinson, "Notetaking Can Aid Juror Recall," 18 *Law & Hum. Behav.* 53 (1994) (study results show that jurors who took notes had superior recall and were more continually attentive to trials compared to jurors who did not take notes).

Related Appendix

Appendix 6: Arizona Rules of Civil Procedure Rule 39 (1996)

§ V-7   Jurors' Questions to Witnesses

Technique

The judge permits the jurors to submit clarifying questions to witnesses through the trial judge. This technique is especially appropriate for situations in which the witness testimony is particularly complex or confusing for the jury. The decision of whether to permit juror questions to witnesses generally lies within the discretion of the judge, although the trial attorneys retain the right to object to the scope or content of any specific jury questions.

Issues

- Under what authority may jurors direct questions to witnesses?

- How should the judge screen for irrelevant or prejudicial juror questions?

- What significance will jurors attach to the fact that some of their questions are posed to witnesses and others are not?

- Does permitting jurors to ask questions of witnesses increase juror comprehension or reduce juror confusion concerning the substance of the witness's testimony?

- Does permitting jurors to ask questions of witnesses increase the length of the trial proceedings?

Procedures

At the beginning of the trial, the judge explains to the jurors that if witness testimony is confusing or complicated, they may submit clarifying questions through the judge. Following direct and cross-examination of a witness, the judge sends the jurors into the jury room for a limited period of time (usually five to ten minutes) with instructions to draft any questions for the witness that they believe will clarify the witness's testimony. Jurors need not sign or otherwise identify themselves as the authors of the questions.

The jury remains in the jury room while the judge and trial attorneys review the jurors' questions. While the jury is sequestered, the judge reads each juror question on the record and permits the trial attorneys to object to the scope or content of any question. The judge rules on the objection at that time.

The judge may instruct the witness that he or she should confine the answers to the scope of the question. The trial judge also may instruct the trial attorneys to refrain from renewing in the presence of the jury any objections that were previously overruled. After the judge has ruled on all of the objections and made any supplemental instructions to the witnesses or parties, the jury returns to the courtroom.

The judge explains to the jury that evidentiary rules may prohibit certain questions from being asked of the witnesses and that the jurors should attach no significance to the fact that some of their questions were asked of the witnesses while others were not. The judge then reads to the witness those questions that have survived any objections. After the witness answers the question, the trial attorneys may re-direct or re-cross-examine the witness.

Judges and attorneys who have used this technique report that the vast majority of juror questions are serious, concise, and relevant to the trial proceedings. There is no evidence that permitting jurors to pose questions to the witnesses has any significant effect on the deliberative role of the jury. Likewise, the fact that irrelevant or prejudicial questions are not posed to witnesses does not appear to affect the jurors' judgment in any significant manner.

ADVANTAGES

1. The nature of juror questions often alerts the trial judge and the attorneys when the jurors have misunderstood an important point of the evidence or testimony, thus giving them the opportunity to correct the misunderstanding with new witness testimony, closing arguments, or jury instructions on the issue.

2. Permitting jurors to ask questions increases the likelihood that the jury will understand the witness testimony and give it appropriate weight during deliberations.

3. Permitting jurors to ask questions helps keep them alert and engaged in the trial proceedings, thus increasing satisfaction with jury service.

DISADVANTAGES

1. Permitting jurors to ask questions may confuse their role as neutral fact finders, assuming instead the role of advocates.

2. Jurors may interpret the trial judge's failure to ask a question as an indication that the witness's testimony should be discounted.

3. Jurors may be offended or angry if all of their questions are not answered.

4. Permitting jurors to ask questions of witnesses adds to the length of the trial proceedings.

AUTHORITY

Michigan v. Heard, 200 N.W.2d 73 (1972) (holding that the questioning of witnesses by jurors and the method of submitting juror questions to the witnesses lie within the sound discretion of the trial judge).

Ratton v. Busby, 326 S.W.2d 889 (Ark. 1959) (holding that multiple questions by jurors to witnesses to obtain explanation about technical terminology used in expert testimony did not deprive the defendant of a fair trial).

Carter v. State, 234 N.E.2d 650 (Ind. 1968) (holding that a preliminary jury instruction that jurors were forbidden to ask questions of witnesses was reversible error).

REFERENCES

Larry Heuer & Steven Penrod, "Increasing Juror Participation in Trials Through Notetaking and Question Asking," 79 *Judicature* 256 (1996) (describing the empirical research and limitations in methodology).

Warren D. Wolfson, "An Experiment in Juror Interrogation of Witnesses," 1 *CBA Report* 12 (Feb. 1987) (a trial judge's assessment of permitting jurors to ask questions of witnesses).

STUDIES

American Judicature Society, *Toward More Active Juries: Taking Notes and Asking Questions* (1991) (finding no prejudicial effect from permitting jurors to ask questions of witnesses).

Larry Heuer & Steven Penrod, "Juror Notetaking and Question Asking During Trials," 18 *Law & Hum. Behav.* 121 (1994) (study findings support the hypothesis that jury questioning promotes juror understanding of facts and issues and that potential disadvantages of questions do not occur).

RELATED APPENDIX

§ V-8   Shadow Juries

Technique

Individuals, selected to closely represent the actual jurors, are recruited to watch a trial for the purpose of evaluating the trial process. These individuals receive the same information as actual jurors and give feedback to attorneys or consultants on a daily basis. Shadow jurors also are called surrogate juries and trial-monitoring response groups.

Issues

- Do shadow juries behave similarly to the actual jury?

- Do shadow juries give an unfair advantage to one side over the other?

- Does the fact that the shadow jurors know their decisions do not "count" distort their perceptions and opinions?

- Are shadow juries effective in short trials when there is limited time to change tactics or approaches?

- Should shadow jury predictions about verdicts be used to assess settlement offers?

Procedures

Shadow juries should be similar to the actual jury in terms of demographics and attitudes. These individuals can be found by a recruiting facility or by phone surveys. Shadow juries usually consist of six individuals. The shadow jurors are seated in the spectator section of the courtroom and attend the entire trial. Some consultants have the jurors sit apart and others seat them together. They are treated as if they were real jurors. For example, when jurors leave the courtroom, so do the shadow jurors. Similarly, shadow jurors are not allowed to discuss the case with anyone. Every night shadow jurors are contacted to review critical aspects of the case and give observations on the proceedings. On occasion, shadow juries are used to evaluate only the opening statements and the first key witnesses.

Usually shadow jurors are paid between $75 and $150 dollars a day.

This procedure is controversial and seldom used. Some trial consultants are opposed to using shadow juries because of their potentially deceptive nature.

Advantages

1. Shadow jury reactions are more realistic than mock juries because the shadow jurors hear live argument, witness testimony, and evidence.

2. Shadow juries provide attorneys with valuable feedback from the trial. They can identify confusing issues and misunderstandings, which the trial attorneys can then address the next day of trial. Attorneys can also see if their strategies are working as planned or if they need to make some technical changes.

3. Shadow juries can be used to evaluate whether to accept or to make a settlement offer.

4. Shadow juries can shed some light on the jurors' decision-making process.

Disadvantages

1. A shadow jury can have a disruptive effect on the real jurors. Discovering that a shadow jury is being used can have a negative effect on jurors' attitudes about the trial process. Jurors have been known to play games, trying to figure out who represents them on the shadow jury.

2. Information gained from shadow juries during trial has limited use. Often it is too late to change a strategy or create a new theme.

3. Although the shadow jury is similar to the real jury, the jurors have had different life experiences and process information differently, thus decreasing the reliability of their reactions.

4. Shadow juries may be prohibitively expensive, especially in longer trials.

5. Using shadow juries widens the gap between rich and poor litigants, giving the appearance that the justice system favors wealthy individuals.

References

Walter F. Abbott, *Surrogate Juries* (1990) (comprehensive overview of the use of shadow juries, the empirical research concerning their reliability for predicting verdicts, and the methodology for employing this technique).

Jeffrey T. Frederick, *The Psychology of the American Jury* 317-18 (1987) (describing the practical methodology involved in impaneling a shadow jury).

STUDY

Donald E. Vinson, "The Shadow Jury: An Experiment in Litigation Science," 68 *A.B.A. J.* 1242 (Oct. 1982) (in-depth description of the methodology and findings of an experiment in juror decision making using shadow juries).

§ V-9   PREINSTRUCTING THE JURY

TECHNIQUE

The judge preinstructs the jury in order to improve its comprehension of both the evidence and the issues that are presented during the course of the trial. The preinstructions are delivered verbally and in writing. They include the basic principles of law that will govern the trial as well as more traditional topics concerning the role and responsibilities of the jury.

ISSUES

- What topics should be included in the preinstructions?

- When should preinstructions be delivered?

PROCEDURES

Preinstructions for the jury consist fundamentally of an introduction to the parties and their claims, a presentation of matters not in dispute, and guidance on the contested issues and the governing legal principles. When preinstructing the jury, the judge explains that these instructions are preliminary instructions only and subject to change. The jury will receive final instructions that are definitive after all the evidence has been presented. Preinstructions are delivered to the jury both verbally and in writing. They may be distributed to the jury as an insert in each juror's notebook, if provided for the trial, for ready reference during the course of the trial proceedings. See § IV-7, "Juror Notebooks."

At the end of the plaintiff's case, the judge and trial attorneys may update the preinstructions to reflect changes in the claims presented during the plaintiff's case in chief. To avoid any prejudicial effect from such a modification, the judge and trial attorneys draft the preinstructions to reflect "black letter law," albeit tailored to the case to avoid excess abstraction. Pattern instructions are a ready source of concise summaries of governing legal principles. See § VI-3, "Improving Pattern Instructions." This synopsis of the law should cover all of the basic elements of the claims and defenses, explaining that some of the elements may be uncontested and emphasizing that the issues may change as the case unfolds. The instructions should *not* include any "verdict directing" type of instructions (e.g., "if you find these elements have been proven, then your verdict should be . . .").

ADVANTAGES

1. Preinstructions help the jury identify, recall, and evaluate the pertinent evidence.

2. Preinstruction enhances jurors' ability to remember information presented at trial and to link the evidence to relevant issues.

3. Preinstruction helps jurors identify personal prejudices that must be put aside.

4. Preinstruction helps jurors assess the credibility of or reasonable inferences from the evidence at the time the evidence is received.

DISADVANTAGES

1. Preinstruction compels the judge to expend greater time at an early stage when he or she may be less than fully informed about the disputed issues that will arise at trial.

2. Preparation of preinstructions is a contentious process given that trial counsel generally prefer instructions that anticipate all possible contingencies that might arise during trial.

REFERENCES

Robert F. Forston, "Sense and Non-Sense: Jury Trial Communication," 1975 *B.Y.U. L. Rev.* 601, 620-23 (recommending jury instruction before and after the presentation of evidence, with interim instructions as needed to address unforeseen issues that arise during trial).

Leonard B. Sand & Steven A. Reiss, "A Report on Seven Experiments Conducted by District Court Judges in the Second Circuit," 60 *N.Y.U. L. Rev.* 423, 437-42 (1985) (describing the results of experimentation in the timing of jury instructions by three federal district court judges in 14 trials and observing that no survey respondent noted any negative effects on the jury).

William W Schwarzer, "Reforming Jury Trials," 132 F.R.D. 575, 583-84 (1990) (discussing the legal authority and practical and theoretical justifications for preinstructions).

Vicki L. Smith, "The Feasibility and Utility of Pretrial Instruction in the Substantive Law," 14 *Law & Hum. Behav.* 235 (1990) (discussing the advantages and disadvantages associated with preinstructions).

STUDIES

American Bar Association, Special Committee on Jury Comprehension, *Jury Comprehension in Complex Cases* (1989) (based on the findings of a study of juror decision making in complex litigation, recommending clear, plain English instructions at the beginning and end of cases).

Amiram Elwork, Bruce D. Sales & James J. Alfini, "Juridic Decisions: In Ignorance of the Law or In Light of It?" 1 *Law & Hum. Behav.* 163 (1977) (study findings revealed that presenting instructions at the beginning and end of the trial gave jurors a greater opportunity to focus their attention on relevant evidence and to remember it).

Larry Heuer & Steven D. Penrod, "Instructing Jurors: A Field Experiment with Written and Preliminary Instructions," 13 *Law & Hum. Behav.* 409 (1989) (study findings revealed that preliminary instructions help jurors follow legal guidelines in decision making and increase juror satisfaction).

Saul M. Kassin & Lawrence S. Wrightsman, *The American Jury on Trial: Psychological Perspectives* 144-46 (1988) (reporting study findings that jurors' adherence to judges' instructions hinges in part on the placement of instructions within the trial proceedings).

Saul M. Kassin & Lawrence S. Wrightsman, "On the Requirements of Proof and the Timing of Judicial Instructions on Mock Juror Verdicts," 37 *J. Personality and Soc. Psychol.* 1877 (1979) (study finding that jurors who were given preinstructions in criminal trials were significantly less likely to view the defendant as guilty of the crime than jurors who received instructions after presentation of the evidence or who received no instructions).

RELATED APPENDIX

Appendix 8: Sample Preliminary Jury Instructions

§ V-10 Mini-Openings/Interim Commentary

TECHNIQUE

The trial attorneys present a brief opening statement to the jury outlining the major theory of the case. At periodic intervals during trial, they then explain to the jury the significance of evidence or testimony about to be presented with respect to how it supports the theory of the case. Opposing counsel has the opportunity to respond to interim commentary. This technique is especially helpful in lengthy or complex litigation.

ISSUES

- When opposing counsel responds to interim commentary, does the response time count against that party's allocated time for interim commentary?

- Should interim commentary come before or after presentation of the evidence?

- Do traditional rules of procedure governing opening and closing argument apply to interim commentary?

- Before presenting interim commentary, must counsel give notice to the court and/or opposing counsel? Must counsel obtain the consent of the court and/or opposing counsel?

PROCEDURES

At the beginning of the trial, each party is allocated a specific amount of time in which to present opening arguments and interim commentary as it sees fit during the course of the trial. See also § IV-1, "Pretrial Limits on Each Party's Time at Trial." An alternative procedure is to allocate a few minutes for each party to present interim commentary at prescheduled times or days during the trial.

The trial attorneys use this time to explain to the jury the significance of testimony or evidence as it is presented throughout the trial. This technique permits counsel to frame the context of their cases in manageable segments that jurors can easily assimilate.

ADVANTAGES

1. Mini opening statements and interim commentary increase juror comprehension by periodically permitting jurors to place the evidence in the context of the theory of the case.

2. Interim commentary buttresses limiting instructions by the judge regarding the purpose of offered evidence.

3. Interim commentary permits the trial attorneys to organize, clarify, emphasize, contextualize, and explain evidence.

4. Interim commentary keeps jurors focused on the evidence, thus preventing them from making premature judgments.

5. Presenting several short interim commentaries throughout the trial (rather than lengthy opening and closing arguments) may shorten the trial overall.

DISADVANTAGES

1. Jurors may focus on the attorneys' commentary rather than the evidence.

2. Jurors may pay less attention to the evidence, relying on the trial attorneys to explain it to them.

REFERENCES

B. Michael Dann, "'Learning Lessons' and 'Speaking Rights': Creating Educated and Democratic Juries," 68 *Ind. L. J.* 1229, 1249-50 (1993) (discussing justifications for preinstructing the jury).

Patrick E. Higginbotham, "Juries and the Complex Case: Observations About the Current Debate," in *The American Civil Jury* 78 (1987) (advocating the use of interim commentary in lengthy trials).

New York State Bar Association, Committee on Federal Courts, "Improving Jury Comprehension in Complex Civil Litigation," 62 *St. John's L. Rev.* 549, 557-58 (1988) (describing the application of permitting counsel to make interim commentary in *Westmoreland v. CBS*).

Study

Saul M. Kassin & Lawrence S. Wrightsman, *The American Jury on Trial: Psychological Perspectives* 144-46 (1988) (reporting study findings that jurors' adherence to judges' instructions hinges in part on the placement of instructions within the trial proceedings).

§ V-11 Plain English at Trial

Technique

The judge, court staff, and trial attorneys use plain English when communicating with the jury.

Issues

- To what extent can juror satisfaction be enhanced by removing the verbal mystique and incomprehensible discourse typically used during the trial process?

- Apart from jury instructions, what opportunities exist for the judge and trial attorneys to make their communications to the jury more understandable?

- What are the appropriate limits for encouraging plain English, recognizing that the trial attorneys should have some freedom to use (or not use) any style of communication that reflects their preferred trial strategies?

Procedures

A strong correlation exists between juror satisfaction with jury service and how well jurors understood the proceedings in which they participated and their role within those proceedings. To maximize jurors' understanding, the judge, court staff, and trial attorneys use plain English in their communications with the jury throughout the trial. For example, the judge should avoid "legalese" vocabulary—replacing, or at least explaining, terms such as "plaintiff," "cause of action," or "indictment."

During voir dire, jurors may perceive the judge's questioning as an inquisition, perhaps even subject to penalties for incomplete responses. Thus, the nature of the questions should be assuring, comforting, and open-ended. The judge also should invite the jurors to ask any questions about the court's voir dire examination. If the trial attorneys conduct voir dire, they also should limit the use of legal jargon. See also § III-1, "Lawyer-Conducted Voir Dire."

Rulings on evidentiary objections and other exchanges between the judge and trial attorneys need be conducted in plain English only if it is appropriate for the jury to understand them. However, both the judge and trial counsel should be aware that the jury may feel deliberately excluded from understanding part of the trial process. Admonitions to the jury, such as to disregard evidence that has been stricken, also should be framed in plain language.

ADVANTAGE

Jurors who understand the trial proceedings are likely to perform their duties well.

DISADVANTAGES

1. Efforts to employ plain English can result in trial judges being too casual, diminishing the dignity of the court.

2. The quest for improved communications with the juror may encroach on the parties' strategic options as to how the case should be presented to the jury.

REFERENCES

Joseph Kimble, *Clarity* (an international periodical reviewing efforts to simplify legal language, published by CLARITY, 74 South St., Dorking, Surrey RH4 2HD England).

Judith N. Levi, *Language and Law: A Bibliographic Guide to Social Science Research in the U.S.A.* (1994) (bibliographic compendium of linguistic research applicable to jury studies).

Judith N. Levi & Anne Graffam Walker, eds., *Language in the Judicial Process* (1990) (compendium of scholarly papers presented at the Conference on Language in the Judicial Process, July 1985).

Chapter VI

Jury Instructions and Deliberations

CONTRIBUTORS AND REVIEWERS

Joel Aronson, Esq.
Ober, Kaller
Washington, D.C.

Robert E. Kehoe, Jr., Esq.
Law Offices of Robert E. Kehoe, Jr.
Chicago, Illinois

Prof. Mark S. Brodin
Boston College
Newton, Massachusetts

Prof. Joe Kimble
Thomas M. Cooley Law School
Lansing, Michigan

Hon. B. Michael Dann
Superior Court of Arizona
Phoenix, Arizona

Hon. Howard McKibben
U.S. District Court,
District of Nevada
Reno, Nevada

David B. Graeven
Trial Behavior Consulting, Inc.
San Francisco, California

Cathy Miller
Trial Behavior Consulting, Inc.
San Francisco, California

Paula L. Hannaford, J.D. M.P.P.
National Center for State Courts
Williamsburg, Virginia

Janice Toran, Esq.
G.D. Searle & Co.
Skokie, Illinois

Hon. Lawrence Waddington (ret.)
Los Angeles County Superior Court
Santa Monica, California

§ VI-1   Jury Instructions Before Closing Arguments

Technique

The judge delivers instructions to the jury before, rather than after, closing arguments. A variation on this technique consists of the judge delivering substantive instruction to the jury before closing arguments, holding instructions on administrative matters until after closing arguments.

Issues

- Does providing final instructions before closing arguments enhance juror understanding about the legal framework in which they must make their decisions?

- Does providing final instructions enhance procedural fairness or increase the number of "legally correct" decisions?

Procedures

Traditionally, the judge has issued final instructions after closing arguments by the trial attorneys. The Federal Rules of Civil Procedure and some state rules reflect this practice. Until they were amended in 1987, the Federal Rules required that the judge instruct the jury after counsel completed closing arguments. Today, the Federal Rules and many state codes are more flexible, permitting the judge to instruct the jury either before or after argument, or both.

The judge may instruct the jury on the law before closing arguments, leaving instructions on administrative matters until after the arguments. This alternative reminds the jurors of the earlier instructions and instructs them about procedures to follow during deliberations, including asking questions about the instructions or deliberations and reporting the verdict.

Advantages

1. Closing arguments are more meaningful within the legal framework provided by instructions and, as a result, may improve jurors' recollection of the evidence.

2. The trial attorneys know the exact wording of the instructions and can tailor their closing arguments accordingly.

3. The trial attorneys can include an explanation of the instructions in their closing arguments and demonstrate how the instructions should be applied to the facts of the case.

4. Jurors spend less time during deliberations attempting to reconstruct the judge's instructions.

5. Jurors are less likely to be swayed inappropriately by closing arguments and are more likely to evaluate the evidence according to legally correct guidelines.

DISADVANTAGES

1. Jurors will focus on the judge's instructions rather than on closing arguments.

2. Jurors will view the trial from the perspective of the trial judge and will fail to consider the perspectives articulated in closing arguments.

AUTHORITY

Fed. R. Civ. Proc. Rule 51 (1996) (giving the trial court discretion to deliver jury instructions before or after closing arguments).

Wis. Stat. § 805.13(4) (1994) (giving the trial court discretion to deliver jury instructions before or after closing arguments).

REFERENCE

New York State Bar Association, Committee on Federal Courts, "Improving Jury Comprehension in Complex Civil Litigation," 62 *St. John's L. Rev.* 549, 553-54 (1988) (survey results finding that the majority of judges and lawyers favored preinstruction).

STUDY

William W Schwarzer, "Communication with Juries: Problems and Remedies," 69 *Cal. L. Rev.* 731, 755-59 (1981) (discussing the importance of timing and delivery of jury instructions).

§ VI-2   Plain English Jury Instructions

Technique

To foster more comprehensible, "plain English" jury instructions, the judge and trial attorneys jointly prepare instructions with specific attention to the overall character and structure of the jury charge. The trial judge uses a conversational tone to deliver the charge. If the instructions are lengthy or complex, the use of "stretch breaks" and audio-visual aids also may increase the jurors' ability to understand and assimilate the charge. See also § VI-3, "Improving Pattern Instructions."

Issues

- Are "plain English" jury instructions more comprehensible to jurors?

- Can trial procedures be revised to encourage more time and attention to refining and clarifying the charge?

- To what extent should greater emphasis be given to the overall structure and composition of the charge?

- Does a multimedia presentation of the jury instructions improve jurors' comprehension of the issues and governing law?

- Do counsel have an opportunity (or responsibility) to include an explanation of the jury instructions in their closing arguments?

Procedures

The frustrations expressed by jurors during deliberations indicate a need to improve the clarity (and, thereby, the efficacy) of jury instructions. To do so, the court carefully considers the message that the jury charge is intended to communicate. Jury instructions are not intended to provide a crash course on governing legal principles so that duly educated jurors can engage in the same decision-making process as a well-trained judge. Rather, jury instructions should present the factual issues to be decided and those legal rules the jury must use in deciding such issues. Most instructions can be clarified by eliminating any unnecessary "legal education."

Before trial, the trial judge requires the parties to identify two types of issues: those that are purely factual ("Was the traffic light red or green?") and those that concern the application of relevant law ("Did the defendant breach his fiduciary duty?"). Based upon these submissions, the trial judge prepares a working list of the issues.

The judge's list of issues (factual and applicable law) serves as the basis for an outline of the jury instructions. In practical terms, the outline is a table of contents that guides the parties in preparing proposed jury instructions that address the same issues. In cases covered by pattern instructions, the outline will indicate which pattern instructions will be given and in what sequence, allowing more time to consider any deviations that might be appropriate. See also § VI-3, "Improving Pattern Instructions." The outline approach also will encourage the appellate courts to examine the propriety of the charge as a whole. Currently, appellate courts tend to consider only whether specific instructions correctly state the governing law and pay little attention to shortcomings in the comprehensibility of the charge as a whole. This procedure enables the trial judge to focus on the text of the individual proposed instructions.

Using a style manual for jury instructions can help the judge and attorneys draft instructions that:

- avoid abstract statements of legal principles;

- use language that is "case-specific" in terms of the parties and the evidence—e.g., "Mrs. Smith" and "the bus company" rather than "plaintiff" and "defendant";

- organize the instructions according to a hierarchical checklist of the applicable legal tests and criteria, including descriptive headings and distinct subtopics to be addressed by the jury;

- summarize text that is important for guiding the jury through the instructions, even though this text may have no substantive legal content;

- include examples to illustrate the application of governing law;

- include a table of suggested "jury-friendly" terms and expressions that might replace traditional legal jargon; and

- use consistent terminology throughout the instructions.

The judge's use of a conversational tone and demeanor, written copies of instructions, modern communications technology (e.g., overhead projectors or video monitors), and appropriate visual aids (e.g., an outline of the charge, a summary of key points, or other graphic presentations) tends to improve juror comprehension. The judge also should encourage jurors to ask questions about the instructions before they begin deliberating. See § VI-6, "Juror Questions About Instructions."

If closing arguments follow the jury instructions, the trial attorneys display the precise text of the jury instructions and discuss the evidence in terms of the instructions. See also § VI-1, "Jury Instructions Before Closing Arguments."

ADVANTAGES

1. By preparing a working outline of disputed factual and legal issues, the judge and trial attorneys avoid the problem of jury charges that are a garbled patchwork of competing submissions by the opposing parties.

2. Greater attention to the overall structure and character of the charge minimizes redundancies, inconsistencies, and omissions in the instructions.

3. Upgrading the quality of jury instructions encourages jurors to consider all of the issues, rather than mistakenly looking to isolated instructions as hit-or-miss guidance on what they are supposed to do.

DISADVANTAGES

1. Formulating an outline of issues to be addressed in jury instructions requires the judge to dedicate additional time becoming familiar with the case before trial.

2. An outline of disputed factual and legal issues necessarily is subject to change during the course of the trial. Some judges may be reluctant to make adjustments to instructions about issues that have been "already decided."

3. Deviations from approved pattern instructions or other jury instructions that have survived prior appeals create more potential grounds for appeal.

REFERENCES

American Bar Association, Special Committee on Jury Comprehension, *Jury Comprehension in Complex Cases* 43-52 (1989) (discussing specific problems encountered by jurors in deciphering jury instructions).

Veda Charrow, "Some Guidelines for Clear, Legal Writing," 8 *U. Bridgeport L. Rev.* 405 (1987) (practitioners' guide to drafting plain English jury instructions).

Amiram Elwork, Bruce D. Sales & James J. Alfini, *Making Jury Instructions Understandable* (1982) (comprehensive practitioners' guide for evaluating jury instructions for comprehensibility and for redrafting instructions).

Edward J. Imwinkelried and Lloyd R. Schwed, "Guidelines for Drafting Understandable Jury Instructions: An Introduction to the Use of Psycholinguistics," 23 *Crim. L. Bull.* 135 (1987) (providing a review of the literature and a practitioner's guide to problem terminology in jury instructions in criminal cases).

Harvey S. Perlman, "Pattern Jury Instructions: The Application of Social Science Research," 65 *Neb. L. Rev.* 520 (1986) (reviewing empirical studies related to jury decision making and their applicability in the redrafting of judicial pattern jury instructions).

Michael J. Saks, "Judicial Nullification," 68 *Ind. L. J.* 1281 (1993) (arguing that by failing to provide comprehensible jury instructions, judges effectively nullify the law).

William W Schwarzer, "Communicating with Juries: Problems and Remedies," 69 *Cal. L. Rev.* 731, 743-55 (1981) (critiquing the language and construction of jury instructions).

Walter W. Steele, Jr. & Elizabeth G. Thornburg, "Jury Instructions: A Persistent Failure to Communicate," 67 *N.C. L. Rev.* 77 (1988) (concluding that improvements in the comprehensibility of jury instructions are unlikely without institutional changes in the incentives for judges and lawyers to draft plain English instructions).

J. Alexander Tanford, "The Law and Psychology of Jury Instructions," 69 *Neb. L. Rev.* 71 (1990) (challenging the assumptions that juries would follow jury instructions even if they understood them).

STUDIES

Robert P. Charrow & Veda R. Charrow, "Making Legal Language Understandable: A Psycholinguistic Study of Jury Instructions," 79 *Colum. L. Rev.* 1306 (1979) (identifying, and testing for reliability and validity, those linguistic features that interfere with jury comprehension).

Shari S. Diamond & Judith N. Levi, "Improving Decisions on Death by Revising and Testing Jury Instructions," 79 *Judicature* 224 (1996) (reporting increases in juror comprehension of jury instructions on the death penalty after redrafting in accordance with established linguistic principles).

Amiram Elwork, Bruce D. Sales & James J. Alfini, "Jurdic Decisions: In Ignorance of the Law or In Light of It?" 1 *Law & Hum. Behav.* 163 (1977) (study finding significant improvements in juror comprehension of pattern instructions after rewriting them to define or eliminate unfamiliar terminology, correct grammar, and improve organization).

Robin Reed, "Jury Simulation: The Impact of Judge's Instructions and Attorney Tactics on Decisionmaking," 71 *J. Crim. L. & Criminology* 68 (1980) (study examining the effects of providing or withholding jury instructions on jury decision making).

Laurence J. Severance, Edith Greene & Elizabeth F. Loftus, "Toward Criminal Jury Instructions That Jurors Can Understand," 75 *J. Crim. L. & Criminology* 198 (1984) (study evaluating improvements in the comprehensibility of jury instructions defining "reasonable doubt," "criminal intent," and "limited use of evidence of prior convictions").

Laurence J. Severance & Elizabeth F. Loftus, "Improving the Ability of Jurors to Comprehend and Apply Criminal Jury Instructions," 17 *Law & Soc. Rev.* 153 (1982) (three studies demonstrating methods for improving the comprehensibility of jury instructions).

§ VI-3   Improving Pattern Instructions

Technique

Drafting committees for pattern jury instructions reduce the texts to plain English statements of core legal concepts. Infrequently applied qualifications or other details of governing rules are omitted from the base instructions with the understanding that the judge and trial attorneys can add them as needed. Using a "style manual" that incorporates well-grounded social science research, field testing draft pattern instructions, and conducting evaluations by professional linguists are additional techniques for improving comprehensibility of pattern instructions.

Issues

- From what areas of expertise should drafting committees draw in revising pattern instructions?

- How should proposed instructions be evaluated for improvements in comprehensibility? for adherence to existing law?

- What steps can drafting committees take to increase the likelihood that the use of redrafted pattern instructions will be approved by appellate courts?

Procedures

In preparing pattern instructions, drafting committees first identify the legal content to be expressed and then consult with linguistic experts to ensure that the text of the proposed instructions reflects "plain English" translations of statutory language and case law. A "style manual" drawing on reliable social science resources can be a valuable aid in this endeavor. The draft patterns are then field tested on potential jurors to confirm empirically that they satisfy some minimum level of comprehensibility. The drafting committee may include commentary with the published instructions emphasizing that comprehensibility is every bit as important as accuracy.

Michigan has done the most extensive and best-documented work in rewriting criminal instructions with the objective of improving juror comprehension. The effort began with a survey of judges to find out which instructions they thought were most troublesome. Jurors' understanding of the instructions was examined by assessing the differences in test scores between jurors who were given and those who were not given a particular instruction. The Michigan committee worked from three formats, presented simultaneously to facilitate comparison. The first format was the existing instruction. The second was the existing instruction with proposed redrafted language placed directly over the applicable current language. The second format was not simply a word-for-word adaptation, but could be a major restructuring of an instruction if the committee felt it was necessary. The third format was the redrafted instruction. The committee rewrote the two volumes of instructions, which with commentary are now three volumes.

ADVANTAGES

1. Plain English pattern instructions provide a sound basis for drafting comprehensible jury instructions for specific cases.

2. Plain English pattern instructions are sufficiently broad and encompassing to be used as preliminary jury instructions. See § V-9, "Preinstructing the Jury."

DISADVANTAGES

1. Redrafting pattern instructions into plain English is a time-consuming task that requires substantial psycholinguistic expertise and testing of proposed instructions to achieve significant improvements in juror comprehension.

2. Appellate courts tend to undervalue comprehensibility in pattern instructions, making efforts to improve them subject to risk of being overturned on appeal.

REFERENCES

Robert P. Charrow & Veda R. Charrow, "Making Legal Language Understandable: A Psycholinguistic Study of Jury Instructions," 79 *Colum. L. Rev.* 1306 (1979) (premier study exposing deficiencies in the comprehensibility of jury instructions and isolating linguistic features that cause comprehension problems).

Edward J. Imwinkelried & Lloyd R. Schwed, "Guidelines for Drafting Understandable Jury Instructions: An Introduction to the Use of Psycholinguistics," 23 *Crim. L. Bull.* 135 (1987) (a practical guide to the application of psycholinguistic research).

Judicial Conference of the United States, Subcommittee on Pattern Instructions, *Pattern Criminal Jury Instructions* (1988) (Appendix A provides guidance on drafting comprehensible jury instructions).

Robert E. Kehoe, Jr., *Jury Instructions for Contract Cases* (1995) (Chapter 5 and the appendices provide plain English, well-referenced, and basic rules for writing understandable instructions).

Koenig, Kerr & Hoeck, "Michigan Standard Criminal Jury Instructions: Judges' Perspectives After Ten Years Use" 4 *Cooley L. Rev.* 347 (1987).

Kramer & Koenig, "Do Jurors Understand Criminal Jury Instructions? Analyzing the Results of the Michigan Juror Comprehension Project," 23 *U. Mich. J. L. Ref.* 401 (1990).

Harvey S. Perlman, "Pattern Jury Instructions: The Application of Social Science Research," 65 *Neb. L. Rev.* 520 (1986) (reviewing empirical studies related to jury decision making and their applicability in the redrafting of federal pattern jury instructions).

Jamison Wilcox, "The Craft of Drafting Plain-Language Jury Instructions: A Study of Sample Pattern Instructions on Obscenity," 59 *Temp. L. Q.* 1159 (1986) (illustrating the application of social science research to jury instructions).

§ VI-4   SUGGESTIONS FOR JURORS ON CONDUCTING DELIBERATIONS

TECHNIQUE

The court provides jurors with suggested procedures for conducting deliberations, including how to use the jury instructions to reach a verdict and how to manage the deliberative process.

ISSUES

- Do suggestions on jury deliberations help jurors organize the deliberative process in a useful manner?

- Do suggestions on jury deliberations assist jurors to render verdicts consistent with evidence presented at trial?

- Do suggestions on jury deliberations increase juror satisfaction with the deliberative process?

- Do suggestions on jury deliberations reduce the amount of time jurors spend deliberating?

PROCEDURES

Immediately before the jury retires to deliberate, the judge provides written and verbal suggestions on how to use the instructions in their deliberations and how to manage the deliberative process. For example, the judge may recommend that jurors consider only one claim or offense at a time and that they use the instructions as a guide to determine whether the parties introduced sufficient evidence to establish all the necessary legal elements for each claim or defense. The judge also provides suggestions on managing the deliberative process, such as selecting a presiding juror (if not previously selected), avoiding early public votes on the verdict, conducting small group discussions that provide all jurors with an opportunity to present their opinions, allocating tasks (such as taking notes on deliberations) among jurors, and handling disagreement or deadlock.

ADVANTAGES

1. Suggestions on deliberations inform jurors about the place of jury instructions in the context of the deliberative process.

2. Suggestions on deliberations help jurors organize their deliberations in a systematic fashion without placing restraints (such as those associated with special verdict forms or general verdicts with interrogatories) on the jury's decision-making discretion.

3. Suggestions on deliberations reduce the amount of time jurors spend in deliberations and decrease the likelihood of deadlock.

DISADVANTAGE

Existing jury instructions are sufficient. Additional jury instructions will be superfluous.

REFERENCES

Reid Hastie, Steven D. Penrod & Nancy Pennington, *Inside the Jury* (1983) (comprehensive examination of jury decision making and the dynamics of the deliberation process).

Nancy S. Marder, "Gender Dynamics and Jury Deliberations," 96 *Yale L. J.* 593 (1987) (observing differences in the participation rates between male and female jurors in deliberations).

Christopher N. May, "'What Do We Do Now?': Helping Juries Apply the Instructions," 28 *Loyola L.A. L. Rev.* 869 (1995) (describing a first-hand experience of a law professor deliberating as a juror).

K. Phillip Taylor, Raymond W. Buchanan, Albert Pryor & David U. Strawn, "Avoiding the Legal Tower of Babel," 19 *Judges' J.* 10 (Summer 1980) (application of process jury instructions in a Florida criminal case).

STUDIES

Norbert L. Kerrand & Robert J. MacCown, "The Effects of Jury Size and Polling Method on the Process and Product of Jury Deliberation," in Lawrence S. Wrightsman, Saul M. Kassin & Cynthia E. Willis eds., *In the Jury Box* 209, 213-214, 229-30 (1987) (study finding that "secret polling" in close cases increased the likelihood of hung juries).

David U. Strawn, Raymond W. Buchanan, Albert Pryor & K. Phillip Taylor, "Reaching a Verdict, Step by Step," 60 *Judicature* 383 (1977) (recommending "process instructions" that advise jurors on a systematic method of conducting deliberations).

RELATED APPENDIX

Appendix 9: Suggestions for Juries About Deliberations

§ VI-5   Written or Recorded Instructions for Jurors

Technique

The judge provides jurors with written copies of the jury instructions before they are read by the judge. As an alternative, the judge records the verbal jury charge and provides jurors with the tape recording.

Issues

- Will jurors misinterpret written instructions or place undue emphasis on instructions?

- Do copies of written instructions increase juror comprehension?

- Do written instructions create a cultural or socioeconomic bias against jurors with less formal education or limited ability to read English?

- Who is responsible for the cost of providing copies of jury instructions?

Procedures

The judge notifies the trial attorneys in advance of trial that jurors will be given written copies of instructions. For drafting purposes, the attorneys supply the judge with two sets of recommended jury instructions, one with relevant citations for consideration by the judge and one without citations for submission to the jury. If the judge or attorneys make any last-minute changes, the instructions should be reprinted and recopied to prevent confusion or bias (e.g., with strike-outs, underlining, or typographical errors). The judge should caution the jury that the instructions should be considered as a whole.

If a tape recording of the judge's instructions will be given to the jurors, the judge should be careful to speak clearly and slowly. Audio recordings are especially helpful for jurors who have difficulty with written text. The tape recorder provided for the jurors should have the record button broken off or otherwise disabled to prevent the jurors from accidentally erasing or recording over the instructions.

Advantages

1. Written instructions increase juror comprehension about the charge and reduce the number of questions by the jury about instructions during deliberations.

2. Written instructions prevent jurors from failing to consider critical elements of the legal claims or offenses.

3. Written instructions provide guidance for structuring the deliberative process.

4. Written instructions increase juror confidence in their verdict.

5. Written instructions reduce deliberation time.

6. Written instructions reduce the likelihood of disputes among jurors regarding the content and application of instructions.

7. Audio recordings of instructions help jurors who have difficulty with written text.

8. Audio recordings of instructions are less logistically cumbersome for courts that lack high-speed printers and copiers.

Disadvantages

1. Written instructions may place jurors with less formal education or limited ability to read English at a disadvantage during deliberations.

2. Written instructions require additional time and effort by the court and counsel.

3. Multiple copies of instructions increase the cost of conducting jury trials.

Authority

U.S. v. Massey, 89 F.3d 1433, 1442-43 (1996) (finding that the trial court did not err in providing only a tape recording of the jury instructions in lieu of written instructions).

Iowa R. Civ. P. Rule 196 (1996) (requiring jury instructions to be provided to jurors in writing except in small claims cases [amounts in controversy less than $2,000] or with the consent of all parties).

Iowa R. Crim. P. Rule 18(5)(f) (1996) (extending the Iowa Rules of Civil Procedure concerning juries to criminal trials).

Tenn. R. Crim. P. 30(c) (1996) (requiring written jury instructions in all criminal trials).

REFERENCES

American Bar Association, *Charting a Future for the Civil Jury System: Report from an American Bar Association/Brookings Symposium* 24 (1992) (recommending that all jurors be provided copies of the final instructions).

B. Michael Dann, "'Learning Lessons' and 'Speaking Rights': Creating Educated and Democratic Juries," 68 *Ind. L. J.* 1229 (1993).

Christopher N. May, "'What Do We Do Now?': Helping Juries Apply the Instructions," 28 *Loyola L.A. L. Rev.* 869 (1995) (a first-hand description of jury deliberations and suggestions for improved guidance by the court).

STUDIES

American Bar Association, Special Committee on Jury Comprehension, *Jury Comprehension in Complex Cases* 51-52 (1989) (unanimous reports by jurors that written copies of instructions were helpful to deliberations).

Larry Heuer & Steven D. Penrod, "Instructing Jurors: A Field Experiment with Written and Preliminary Instructions," 13 *Law & Hum. Behav.* 409 (1989) (study found that providing written instructions tended to reduce juror disagreements about instructions and found no support for contention that written instructions lengthen deliberations or place excessive demands on court resources).

New York State Bar Association, Committee on Federal Courts, "Improving Jury Comprehension in Complex Civil Litigation," 62 *St. John's L. Rev.* 549, 564-65 (1988) (reporting survey responses of lawyers and judges concerning written and recorded instructions for the jury).

Leonard B. Sand & Steven A. Reiss, "A Report on Seven Experiments Conducted by District Court Judges in the Second Circuit," 60 *N.Y.U. L. Rev.* 423, 453-56 (1985) (study found mixed reactions by judges and lawyers to providing written instructions to jurors, but generally found increased favor for this practice for complex or lengthy instructions).

§ VI-6   JUROR QUESTIONS ABOUT INSTRUCTIONS

TECHNIQUE

In the final instructions to the jury, the judge gives clear guidance to the jury on the procedures for requesting clarification of instructions.

ISSUES

- Should the judge respond to all questions?

- What form should questions take and in what form should the judge respond?

- What type of cautionary instructions should the judge give to the jury about asking questions during deliberations?

- Should the judge consult with the parties prior to responding to all questions?

PROCEDURES

As part of the final jury instructions, the trial judge advises the jury to submit in writing and in a sealed envelop through the bailiff any questions about the instructions arising during deliberations. Any questions submitted by the jury are then numbered, designated by time and date, and filed and marked as a court exhibit. The judge also permits the jurors to ask clarifying questions about the instructions before they retire to deliberate. This permits early clarification of questions while all parties are still present in the courtroom.

If questions arise during deliberations, the trial judge advises all counsel that the jury has submitted a question and directs that they assemble in the courtroom or by telephone to review it. The judge reads the question on the record and solicits comments from the attorneys regarding any appropriate response. In responding to questions by the jury, the judge advises the jury that instructions should be considered as a whole and that supplemental instructions should be viewed in light of previous instructions.

Whether the judge provides the jury with a specific response to its question is a matter within the sound discretion of the trial judge. Responses need not address more than the specific question asked by the jury. Nonetheless, the judge responds to all questions, even if the response consists of a directive for the jury to continue its deliberations.

Responses to jury questions are delivered either in writing or to the jury in open court. The judge ensures that any additional instructions are not coercive or prejudicial to either party.

ADVANTAGES

1. By carefully screening and reviewing juror questions with counsel and responding to all jury questions, the judge eliminates any potential taint to the jury deliberation process and ensures that supplemental instructions are accurate, clear, neutral, and nonprejudicial.

2. Jurors will take comfort from the fact that they are free to communicate with the judge for supplemental instructions if they find the original instructions confusing or inadequate to address concerns that develop during deliberations.

DISADVANTAGE

Instructing the jury on the procedure to follow when asking questions may invite unnecessary questions.

AUTHORITY

U.S. v. Bay, 820 F.2d 1511, 1514-15 (9th Cir. 1987) (holding that the trial court did not abuse its discretion by limiting the scope of its response to a jury question about the instructions to the definition of "reasonable doubt").

U.S. v. Warren, 984 F.2d 325, 329-30 (9th Cir. 1993) (holding that the trial court's failure to issue supplemental instructions to clarify an apparent misunderstanding by the jury concerning the definition of *premeditated* was reversible error).

REFERENCES

B. Michael Dann, "'Learning Lessons' and 'Speaking Rights': Creating Educated and Democratic Juries," 68 *Ind. L. J.* 1229, 1260-61 (1993) (surveying the literature on jury questions during deliberations).

Vincent J. O'Neill, Jr., "Famous Last Words: Responding to Requests and Questions of Deliberating Jurors in Criminal Cases," 11 *Crim. Just. J.* 381 (1989) (summarizing rules and procedures on judges' responses to jury questions during deliberations).

STUDY

Laurence J. Severance & Elizabeth F. Loftus, "Improving the Ability of Jurors to Comprehend and Apply Criminal Jury Instructions," 17 *Law & Soc. Rev.* 153, 161 (1982) (discussing a study of questions asked by deliberating juries).

§ VI-7   PERMITTING ALTERNATES TO OBSERVE DELIBERATIONS

TECHNIQUE

With the consent of all parties, the judge permits alternates to retire with the jury and observe, but not actively participate in, deliberations. This technique facilitates deliberations in the event that a juror must be excused for illness or other good cause. See also § III-9, "Nondesignation of Alternates and Jurors."

ISSUES

- If present in the jury room during jury deliberations, will alternates actually refrain from participating in the discussions?

- How does the presence of a "nonparticipating" alternate affect jury deliberations?

- Does this practice raise any particular problems for criminal cases?

- Will alternates who are directed to observe jury deliberations resent that they are being held over with no active role to play?

PROCEDURES

In those jurisdictions that permit the trial judge to replace a juror after deliberations have commenced, case law typically requires the jury to begin its deliberations again with the substituted juror (alternate) from the beginning. Alternates who have observed the jury's original deliberations are able to join in the discussion without requiring the jury to retrace all of the steps in its decision-making process in detail.

To implement this technique, the judge obtains the consent of the parties for alternates to observe the jury's deliberations. The judge then instructs the retiring jurors and alternates that the alternates may observe the jury's discussions, but may not vote on specific issues or otherwise participate in these discussions. If circumstances then require the judge to replace a juror (e.g., because of absence, illness, or other good cause), the judge instructs the "new jury" that it should begin its deliberations again from the beginning. If the number of jurors and alternates does not exceed the total number of jurors permitted under statute or court rule, counsel can stipulate and the judge can order that all jurors and alternates participate in deliberations. See also § III-10, "Variable Jury Size/No Alternate Jurors."

As a matter of practice in southern California, counsel in civil cases regularly consent to alternate observation of jury deliberations.

ADVANTAGES

1. Alternates who have observed jury deliberations are able to join in renewed deliberations without requiring the jury to go through its decision-making process in detail.

2. After being presented with all of the evidence, most alternates prefer to observe deliberations rather than be excluded or banished from the court altogether.

3. In bifurcated trials in which the same jury sits on all segments of the trial, having alternates observe the deliberations from the first segment facilitates their substitution in later segments.

DISADVANTAGES

1. Even when not actively participating, alternates who are present for jury deliberations influence the jury's discussions through body language and other signals.

2. Many jurisdictions require the court to dismiss alternates after the jury retires to deliberate.

AUTHORITY

U.S. v. Olano, 113 S. Ct. 1770 (1993) (holding that in the absence of demonstrated prejudice, substitution of an alternate juror during deliberations is permissible).

California v. Collins, 17 Cal.3d 687 (1976) (prohibiting alternates to observe jury deliberations in the absence of consent by counsel).

REFERENCES

Joshua G. Grunat, Note, "Post-Submission Substitution of Alternate Jurors in Federal Criminal Cases: Effects of Violations of Federal Rules of Criminal

Procedure 23(b) and 24(c), 55 *Fordham L. Rev.* 861 (1987) (arguing that substitution of an alternate juror after submission to the jury is plain error under Rule 24(c)).

Valeree D. Marek, Comment, "The Silent Alternate Juror: A Violation of the Constitutional Right to Trial by Jury?" 58 *Chi.-Kent L. Rev.* 765 (1982) (reviewing the history of alternate juror observation of deliberations in the context of *Johnson v. Duckworth*, 650 F.2d. 122 (7th Cir. 1982)).

§ VI-8   SCHEDULING JURY DELIBERATIONS

TECHNIQUE

The judge informs jurors, as part of the regular jury instructions, about what to expect during the deliberative process. When deliberations are expected to be especially lengthy or to require special arrangements (e.g., sequestration), the judge solicits juror input concerning scheduling decisions.

ISSUES

- Should jurors be permitted or required to deliberate beyond normal working hours?

- If extended hours are required, does the judge need the consent of the jurors?

- Who (among court staff) is responsible for arranging security (e.g., escorts to transportation), meals/refreshments, and communications with the judge when the jury deliberates into extended hours?

- How should the judge respond when the jury has a question after hours? Wait until the next court day? Hold a telephone conference call with attorneys? Allow the defendant to appear in court after hours?

PROCEDURES

The court establishes routine policies to address questions such as the length of time jurors will be expected to deliberate each day; where deliberations will take place; when breaks will be scheduled; under what conditions jurors will be sequestered; what resources (e.g., dining) will be made available to jurors during extended hours; and how jurors may communicate with the court. The judge informs the jury of all relevant policies in the process of providing the regular jury instructions. The judge should consult with jurors to determine appropriate deliberation times given jurors' special needs (e.g., personal commitments, child care obligations), especially if deliberations are expected to be lengthy.

ADVANTAGES

1. Advance notice to jurors about deliberation policies permits them, as well as court staff and litigants, to plan their schedules accordingly.

2. Advance notice to jurors about deliberation policies reduces juror anxiety that would otherwise result from uncertainty about deliberation scheduling.

DISADVANTAGE

Court staff must be assigned to accommodate juror needs during extended deliberations.

AUTHORITY

U.S. v. Sanders, 641 F.2d 659, 662-63 (9th Cir. 1981) (holding that a magistrate's determination that the jury should continue to deliberate past working hours and into the weekend did not prejudice the defendant's right to a jury trial).

REFERENCES

American Bar Association, *Standards for Criminal Justice: Trial by Jury,* Standard 15-5.4(b) (1986).

American Bar Association, Committee on Jury Standards, *Standards Relating to Juror Use and Management* 168, 170-71 (1993) (Standard 18(d) advises against requiring jurors to deliberate after normal working hours).

National Conference of Commissioners on Uniform State Laws, *Uniform Rules of Criminal Procedure,* Rule 523(d) (1987).

§ VI-9   SCHEDULING VERDICT ANNOUNCEMENTS

TECHNIQUE

In notorious trials, the trial judge delays announcing the verdict. This delay provides court staff with the opportunity to plan for jury security, media conferences with litigants or jurors, crowd control and police response, and other considerations.

ISSUES

- If the jury reaches a verdict during extended hours, should the verdict announcement be delayed until the next day?

- How much delay is permissible between the jury's notice to the court that it has reached a decision and the verdict announcement in open court?

PROCEDURES

Notorious trials require additional planning by the court to prepare for media reaction and court security, including the post-verdict security of the jurors. After the verdict is returned, the judge sequesters the jury (or temporarily dismisses the jury) for a period of time sufficient to make necessary preparations for court security and media relations. During this delay, the judge may inform jurors about any special security considerations that may be appropriate under the circumstances.

In cases that are likely to provoke widespread public reaction, the court may consider scheduling the verdict announcement for a time at which crowd control is more easily managed. For example, in the second Rodney King trial, the court scheduled the verdict announcement for early Saturday morning to give police an opportunity to prepare for civil disturbances in the event of an unpopular verdict.

ADVANTAGES

1. A short delay before announcing the verdict gives court security and the media an opportunity to make adequate preparations.

2. During the delay, the jurors can be informed about any special security considerations that are appropriate under the circumstances.

DISADVANTAGE

A delay before the verdict announcement gives jurors an opportunity to change their minds.

REFERENCE

Timothy Murphy, Kay Genevra Loveland & G. Thomas Munsterman, *A Manual for Managing Notorious Cases* 75 (National Center for State Courts, 1992) (providing a planning checklist for announcing the verdict in notorious cases).

§ VI-10 SPECIAL VERDICTS AND WRITTEN INTERROGATORIES TO GENERAL VERDICTS

TECHNIQUE

The judge instructs jurors to return a "special verdict" or respond to written interrogatories to a general verdict that articulate answers to specific questions concerning disputed facts in the case and the jury's application of the law to those facts.

ISSUES

- In what types of cases are special verdicts or written interrogatories particularly useful or problematic?

- How specific should special verdicts be? For example, should the jury be required to decide only issues of fact (e.g., did the defendant fail to stop at the intersection?), leaving the judge to apply the controlling law to their findings? Or should the jury be asked broader questions mixing fact and law (e.g., was the defendant negligent?)?

- Do special verdicts deprive the jury of its legitimate role?

- Do special verdicts violate federal or state constitutional provisions guaranteeing the right to jury trials?

- Should the judge instruct the jury on the legal consequences of its answers to the specific verdict questions?

PROCEDURES

When rendering general verdicts, juries merely provide a bottom-line and impenetrable resolution to the case. Requiring jurors to articulate the specific conclusions at which they arrived during their deliberations provides the judge and trial attorneys with a written record that allows them to determine whether the jury has applied the governing law to the facts correctly. This technique is useful for cases in which the governing law is particularly complicated, counterintuitive, or otherwise difficult to apply. In addition, special verdicts or written interrogatories are useful for determining whether a specific issue was fully litigated for the purposes of collateral estoppel in future cases.

To implement this technique, the judge and trial attorneys prepare a special verdict form with specific questions pertinent to each of the disputed factual or applied legal issues in the case. A useful method of organizing the special verdict questions is to follow the general organization of the jury instructions. See § VI-2, "Plain English Jury Instructions." The judge then instructs the jury to provide written answers to each question when returning its verdict. The instructions should clarify which questions require unanimous answers.

ADVANTAGES

1. Special verdicts and written interrogatories to general verdicts record the precise findings of the jury, thus permitting more meaningful review of jury verdicts by trial and appellate courts, as well as more effective use of issue preclusion (collateral estoppel) in future cases that raise common issues.

2. Special verdicts focus the jury's attention on the pivotal issues in the case, potentially making the deliberations more efficient and the result more accurate.

3. Special verdicts can reserve the task of law application to the trial judge, thus decreasing the risk of jury confusion or error.

4. Special verdicts minimize the necessity for elaborate instructions to the jury on legal doctrine, as well as the reliance on lay persons to understand and follow such instructions.

5. Special verdicts reduce the risk of jury nullification, compromise verdicts, and verdicts resulting from prejudice or emotion.

6. Special verdicts can localize error, or demonstrate the error was harmless, and thus avoid the necessity for retrial of the entire case.

7. When there are reasons to doubt the jurors' willingness to apply a "technical" or counterintuitive rule of law, a special verdict can be used to obtain a fact determination from the jury that the judge can then apply in the context of the rule.

8. Written instructions and legal definitions can be combined with the special verdict form to further assist jurors.

9. In multiparty cases, special verdicts can prevent prejudicial spillover from one defendant to another by requiring the jury to delineate the acts of each defendant.

10. Special verdicts document unanimous decisions of the jury and avoid verdicts based on agreements among minorities on different facts that combine to produce the illusion of unanimity.

11. Written interrogatories accompanying a general verdict can test the reliability of the general verdict against the underlying factual findings.

DISADVANTAGES

1. Special verdicts constrain the jury's prerogatives and its ability to dispense a "people's justice."

2. Special verdicts and written interrogatories to general verdicts risk inconsistent or contradictory answers, and thus increase the probability of a new trial.

3. By multiplying the number of points on which the jurors must agree, special verdicts increase the risk of hung juries.

4. A substantial amount of time often must be spent drafting special questions that are not ambiguous or incomprehensible.

5. Special verdicts increase the grounds upon which appeals can be made.

AUTHORITY

Federal Rules of Civil Procedure Rule 49 (1996) (authorizing special verdicts and written interrogatories to general verdicts).

McGuire v. Russell Miller, Inc., 1 F.3d 1306, 1310 (2d Cir. 1993) (holding that the trial court has a duty to reconcile the jury's answers on a special verdict form with any reasonable theory consistent with the evidence presented at trial).

Constilla v. Aluminum Co. of America, 826 F.2d 1444, 1446 n.3 (5th Cir. 1987) (vacating a jury verdict on grounds that the jury's answers to written interrogatories were irreconcilably inconsistent as to manufacturer liability and award of compensatory and punitive damages).

State v. Hart, 477 N.W.2d 732, 739 (Minn. App. 1991) (holding that "either/or" language in jury instructions may infringe on defendant's right to a unanimous verdict and that separate jury instructions and verdict forms for each criminal court are a preferable method for addressing multiple changes or lesser-included offenses in jury instructions).

Binder v. Long Island Lighting Co., 57 F.3d 193, 199 (2d Cir. 1995) (case in which district judge, over objection of plaintiff and without prior notice to counsel, submitted supplemental interrogatories to jury after they returned general verdict for plaintiff, and the court ruled that "there is no authority upholding the submission of fact-specific interrogatories to a jury after a general verdict has been returned, and we note our disapproval of this procedure absent extraordinary circumstances").

REFERENCES

Brodin, Mark S., "Accuracy, Efficiency, and Accountability in the Litigation Process—The Case for the Fact Verdict," 59 *U. Cin. L. Rev.* 15 (1964) (advocating greater use of special verdicts to distinguish factual from legal disputes and thus preserve the separate roles of judge and jury).

Comment, "Special Verdicts: Rule 49 of the Federal Rules of Civil Procedure," 74 *Yale L. J.* 483 (1964) (criticizing the drafters' failure to provide guidelines or standards to trial judges for choosing between general verdicts, special verdicts, and written interrogatories in civil jury cases).

Elizabeth A. Faulkner, Comment, "Using the Special Verdict to Manage Complex Cases and Avoid Compromise Verdicts," 21 *Ariz. St. L. J.* 297, 316-20 (1989) (two case studies of the use of special verdicts in complex, commercial litigation).

David U. Strawn, Raymond W. Buchanan, Bert Pryor & K. Phillip Taylor, "Reaching a Verdict, Step by Step," 60 *Judicature* 383 (1977).

STUDY

Elizabeth C. Wiggins & Steven J. Breckler, "Special Verdicts as Guides to Jury Decision Making," 14 *Law & Psychol. Rev.* 1 (1990) (discussing the relative advantages and disadvantages of special verdicts in light of a study of their impact on juror decision making).

RELATED APPENDIX

Appendix 10: Sample Verdict Forms

§ VI-11 "Reclosing": A Dialogue with the Jury at Impasse

Technique

When deliberating jurors report an apparent impasse, the judge offers the assistance of the judge and trial attorneys through a dialogue with the jury, followed by further proceedings as the court deems appropriate.

Issues

- Should the trial judge ever invite deliberating jurors to disclose issues or questions that they are debating? If so, when? In writing or orally? In open court?

- How should the judge phrase his or her invitation to dialogue?

- How does the judge decide which, if any, issues disclosed by the jurors warrant further proceedings?

- What further proceedings are appropriate? Additional instructions? Reclosing by counsel? More evidence? Some combination of these?

- How should the jury be instructed after such further proceedings and prior to returning to deliberations?

Procedures

After receiving word from a deliberating jury that the jurors feel they are approaching or are at an impasse, the judge consults with the trial attorneys before deciding whether to offer any assistance to the jurors. If the judge decides to ask the jurors if the judge and counsel might be of help, the judge offers in writing or orally in open court a noncoercive invitation to the jurors to list the issues of fact or law that divide them.

If the jury responds, the judge discusses the response with the attorneys before deciding whether and how further proceedings could be productive. Options include providing new or clarifying instructions, additional closing arguments by the attorneys, reopening the trial for more evidence, or a combination of these procedures.

Following any additional proceedings, the jury returns to deliberate with the customary admonitions about deliberations. If the jurors request still more help, the supplement request receives the same serious consideration. If the jurors report deadlock without asking for more assistance, the usual procedures for confirming a hopeless deadlock and deciding upon a mistrial are followed.

ADVANTAGES

1. Assisting deliberating jurors who request help will improve the chances of a verdict and avoid needless mistrials.

2. This procedure enhances the truth-seeking and educational aspects of the trial.

3. Jurors who are allowed to define the issues that divide them, to ask their unanswered questions, and to receive an appropriate response will more likely reach an accurate verdict, or know they have done their best to do so, and will be more satisfied with their effort.

4. At any point in the dialogue or additional proceedings, the judge may, after appropriate inquiry, declare a mistrial due to deadlock.

DISADVANTAGES

1. The technique amounts to an unwarranted invasion into the privacy and confidentiality of jury deliberations.

2. The invitation by the judge to list issues may have a coercive effect.

3. Some jurors' issues or questions may not find their way onto the list returned to the judge.

4. The trial will be protracted as a result of the dialogue and any ensuing supplemental proceedings.

AUTHORITY

Arizona's Civil Rule 39(h).

Withers v. Ringlein, 745 F. Supp. 1271, 1274 (E.D. Mich. 1990) (finding the court's inherent power to be sufficient to authorize additional assistance to the jury after deliberations had commenced).

REFERENCES

Arizona Supreme Court Committee on More Effective Use of Juries, *Jurors: The Power of 12: Report of the Arizona Supreme Court Committee on More Effective Use of Juries* (1994).

B. Michael Dann, "'Learning Lessons' and 'Speaking Rights': Creating Educated and Democratic Juries," 68 *Ind. L. J.* 1229, 1269-77 (1993) (describing techniques for communicating with juries at or near impasse to improve the likelihood of a verdict).

RELATED APPENDIX

Appendix 6: Arizona Rules of Civil Procedure Rule 39 (1996)

Chapter VII

Post-Verdict Considerations

CONTRIBUTORS AND REVIEWERS

Beth Bonora
National Jury Project, West
Oakland, California

Paula L. Hannaford, J.D., M.P.P.
National Center for State Courts
Williamsburg, Virginia

Curtis E. von Kann, Esq.
Ross, Dixon & Masback, L.L.P.
Washington, D.C.

§ VII-1   Advice Regarding Post-Verdict Conversations

Technique

The trial judge provides information to jurors about engaging in post-verdict conversations, including their right to refrain from discussing the case with parties or their attorneys, the media, and researchers.

Issues

- Do post-verdict discussions of the case by jurors increase attempts by the parties to impeach jury verdicts?

- Does the fact that jurors may discuss the trial publicly in post-verdict conversations tend to chill the deliberative process?

- Does judicial advice about post-verdict conversations excessively influence jurors?

Procedures

Post-verdict admonitions are delivered by the judge prior to dismissing the jury. The judge informs jurors that they are no longer prohibited from discussing the case with outside parties, but that they retain the right not to discuss the case with anyone if they so choose. As part of this advice, the judge may inform jurors about the requirements of Federal Rules of Evidence Rule 606(b) and corresponding state statutes regarding inquiries into the validity of jury verdicts. He or she may also ask jurors to respect the deliberative process and the candor of their fellow jurors.

The judge informs jurors about any constraints that he or she will impose on the parties or their attorneys regarding their future contact with jurors. For example, some state and federal jurisdictions bar post-verdict contact with jurors by attorneys or the parties without the consent of the trial court for good cause shown. The judge reassures jurors that the court will continue to be available to protect them from post-trial harassment and instructs them how to contact the court in case they wish to invoke its protection.

Advantages

1. Judicial advice regarding post-verdict conversations protects jurors from post-trial harassment by the parties, their attorneys, and the media.

2. Judicial advice regarding post-verdict conversations protects jurors' privacy rights.

3. Judicial advice regarding post-verdict conversations protects the confidentiality and inviolability of the deliberative process.

4. Judicial advice regarding post-verdict conversations may deter frivolous attempts to impeach jury verdicts.

DISADVANTAGES

1. Judicial advice regarding post-verdict conversations may prevent the parties from investigating possible juror misconduct or interfering with the ability of attorneys to solicit feedback about their trial performance.

2. Judicial advice regarding post-verdict conversations may discourage jurors from speaking with media or researchers, making it difficult to conduct legitimate inquiries into juror decision making either generally or concerning a specific case.

AUTHORITY

Fed. R. Evid. Rule 606(b) (1996) (limiting juror testimony concerning verdicts to statements about extraneous information or outside influences that may have affected the jury's deliberations).

United States v. Giraldi, 858 F. Supp. 85 (Tex. 1994) (establishing procedures for the court to inform jurors of media interest in conducting interviews with jurors and to advise jurors of their rights to grant or deny interviews with the media).

REFERENCES

American Bar Association, Committee on Jury Standards, *Standards Relating to Juror Use and Management* 141-43, 151-52 (1993) (Standard 16(d) describes information to be conveyed to jurors prior to dismissing them from deliberations).

Susan Crump, "Jury Misconduct, Jury Interviews, and the Federal Rules of Evidence: Is the Broad Exclusionary Principle of Rule 606(b) Justified?" 66 *N.C. L. Rev.* 509 (1988) (proposing amended language to FRE 606(b) and a uniform rule to govern post-trial juror interviews in federal trials).

Abraham S. Goldstein, "Jury Secrecy and the Media: The Problem of Postverdict Interviews," 1993 *U. Ill. L. Rev.* 295 (arguing for greater judicial oversight of post-verdict media interviews with jurors).

Nancy S. Marder, "Deliberations and Disclosures: A Study of Post-Verdict Interviews of Jurors," 82 *Iowa L. Rev.* (forthcoming 1997) (analyzing press reports of juror interviews appearing in major newspapers between 1980 and 1995).

Note, "Public Disclosures of Jury Deliberations," 96 *Harv. L. Rev.* 886 (1983) (urging trial judges to place greater emphasis on moral persuasion to discourage jurors from discussing their deliberations).

RELATED APPENDIX

Appendix 11: Suggested Concluding Jury Admonition

§ VII-2 Informal Meetings Between the Judge and Jury

Technique

The judge meets informally with the jurors after the verdict to offer personal thanks for their participation. This technique offers the judge the opportunity to answer general questions from jurors about trial or post-trial procedures (e.g., evidentiary or sentencing issues). The judge may also solicit feedback from the jurors about their reactions to jury service and any suggestions for improving jury administration and management.

Issues

- When and where should the trial judge conduct informal meetings with the jurors?

- Should the parties or their attorneys attend this meeting? Should court staff?

- What precautions should the judge take to avoid violations of judicial ethics (e.g., commenting on the verdict) when meeting with jurors?

- What is the judge's responsibility if he or she becomes aware of jury misconduct?

- Should judges refrain from these meetings if some or all of the jurors will be retained for additional trials?

Procedures

After formally excusing the jury from service, the trial judge invites any jurors who are interested to meet with the judge informally. The judge generally meets with the jurors in the jury deliberation room; however, the courtroom (after the parties, attorneys, and spectators have left) or the judge's chambers (if space permits) are acceptable alternatives. Typically, the parties and their attorneys are not invited to participate in these meetings, although some judges favor their participation in the interest of the attorneys' education. See also § VII-4, "Post-Verdict Interviews by Attorneys and Researchers."

At the beginning of the meeting, the judge should thank the jurors for their participation in the trial. He or she may explain that judges are not permitted to comment on the verdict, but are permitted to answer general questions about the trial process. Informal meetings with jurors also provide an opportunity for the judge to ask about the jurors' perception of jury service and to solicit their suggestions for improving jury administration and management. For example, the judge can ask whether there were specific parts of jury service that they found particularly confusing or irritating.

Trial judges who have used this technique report that they learn a great deal from jurors during these meetings, and almost never find themselves in detailed discussions about the jury's deliberative process or in situations that might permit a new trial. Jurors generally stay for these meetings and appreciate the personal touch from the judge.

ADVANTAGES

1. Informal meetings with the trial judge provide a sense of closure to the jury experience.

2. Informal meetings with the trial judge communicate to jurors that the court values the jurors' participation in the trial and reinforce the importance of jury service as a civic responsibility.

3. Informal meetings with the trial judge provide an opportunity for jurors to ask questions about the trial process, especially questions not answered during jury orientation.

4. Informal meetings with jurors provide an opportunity for the judge to engage in public education about the legal and judicial system.

5. Informal meetings with jurors provide an opportunity for judges to learn about jury conditions and jurors' concerns about jury service.

DISADVANTAGES

1. Informal meetings with jurors run the risk that the trial judge will comment inadvertently on the verdict or will otherwise violate judicial ethics.

2. Informal meetings with jurors run the risk that the trial judge will become aware of juror misconduct.

3. Informal meetings with jurors take additional time.

4. Some judges are uncomfortable meeting with jurors in an informal setting.

AUTHORITY

Model Code of Judicial Conduct Canon 3(B)(9) (1992) (prohibiting judges from making comments that might reasonably affect the outcome or substantially interfere with judicial proceedings).

Model Code of Judicial Conduct Canon 3(B)(10) (1992) (prohibiting judges from commenting on a jury's verdict in a form other than a court order or formal opinion).

REFERENCES

James E. Kelley, "Addressing Juror Stress: A Trial Judge's Perspective," 43 *Drake L. Rev.* 97, 116-22 (1994) (describing ground rules and their basis for jury debriefings conducted by the trial judge).

Timothy R. Murphy, Genevra K. Loveland & G. Thomas Munsterman, *A Manual for Managing Notorious Cases* 77-78 (National Center for State Courts, 1992) (describing various approaches and styles of post-verdict meetings between the judge and jury).

§ VII-3   Debriefing Sessions to Alleviate Juror Stress

Technique

For trials in which jurors are likely to experience severe emotional distress, the court employs a professional psychologist or social worker to "debrief" the jurors following the verdict. This technique is particularly appropriate for trials in which the evidence or testimony is especially gruesome, the trial provokes a great deal of media attention, or the trial is exceptionally lengthy or requires extraordinary measures (e.g., sequestration) to help jurors handle post-verdict stress. For trials that cause less severe stress, trained judges or court staff can conduct jury debriefings.

Issues

- What kinds of cases require professional debriefing?

- Under what authority do courts call for professional assistance?

- What training and expertise should the people who conduct juror debriefings have?

- How do courts locate or train these individuals?

- Who is responsible for the costs of juror debriefings?

- Should a professional psychologist or social worker be available to jurors during deliberations? Should debriefing sessions be offered to alternates?

- Should the jurors be informed that a post-verdict debriefing is available before they retire to deliberate?

- Do post-verdict debriefings affect the validity of the verdict?

- Does the doctor-patient privilege apply to debriefings conducted by professional psychologists, psychiatrists, or social workers?

- Who should attend the debriefing sessions? The judge? Court personnel? Attorneys?

PROCEDURES

The debriefing consists of a short group session in which the jurors have an opportunity to explore and better understand their emotional reaction to the trial and to jury service. The debriefings also include a description of the symptoms commonly associated with juror stress (e.g., nightmares, depression, insomnia) and make recommendations to the jurors about appropriate stress management techniques.

The debriefing session typically is held after the jury returns its verdict and is released from service by the trial judge. At that time, the judge explains that he or she recognizes that the jurors have been under a great deal of stress and invites any jurors that are interested to attend a short debriefing session. Alternates, regardless of whether they participated in the deliberations, may also be invited to participate in debriefings. In some cases, the trial judge participates. If the jury returns its verdict late in the day, the debriefing session may be held the following day.

A professional psychologist, psychiatrist, or social worker with expertise in post-traumatic stress disorder (PTSD) generally conducts the debriefing. The court can inquire at local mental health centers, nearby medical schools, or other community or regional resources for information about qualified professionals. The court is responsible for the costs of debriefing, although many professionals will conduct debriefings on a pro bono basis. With proper training, judges or other court staff may be able to conduct debriefings for routine trials that provoke less severe emotional stress.

ADVANTAGES

1. Jury debriefings reduce the post-verdict stress associated with jury service in emotionally trying cases.

2. Jury debriefings provide closure to the experience of jury service.

3. Jury debriefings safeguard the mental health of jurors, thus promoting public confidence in the judicial system.

4. Jury debriefings enhance juror satisfaction with the judicial process.

DISADVANTAGES

1. Informing jurors that a post-verdict debriefing is available may cause or increase juror stress.

2. Informing jurors that a post-verdict debriefing is available may influence the verdict.

REFERENCES

Leigh B. Bienen, "Helping Jurors Out: Post-Verdict Debriefing for Jurors in Emotionally Disturbing Trials," 68 *Ind. L. J.* 1333 (1993) (describing the trial experience from the juror's perspective and recommending post-verdict counseling for jurors in some trials).

Pamela Casey & Shelley Gable, *Judicial Benchbook on Juror Stress* (National Center for State Courts, forthcoming 1997) (describing sources of juror stress and providing practical guidance on techniques to alleviate stress).

Thomas L. Hafemeister & W. Larry Ventis, "Juror Stress: What Burden Have We Placed on Our Juries?" 56 *Tex. B. J.* 586 (1993) (describing the psychological and physiological effects of jury service in notorious cases).

Timothy R. Murphy, Genevra K. Loveland & G. Thomas Munsterman, *A Manual for Managing Notorious Cases* 79-81 (National Center for State Courts, 1992) (proposing criteria for assessing whether a post-verdict debriefing or counseling would be advisable for jurors in high-profile trials).

STUDIES

Stanley M. Kaplan & Carolyn Winget, "Occupational Hazards of Jury Duty," 20 *Bull. Am. Acad. Psychiatry & L.* 325 (1992) (describing the sources of juror stress in criminal trials and the incidence of symptomatic expression in jurors).

James E. Kelly, "Addressing Juror Stress: A Trial Judge's Perspective," 43 *Drake L. Rev.* 97 (1994) (reporting that jurors in murder trials exhibited significantly higher symptoms of stress than jurors in other types of trials).

RELATED APPENDICES

Appendix 12: Suggested Procedures for Judges Conducting Juror Debriefings

Appendix 13: Letter from a Juror in a High-Profile Case

Appendix 14: "Tips for Coping After Jury Duty," Brochure Distributed by the Maricopa County (Arizona) Superior Court

§ VII-4 Post-Verdict Interviews by Attorneys and Researchers

Technique

After the jury returns its verdict, the attorneys or researchers conduct interviews with the jurors. In jurisdictions that permit attorney interviews, this technique provides attorneys with an opportunity to improve their advocacy skills with constructive feedback about their trial practice techniques. Interviews conducted by researchers provide valuable insight into juror decision making.

Issues

- Where should juror interviews take place?

- If consent of court is necessary to conduct post-trial interviews, should the court supervise interviews? Should the court place any restrictions on the scope of the interviews?

- Who should be present during interviews?

- Should post-trial juror interviews be conducted as individual or group interviews?

- Who should conduct post-trial interviews?

- How long after the trial should post-trial interviews be conducted?

- What topics should be covered?

Procedures

In most jurisdictions, the names and addresses of former jurors are a matter of public record. In some jurisdictions, courts prohibit or limit post-verdict interviews by attorneys or researchers to prevent frivolous efforts to impeach jury verdicts and to protect juror privacy and the inviolability of the deliberative process. Other jurisdictions require prior consent of the judge as an ethical or statutory limitation on post-trial contacts by attorneys. In these jurisdictions, post-verdict interviews are often held at the courthouse and arranged by the court.

The person who contacts the former juror to request an interview should inform the juror of his or her right to refuse to participate in the interview. See also § VII-1, "Advice Regarding Post-Verdict Conversations." Juror interviews may be conducted as telephone interviews, as one-on-one in-person interviews, or as group interviews. The person conducting the interview should be well acquainted with both sides of the trial presentation. Jurors may be more candid and forthcoming with "neutral" interviewers, rather than the trial attorneys themselves.

ADVANTAGES

1. Post-trial juror interviews permit trial attorneys to learn the relative strengths and weaknesses of trial strategies.

2. Post-trial juror interviews permit trial attorneys to receive a fair evaluation of their communication and presentation skills.

3. Post-trial juror interviews permit jury researchers to develop and test emerging theories about juror decision making in real, as opposed to simulated, situations.

4. Jurors often appreciate the opportunity to share their insights and experiences from the trial during post-trial interviews.

5. Post-trial juror interviews often confirm for jurors that their service was an important and valuable contribution to the judicial process.

DISADVANTAGE

Post-trial juror interviews may infringe on jurors' privacy rights or jeopardize the inviolability of the deliberative process.

AUTHORITY

Cal. Civ. Proc. § 206 (Deering 1996) (establishing procedures for post-verdict contact with jurors by the attorneys and parties in criminal cases).

Del. Prof. Cond. R. 3.10 (1995) (prohibiting post-verdict contact with jurors by the trial attorneys).

U.S. Dist. Ct. (N.D. Ind.) Local Rule 47.2 (1996) (prohibiting post-verdict contact with jurors by the trial attorneys except by leave of court and for good cause shown).

REFERENCES

Elissa Krauss & Beth Bonora, eds., *Jurywork: Systematic Techniques* (1995) (Chapter 13 provides a comprehensive overview of post-verdict interview techniques).

Howard Varinsky & Laura Nomikos, "Post-Verdict Interviews: Understanding Jury Decision Making," 26 *Trial* 64 (Feb. 1990) (proposing methodology for conducting post-verdict jury interviews).

§ VII-5 Juror Exit Questionnaires

Technique

The court uses exit questionnaires to monitor juror reaction to jury service and to identify areas of juror dissatisfaction.

Issues

- Who is responsible for distributing exit questionnaires?

- At what point should jurors receive exit questionnaires?

- Who is responsible for tabulating exit questionnaires?

- How often should exit questionnaires be administered?

- Which jurors should receive exit questionnaires? Only sworn jurors? All persons called for voir dire? All jurors or a random sample?

- What questions should be asked of jurors? How should they be phrased?

Procedures

The court selects a distribution system for exit questionnaires and follows it consistently. It may not be necessary to administer exit questionnaires on a daily basis, but they should be distributed on a sufficiently frequent basis to determine juror attitudes toward jury service during periods of high and low jury usage. The court should administer exit questionnaires to a representative sample of persons called for jury service, including those individuals who do not serve as jurors (e.g., alternates, members of the jury panel who are not selected as jurors, and individuals who are subsequently excused from jury service). Use of pretested questions that require fixed (not open-ended) answers avoids biased or ambiguous questions. Pretested questions also facilitate comparison of jurors' responses with responses collected in other courts.

Advantages

1. Consistent and regular use of juror exit questionnaires provides courts with a baseline juror evaluation as well as a perspective on trends in juror attitudes over time.

2. Juror exit questionnaires identify problem areas (e.g., excessive "down-time" for jurors, uncomfortable waiting rooms, etc.) to help courts improve juror satisfaction and the efficiency of jury administration.

DISADVANTAGES

1. Juror exit questionnaires require additional expenditures for copying and personnel time.

2. Accurate analysis of jurors' responses may require expertise that is not routinely available through court personnel.

REFERENCES

American Bar Association, Committee on Jury Standards, *Standards Relating to Juror Use and Management,* Standard 12 (Monitoring the Jury System) (1993).

Brookings Institution, *Charting a Future for the Civil Jury System: A Report from an American Bar Association/Brookings Symposium* 30 (1992).

G. Thomas Munsterman, *Jury System Management* (National Center for State Courts, 1996).

RELATED APPENDIX

Appendix 15: Sample Jury Exit Questionnaires

Appendix 1

Sample Jury Summons Form (Dallas, TX)

STATE OF TEXAS
COUNTY OF DALLAS

CERTIFICATE NO.
DL OR ID NO.
𝔊reetings,

JUROR NO.

Jury Summons

TIME:
DATE:
PLACE:

BY ORDER OF

**YOU ARE CAUTIONED UNDER THE PENALTIES OF LAW
NOT TO FAIL TO ANSWER THIS SUMMONS**

PLEASE READ BOTH SIDES OF SUMMONS CAREFULLY

If claiming exemption or disqualification read the instructions on the back of this form. If the name and/or address above is incorrect, fill out the Voter Registration update on the back of form. Should you have any further questions please direct your inquiries as follows:

PLEASE DIRECT CALLS TO:	MAILING ADDRESS:

TELEPHONE INQUIRIES WILL BE
ANSWERED MONDAY THROUGH FRIDAY
FROM 10:00 A.M. TO 4:00 P.M.

FREE BUS RIDE COUPON - INBOUND ONLY

Detach coupon and present to bus operator upon boarding. Good for one total fare, including transfer, TO DOWNTOWN Dallas. Valid on all DART scheduled bus lines, including Suburban Express routes. Dial 979-1111 for schedule information. Time tables will be available in the courthouse for return trip information.

(over)
VALID ONLY ON:

FREE BUS RIDE COUPON - OUTBOUND ONLY

Detach coupon and present to bus operator upon boarding. Good for one total fare, including transfer, FROM DOWNTOWN Dallas. Valid on all DART scheduled bus lines, including Suburban Express routes. Time tables are available in the courthouse.

(over)
VALID ONLY ON:

PARKING: WE ENCOURAGE JURORS TO PARK IN COUNTY GARAGES MARKED ON THE BACK OF THIS SUMMONS. IF YOU CHOOSE A PREPAY PARKING LOT, PLEASE PAY IN ADVANCE OR YOUR CAR WILL BE TOWED. THERE IS A FEE FOR ALL PARKING, PARKING TICKETS WILL NOT BE VALIDATED.

IMPORTANT: COMPLETE FORM AND BRING WITH YOU

PLEASE TYPE OR PRINT IN BLACK INK   JUROR INFORMATION FORM

NAME	DATE OF BIRTH	DRIVERS LICENSE NO	CIRCLE ONE	NUMBER CHILDREN
			SINGLE MARRIED DIVORCED WIDOWED	
YOUR OCCUPATION	YOUR PRESENT EMPLOYER	YRS	HOW LONG HAVE YOU LIVED IN DALLAS COUNTY	PLACE OF BIRTH
SPOUSE'S OCCUPATION	SPOUSE'S PRESENT EMPLOYER	YRS	SPOUSE'S NAME	

HAVE YOU EVER SERVED ON A CIVIL JURY?	HAVE YOU EVER BEEN PARTY TO A LAW SUIT?
YES ☐ NO ☐ IF SO, WHERE? _____	YES ☐ NO ☐ IF SO, WHAT TYPE?
HAVE YOU EVER SERVED ON A CRIMINAL JURY?	RELIGIOUS PREFERENCE	PHONE NUMBER
YES ☐ NO ☐ IF SO, WHERE? _____		HOME _____ WORK _____

CERT. NO.

DATE

DL NO.

TIME

JUROR NO.

ENTER CORRECT NAME AND/OR ADDRESS BELOW

PLEASE CHECK THE FOLLOWING BOX IF YOU DESIRE TO DONATE YOUR JURY FEE TO THE JUVENILE DEPARTMENT AND HOLIDAY GIFTS FOR CHILDREN IN FOSTER CARE.

YES ☐

SIGNATURE _______________________   NO ☐

On behalf of our youth, the Dallas County Juvenile Board thanks you for your generous contribution.

DISQUALIFICATION OR POSTPONEMENT AFFIDAVIT

IF CLAIMING A DISQUALIFICATION LISTED BELOW OR REQUESTING A POSTPONEMENT, PLEASE FILL IN THIS AFFIDAVIT, DETACH, AND MAIL TO THE REPORTING ADDRESS ON THE FRONT OF THIS FORM. AFFIDAVIT MUST BE NOTARIZED.

AFFIDAVIT

I DO SOLEMNLY SWEAR THAT I AM DISQUALIFIED OR AM REQUESTING A POSTPONMENT FOR THE FOLLOWING REASON: _______________
____
____

I FURTHER SWEAR THIS REQUEST IS NOT FOR BUSINESS REASONS.

____
    YOUR SIGNATURE

SUBSCRIBED TO AND SWORN TO BEFORE ME

THIS _________ DAY OF ____________________ , 19 ____ .
                                        STATE OF TEXAS
                                        COUNTY OF DALLAS

____
    NOTARY   SEAL

DISQUALIFICATIONS

Section 62.102 of the Government Code of the State of Texas states the General Qualifications for Jury Service. A person is disqualified to serve as a petit juror unless he:

(1) is at least 18 years of age;
(2) is a citizen of this state and of the county in which he is requires as a juror;
(3) is qualified under the constitution and laws to vote in the county in which he is to serve as a juror;
(4) is of sound mind and good moral character;
(5) is able to read and write;
(6) has not served as a petit juror for six days during the preceding three months in the county court or during the preceding six months in the district court;
(7) has not been convicted of a felony; and
(8) is not under indictment or other legal accusation of misdemeanor or felony theft, or any other felony.

VOTER REGISTRATION UPDATE
ENTER NAME AND ADDRESS CHANGES BELOW

VOTER REGISTRATION CERTIFICATE NO. ________________

*DRIVERS OR ID NO. ________________________________

*SOCIAL SEC. NO. _________________________________

NAME: ____

ADDRESS: ____

CITY: _________________ STATE: __________ ZIP: ____

*OPTIONAL

EXEMPTIONS

IF CLAIMING AN EXEMPTION LISTED BELOW, FILL IN THE NUMBER OF THE EXEMPTION AND YOUR SIGNATURE. DETACH AND MAIL TO THE REPORTING ADDRESS ON THE FRONT OF THIS FORM.

EXEMPTION NUMBER: _______________________________

SIGNATURE: ______________________________________

EXEMPTIONS

Section 61.106 of the Government Code of the State of Texas states the exemptions from Jury Service as follows:

A person qualified to serve as a juror may establish an exemption from jury service if he:

(1) is over 65 years of age; *for over 65 permanent exemption see #7.
(2) has legal custody of a child or children younger than 10 years of age and his service on the jury requires leaving the child or children without adequate supervision;
(3) is a student of a public or private secondary school;
(4) is a person enrolled and in actual attendance at an institution of higher education;
(5) is an officer or employee of the Senate, House of Representatives or any department, commission, board, office or any other agency in the legislative branch of state government;
(6) is the primary caretaker of a person who is an invalid unable to care for himself.

Section 62.108 of the Government Code of the State of Texas establishes eligibility for exemption if he
*(7) is over 65 years of age who wishes to claim permanent exemption.

INFORMATION TO JURORS

PARKING: Your Parking ticket WILL NOT be validated by a member of the Jury Staff.
JUROR FEE: You will receive $6.00 each day you report.
ATTIRE: Please dress appropriately.

To assist DART in monitoring the success of this free ride offer, please check the appropriate boxes below:

If you are required to return to the courthouse tomorrow, or on successive days, do you plan to ride the bus again?   Yes ☐ No ☐

To assist DART in monitoring the success of this free ride offer, please check the appropriate boxes below:

If called to return to the courthouse on successive days, do you plan to ride the bus again?   Yes ☐ No ☐
Are you a regular transit rider?   Yes ☐ No ☐

THIS IS THE ONLY COMPLIMENTARY SET
OF BUS PASSES THAT YOU WILL BE ISSUED.

REFER TO ADDRESS ON THE FRONT SIDE OF FORM FOR CORRECT REPORTING LOCATION

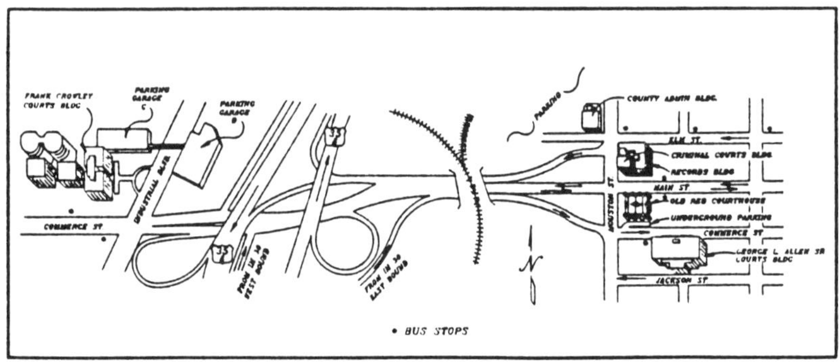

Appendix 2

Modification to the Second Restated Plan for Random Selection of Grand and Petit Jurors Pursuant to Jury Selection and Service Act of 1968 (as Amended)

UNITED STATES DISTRICT COURT
DISTRICT OF CONNECTICUT

MODIFICATION TO THE
SECOND RESTATED PLAN FOR RANDOM SELECTION
OF GRAND AND PETIT JURORS PURSUANT TO JURY SELECTION
<u>AND SERVICE ACT OF 1968 (AS AMENDED)</u>

Pursuant to Article XVI of the Second Restated Plan for Random Selection of Grand and Petit Jurors Pursuant to Jury Selection and Service Act of 1968 (as Amended) ["the Jury Selection Plan"], The Jury Selection Plan is hereby modified as follows:

1. On page 18, insert a new subparagraph e., entitled <u>Additional Questionnaires for Designated Municipalities</u>, at the end of Article XVII, "**AUTOMATION**":

"After the Qualified Jury Wheels have been constructed, in accordance with Articles X, XII, and XVII of the Jury Selection Plan, including the second questionnaires described in Article XVIII of the Jury Selection Plan, additional questionnaires shall be forwarded to designated municipalities ["designated municipalities"] pursuant to the formula set forth below. Such designated municipalities shall consist of such municipalities within each Division whose Hispanic population is equal to or greater than ten percent of its total population. The formula is as follows:

$A = N(y/x-1)$, where

A = number of additional questionnaires to be sent to the designated municipality;

N = number of additional questionnaires originally sent to the designated municipality pursuant to Articles X, XII, and XVII of the Jury Selection Plan;

y = percentage of potential jurors sent questionnaires in the Division excluding all designated municipalities in the Division who returned nondisqualifying questionnaires, as defined in Article VII of the Jury Selection Plan; and x = percentage of potential jurors sent questionnaires in the designated municipality who returned nondisqualifying questionnaires, as defined in Article VII of the Jury Selection Plan.

After such additional questionnaires have been mailed in accordance with this subparagraph, a written certification thereof shall be filed in the public records maintained by the Clerk of the Court in accordance with Article XVIII of the Jury Selection Plan. Such certification, which shall be filed by the Federal Magistrate Judge, Jury Systems Supervisor, or Computer Contractor (as defined in Article XVIII of the Jury Selection Plan), shall indicate each designated municipality within each Division, the number of additional questionnaires sent, and the arithmetical application of the formula.

This modification has been adopted to further enhance the policy of the Jury Selection Plan, as stated in Article II of the Jury Selection Plan, with respect to the participation of Hispanics in federal juries."

Modification of Jury Selection Plan adopted at New Haven, Connecticut, this ___ day of ____, 1995.

Peter C. Dorsey
Chief Judge

T.F. Gilroy Daly
U.S. District Judge

Alan H. Nevas
U.S. District Judge

Alfred V. Covello
U.S. District Judge

Robert N. Chatigny
U.S. District Judge

Dominic J. Squatrito
U.S. District Judge

Alvin W. Thompson
U.S. District Judge

Janet Bond Arteron
U.S. District Judge

Appendix 3

United States v. Soghanalian,
777 F. Supp. 17 (1991)

(Defendants' Motion Requesting Permission to Question Jurors Individually and Out of the Presence and Hearing of Other Jurors)

UNITED STATES DISTRICT COURT
SOUTHERN DISTRICT OF FLORIDA

UNITED STATES OF AMERICA,   )

      Plaintiff,   )

vs.   ) **CASE NO. 87-893-CR-MORENO**

SARKIS G. SOGHANALIAN   )
and PAN AVIATION, INC.,

)

_________________________________   )

DEFENDANTS' MOTION REQUESTING PERMISSION TO QUESTION JURORS INDIVIDUALLY AND OUT OF THE PRESENCE AND HEARING OF OTHER JURORS

The Defendants, Sarkis G. Soghanalian and Pan Aviation, Inc., request that this court permit the questioning of jurors individually and out of the presence and hearing of other jurors. In support of this motion, the Defendants state:

I.

SUMMARY OF THE FACTS

Because this case involves issues of armaments and Iraq, there has been substantial publicity about the case and the Defendants. Moreover, the mere mention of the Nation of Iraq promotes immediate and negative recognition throughout the world, and certainly within the Southern District of Florida. Not only was the Persian Gulf War the subject of the most vigorous and extensive press attention in our history, vastly overwhelming the coverage of the Vietnam War in the 1960's and 1970's, but the conflict with Iraq continues to this day. During the last ten days, concern about world safety and the possibility that Saddam Hussein may be hiding nuclear secrets, have been the talk of the town, the headlines in the newspaper, and the most important world story on television news.

Within this atmosphere of highly charged publicity, the Defendants must fight to obtain a fair trial. While this case has nothing whatsoever to do with the Iraqi conflict or the current atmosphere of hostility between the United States and Saddam Hussein, jurors will have to be questioned about this reality. Because of the extensive and prejudicial publicity, some of which has been directed against Defendant Sarkis Soghanalian, and the virtually certain likelihood that every juror has been exposed to this publicity and may have formulated opinions about the Defendant, the questioning of jurors in each other's presence may expose prejudicial facts which will taint other jurors. There can be little doubt that group voir dire has the potential to poison the entire venire.

This motion is made for three purposes. The first purpose is to permit the selection of fair-minded jurors in an atmosphere of intense publicity. The second purpose is to eliminate the prejudicial influences and effect on other members of the jury panel by reason of questions asked of one prospective juror and the answers given by that juror. Third, individual voir dire is the only effective mechanism to avoid a long delay of the trial to permit the dissipation of the effects of the Iraqi conflict. Because of these issues, the Defendants request that the following procedures be instituted:

1.   Individual voir dire of the jury should be conducted by counsel as to issues of publicity, the Iraqi conflict, the Persian Gulf War, the international sale of armaments and munitions, and Saddam Hussein.

2.   This court should not permit any other prospective juror to be present during the questioning, except those jurors being questioned.

3.   Juror voir dire for all remaining issues should be conducted in groups of no more than six prospective jurors.

II.

REASONS FOR THE REQUEST FOR
INDIVIDUAL VOIR DIRE

1.   There has been and will continue to be, considerable publicity and public discussion about the Iraqi conflict and even about this case. The local, national, and world media coverage of the Iraqi conflict, Sarkis Soghanalian, international arms sales, and the "Merchant of Death" has not been favorable to the Defendant. It would be an understatement to say that the news media attention on these issues has completely saturated the community. There has been, to date, round-the-clock electronic media, daily newspaper, and weekly news magazine coverage of matters which may be discussed during this trial. The publicity certainly raises a legitimate concern regarding the ability of jurors to be fair.

2.   Jurors questioned in large groups are less likely to divulge their true feelings and prejudices for fear of being branded an "unacceptable" juror and to avoid having to voice their opinions and prejudices publicly for fear of being struck from the jury panel. See Murphy v. Florida, 421 U.S. 794, 800, 95 S. Ct. 2031, 2036 (1975) (prospective juror's own "assurances that he is equal to the task cannot be dispositive of the accused's rights."); United States v. Shavers, 615 F.2d 266, 268 (5th Cir. 1980) ("[i]nquiring generally about one's impartiality or participation in a criminal case as a witness or defendant fails to reach the important concerns highlighted in [the defendant's] proposed questions and might not reveal latent prejudice.")

3.   Prospective jurors may respond to questions in ways that would taint the attitudes and answers of other prospective jurors. This will necessitate a mistrial or an entire venire having to be stricken. This factor is most commonly present when there has been extensive pretrial publicity about a case or about issues in a case. Permitting individual voir dire will prevent such problems and will promote the open and honest answers which are sought by voir dire questioning.

4.   In a case such as this, where the issues are serious and complex, the jury selection process should be extensive enough to ensure that the parties are able to intelligently use their peremptory challenges and intelligently challenge prospective jurors for cause, in order to assure the likelihood that a fair and impartial jury will be selected. The selection procedures suggested in this motion will better assure the selection of a fair and impartial jury panel.

5.   This case raises significant problems which will be encountered in attempting to determine whether prospective jurors have become so prejudiced by the pervasive publicity that they are unable to render a fair and impartial judgment based upon the merits of the case. Lawyer-conducted voir dire will allow the type of questioning calculated to effectively probe the possibility that such prejudice exists.

6.   The procedures requested will not take any unnecessary time for the court or the parties, and will prove a more efficient use of time, especially for those prospective jurors not required to sit through the questioning of other jurors. It is imperative that every precaution be taken to select the fairest jury possible, and the procedures requested will provide a very fair method of selecting a jury under the circumstances of this case.

7.   The requested procedures are necessary to protect the Defendants' rights under the Sixth Amendment to the United States Constitution.

III.

<u>LEGAL SUPPORT</u>

The allowable limits of voir dire examination fall within a court's discretion, subject to the element of fairness. <u>Aldridge v. United States</u>, 283 U.S. 308, 310 (1931). Courts have recognized that individual, privately-conducted voir dire promotes candor. <u>Irvin v. Dowd</u>, 366 U.S. 717, 728 (1961). While collateral and unrelated issues are not a proper part of the voir dire process, the necessary inquiry varies in each particular case, depending on the specific facts involved. "Some questions may appear tangential for the trial but are actually so integral to the citizen juror's view of the case, especially one with publicly controversial issues, that they must be explored." United States v. Dellinger, 472 F.2d 340 (7th Cir. 1972).

The nature and type of extensive media comment about issues and facts which may appear in this case signal the need for the type of procedure suggested in this motion. The Fifth and Sixth Amendments to the United States Constitution require that a criminal defendant be afforded a fair trial by a jury "free of the probability of prejudice." Rideau v. Louisiana, 373 U.S. 723 (1963); Estes v. Texas, 381 U.S. 532 (1965).

Recently, the Supreme Court explored the voir dire process in Mu'Min v. Virginia, _____ U.S. _____, 111 S. Ct. 1899 (1991). The Court explained that "[v]oir dire examination serves the dual purposes of enabling the court to select an impartial jury and assisting counsel in exercising peremptory challenges." Id. at 1908. Although the Court rejected a claim that due process requires the individual questioning of jurors about matters pertaining to bias, the Court nevertheless noted in that case that the "subject of possible bias from pretrial publicity" was covered extensively during the voir dire. Id.

A.   Individual Voir Dire Will Permit Free And Uninhibited Communication Between Defense Counsel and Prospective Jurors

Individual and privately-conducted voir dire serves to enhance the obtaining of a jury comprised of a non-biased, uninfluenced cross-section of the community. As the District of Columbia Circuit state in Coppedge v. United States, 272 F.2d 504, 508 (D.C. Cir. 1979):

> It is too much to expect of human nature that a juror would have volunteered, in open court, before his fellow jurors, that he would be influenced in his verdict by a newspaper story of the trial.

Many federal courts have authorized individualized, privately-conducted voir dire in order to promote candor on the part of prospective jurors. See, e.g., United States v. Addonizio, 450 F.2d 49 (3d Cir. 1971); United States v. McKinney, 429 F.2d 1019, 1028, n.9 (5th Cir.) cert. denied, 401 U.S. 922 (1971); United States v. Colovella, 448 F.2d 1299 (2nd Cir. 1971).

Conducting group voir dire in this case is the surest way to "taint" other members of the panel. This concern most commonly arises when there has been extensive pretrial publicity. See, e.g., United States v. Shropshire, 498 F.2d 137 (6th Cir. 1974); United States v. Ridley, 412 F.2d 1126 (D.C. Cir. 1969). Individual voir dire, conducted out of the presence and hearing of other prospective jurors, will best insure that the Defendants receive a fair and impartial trial by a jury that is free from extraneous influences and has no preconceived conclusions regarding guilt.

B.   Individual Voir Dire Promotes Intelligent Use Of Peremptory Challenges

Besides insuring that the voir dire satisfies constitutional standards, individual examination of each prospective juror will facilitate counsels' intelligent use of peremptory challenges exercised pursuant to Rule 24(b). Peremptory challenges remain one of the most important rights of the accused. See Batson v. Kentucky, 476 U.S. 79 (1986); Swain v. Alabama, 380 U.S. 202 (1965); United States v. Blanton, 719 F.2d 815, 823 (6th Cir. 1983)(en banc). In view of the intricate and sensitive issues involved in this case and in view of the extensive prejudicial publicity, individual questioning of prospective jurors by counsel would enable counsel to make individualized judgments regarding the exercise of peremptory challenges. This would minimize the possibility of impairing the peremptory challenge right: Appellate courts have instructed trial courts to "spare no effort to secure an impartial panel." United States v. Dennis, 183 F.2d 201, 226 (2nd Cir. 1950), aff'd. 341 U.S. 494 (1951). In a case like this, "voir dire examination that calls only for the jurors' subjective assessment of their own impartiality is inadequate and ... general questions addressed to the entire panel do not adequately protect the defendant." United States v. McDonald, 576 F.2d 1350, 1355 (9th Cir. 1978).

Individual jurors will adapt better to attorney-conducted voir dire, and are more likely to respond in an inhibited manner. Attorney-conducted voir dire will more easily elicit honest responses from prospective jurors.

IV.

<u>CONCLUSION</u>

The court has considerable discretion in determining the procedures to be utilized at voir dire. In exercising that discretion, this court must be guided by the "demands of essential fairness." United States v. McGregor, 529 F.2d 925, 931 (9th Cir. 1976). "Rigorous voir dire of prospective jurors is required where pretrial publicity is great." MacDonald, 570 F.2d at 1355. This court should exercise its discretion, especially with regard to aspects of the case relating to publicity, and allow defense-conducted individual voir dire of prospective jurors out of the hearing and presence of other jurors.

Respectfully submitted,

SONNETT SALE & KUEHNE, P.A.
Attorneys for Defendant
  SARKIS SOGHANALIAN
26th Floor, One Biscayne Tower
Two South Biscayne Boulevard
Miami, Florida 33131-1802
(305) 358-2000

By______________________________
  NEAL R. SONNETT
  Florida Bar #105986

FLOYD PEARSON RICHMAN GREER
WEIL BRUMBAUGH and RUSSOMANNO, P.A.
Attorneys for Defendant
    PAN AVIATION, INC.
26th Floor, Courthouse Center
175 N.W. First Avenue
Miami, Florida 33128
(305) 373-4000

By________________________________
    GERALD F. RICHMAN
    Florida Bar #066457

Appendix 4

Number of Peremptory Challenges by State and Case Type

PEREMPTORY CHALLENGES
FELONIES/NON-CAPITAL

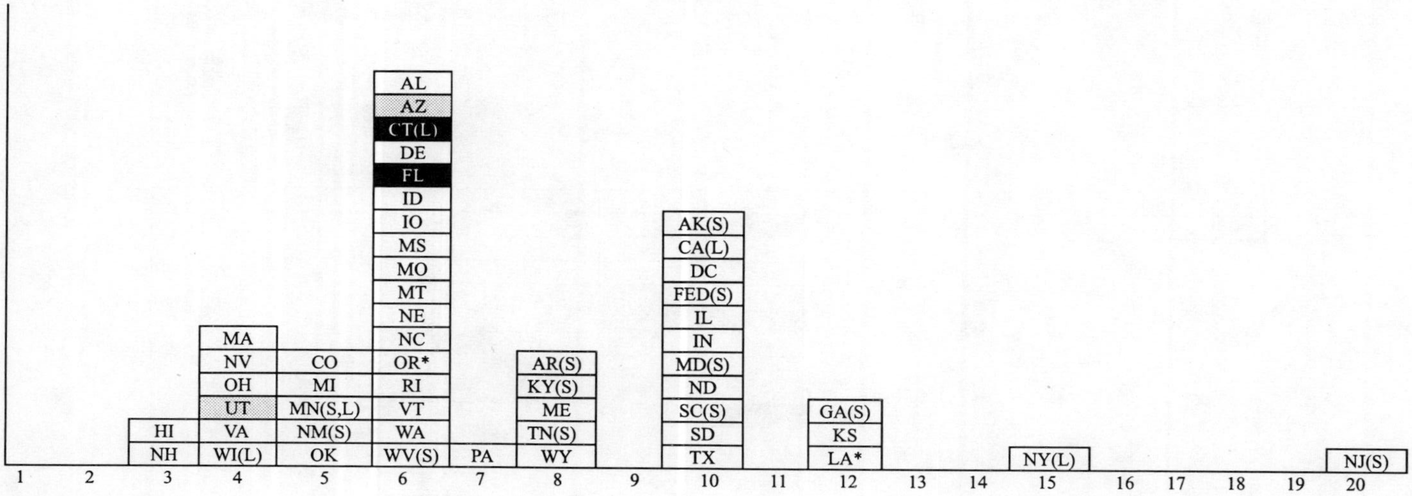

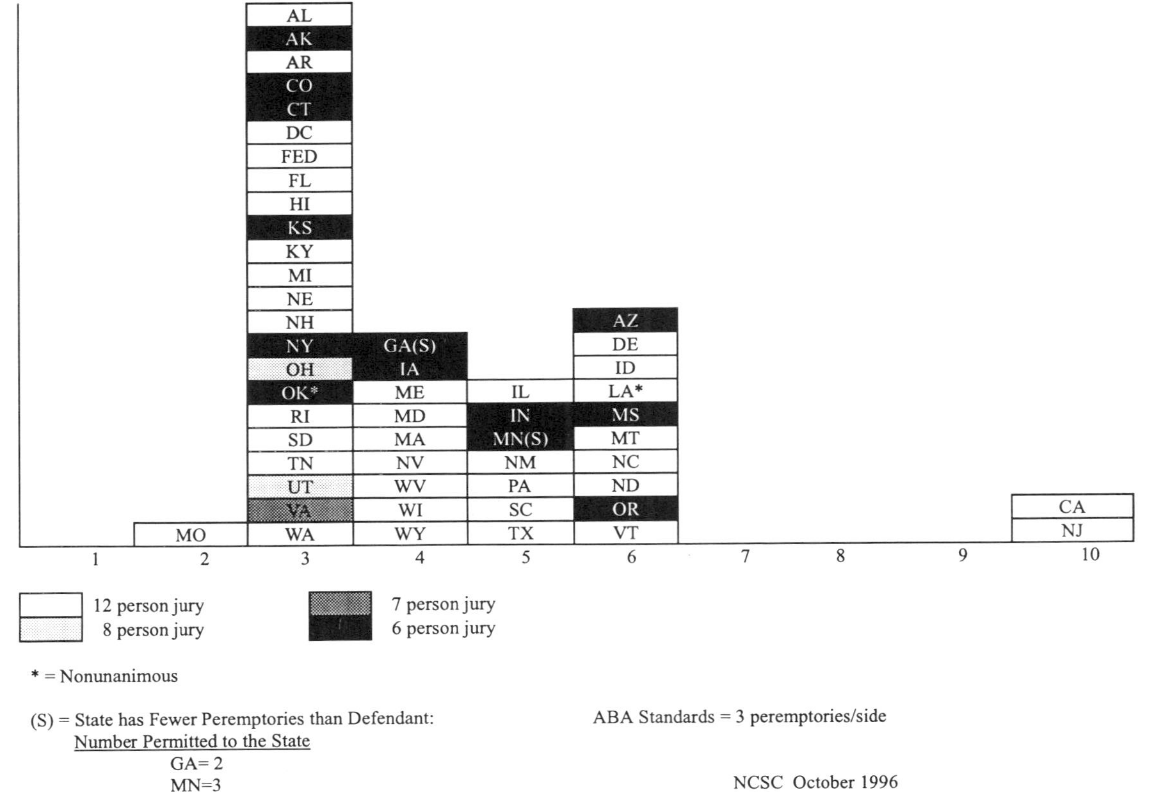

PEREMPTORY CHALLENGES
MISDEMEANOR
AL
AK
AR
CO
CT
DC
FED
FL
HI
KS
KY
MI
NE
NH
NY   GA(S)
OH   IA
OK*   ME   IL   AZ
RI   MD   IN   DE
SD   MA   MN(S) ID
TN   NV   NM   LA*
UT   WV   PA   MS
VA   WI   SC   MT
MO   WA   WY   TX   NC   CA
                         ND   NJ
                         OR
                         VT
1   2   3   4   5   6   7   8   9   10
12 person jury
8 person jury
7 person jury
6 person jury
* = Nonunanimous
(S) = State has Fewer Peremptories than Defendant:
Number Permitted to the State
GA= 2
MN=3
ABA Standards = 3 peremptories/side
NCSC October 1996

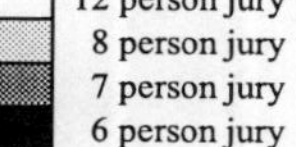

PEREMPTORY CHALLENGES
CIVIL CASES 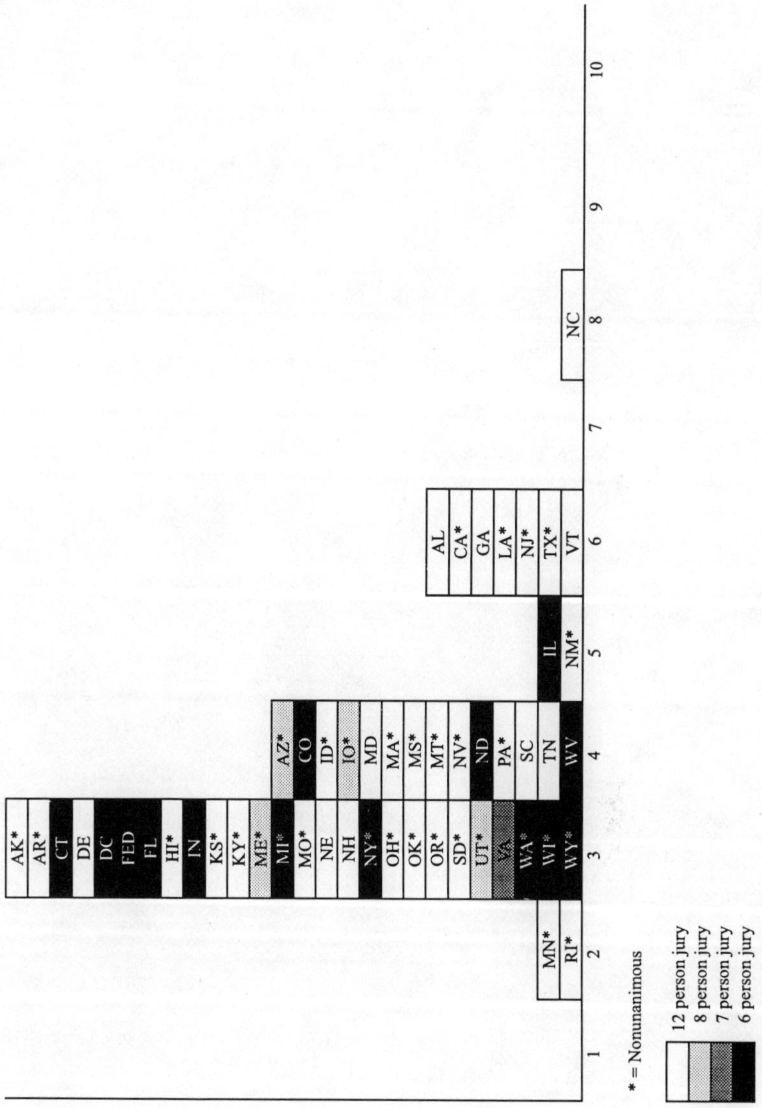
AK*
AR*
CT
DE
DC
FED
FL
HI*
IN
KS*
KY*
ME*
MI*
MO*
NE
NH
NY*
OH*
OK*
OR*
SD*
UT*
VA
WA*
WI*
WY*
AZ*
CO
ID*
IO*
MD
MA*
MS*
MT*
NV*
ND
PA*
SC
TN
WV
MN*
RI*
IL
NM*
AL
CA*
GA
LA*
NJ*
TX*
VT
NC
1 2 3 4 5 6 7 8 9 10
* = Nonunanimous
12 person jury
8 person jury
7 person jury
6 person jury
ABA Standards = 3 per side
NCSC October 1996

Appendix 5

Suggested Procedures for the Management of Anonymous Juries

From Jury Committee of the Ninth Circuit,
A Manual on Jury Trial Procedures, Appendix 8 (1993).

<u>ANONYMOUS JURY PANELS</u>

Anonymous jury panels often become desirable for two reasons. First, due to the nature of the case, the physical security of the jurors becomes a consideration and second, the court may wish the jurors to be protected from an invasion of their privacy from undue publicity.

Often both justifications for anonymity simultaneously apply. Anonymity may also be particularly warranted where the threat of jury tampering is a concern. For example, where the defendants have a prior conviction for jury tampering or where jury tampering is charged in the indictment.

The authority to order an anonymous jury is contained in 27 § 1863 (b) (7) which allows a provision for anonymity to be included in the district's jury selection plan.

The following will outline the method used in the Southern District of New York to derive an anonymous jury. This system is most effective when integrated with the management principles discussed above (e.g., juror questionnaire). The system under discussion provides for all but absolute anonymity meaning that no individual, including the judge and other jurors, will know the name, address, employer's identity, etc., of any given juror. The sole exception to the above will be the jury payroll clerk who will maintain the corresponding records as will be explained below. The jury administrator/clerk should have <u>access</u> to the records routinely. At first blush the above may seem to exceed plausible bounds, but in fact, considerable flexibility is provided by available variations as will be explained. It is generally recognized, however, that the above in practice has worked to the advantage of all parties.

<u>PROCEDURES FOR PROCESSING OF ANONYMOUS JURORS</u>

Assuming 100 anonymous jurors are required:

A)   The anonymous jurors are selected as they come in the door, i.e., the first 100 people in the door are the anonymous panel. (This method avoids having to publicly call names from the wheel. See also <u>Qualifying, Summoning and Excusing Jurors</u>, Administrative Office of the United States Courts, p. 46.)

B)   Three sets of numbered cards (001 to 100) are prepared and used as follows:

       1)   One card is given to the juror as his/her identifying card as they come in the door.

    2)   One card is stapled to the summons as it is handed in by the juror at the door.

    3)   One set, included with the panel sheet, is sent to the courtroom. (The panel sheet does <u>not</u> include the juror's names.)

C)   After the summonses are collected and cards are stapled to the summonses they are <u>alphabetized</u> and secured.

D)   After the jury is selected, the numbered cards of those jurors who were <u>not</u> selected are matched with the corresponding summons.

E)   These summons are in turn matched with the original wheel cards (the cards with the juror's name on it) and these are returned to the wheel for further use.

F)   The summonses and wheel cards of the anonymous jurors are matched and secured.

PAYROLL AND ATTENDANCE

All pertinent papers including name and address forms, mileage sheets, etc., are forwarded to the payroll clerk who maintains a separate and secure record. Attendance is kept by the jury assembly room clerk and courtroom deputy using numbers only, which is in turn transmitted to the payroll clerk who knows the jurors names. The payroll clerk may maintain a separate manual payroll wherein he/she types the checks. Alternatively, a check produced by a computer should have only the anonymous juror's number on it with the address of the courthouse used in lieu of the anonymous juror's address. In this instance the payroll clerk matches the numbered check with the secured records and types in the juror's name manually and then hand delivers the check to the juror at the courthouse. The distribution may be done with the assistance of the Marshal's service. It is assumed that differences among the various districts may obtain regarding payroll processing and the required degree of security and method of processing should be ascertained by the court beforehand. Further, it will be necessary to determine the degree of security required for the various records after the trial is completed.

Interestingly, keeping the records separate may not always be the best method for their security. In some large automated systems integrating them with other petit and grand juror records, as long as they are indistinguishable, would make them virtually impossible to identify, whereas, keeping them separate, with the attendant logistical problems, may make them easier to identify. As noted, each district will have to make a determination in this regard.

TRANSPORTATION OF ANONYMOUS JURORS

In the Southern District of New York, transportation is provided to anonymous jurors from the courthouse to home. These jurors are maintained in a semi-sequestered status and as such are protected from any outside contacts and are escorted by Marshal's from the courtroom to the transportation terminus. Transportation is provided either to a fixed point, such as a specific subway or train station, or portal-to-portal. It is provided one-way only. It is monitored by the Marshal's Service, but is paid for out of Clerk's office funds.

Appendix 6

Arizona Rules of Civil Procedure
Rule 39 (1996)

RULE 39. TRIAL BY JURY OR BY THE COURT

(a) Trial by Jury. When trial by jury has been demanded as provided in Rule 38, the action shall be designated upon the docket as a jury action. The trial of all issues so demanded shall be by jury, unless:

1. The parties or their attorneys of record, by written stipulation filed with the court or by an oral stipulation made in open court and entered in the record, consent to trial by the court sitting without a jury, or

2. The court upon motion or of its own initiative finds that a right of trial by jury of some or all of those issues does not exist.

(b) Order of Trial by Jury; Questions by Jurors to Witnesses or the Court. The trial by a jury shall proceed in the following order, unless the court for good cause stated in the record, otherwise directs:

1. Immediately after the jury is sworn, the court shall instruct the jury concerning its duties, its conduct, the order of proceedings, the procedure for submitting written questions of witnesses or of the court as set forth in Rule 39(b)(10), and the elementary legal principles that will govern the proceeding.

2. The plaintiff or the plaintiff's counsel may read the complaint to the jury and make a statement of the case.

3. The defendant or the defendant's counsel may read the answer and may make a statement of the case to the jury, but may defer making such statement until after the close of the evidence on behalf of the plaintiff.

4. Other parties admitted to the action or their counsel may read their pleadings and may make a statement of their cases to the jury, but they may defer making such statement until after the close of the evidence on behalf of the plaintiff and defendant. The statement of such parties shall be in the order directed by the court.

5. The plaintiff shall then introduce evidence.

6. The defendant shall then introduce evidence.

7. The other parties, if any, shall then introduce evidence in the order directed by the court.

8. The plaintiff may then introduce rebutting evidence.

9. The defendant may then introduce rebutting evidence in support of the defendant's counterclaim(s), if any. Rebuttal evidence from other parties or with respect to cross-claims or third party complaints may be introduced with the permission of the court in an order to be established at the court's discretion.

The statement to the jury shall be confined to a concise and brief statement of the facts which the parties propose to establish by evidence on the trial, and any party may decline to make such statement.

10. Jurors shall be permitted to submit to the court written questions directed to witnesses or to the court. Opportunity shall be given to counsel to object to such questions out of the presence of the jury. Notwithstanding the foregoing, for good cause the court may prohibit or limit the submission of questions to witnesses.

> [Court Comment 1995 Amendments. Rule 39(b)(10). The court should instruct the jury that any questions directed to witnesses or the court must be in writing, unsigned and given to the bailiff. The court should further instruct that, if a juror has a question for a witness or the court, the juror should hand it to the bailiff during a recess, or if the witness is about to leave the witness stand, the juror should signal to the bailiff. If the court determines that the juror's question calls for admissible evidence, the question should be asked by the court or counsel in the court's discretion. Such question may be answered by stipulation or other appropriate means, including but not limited to additional testimony upon such terms and limitations as the court prescribes. If the court determines that the juror's question calls for inadmissible evidence, the question shall not be read or answered. If a juror's question is rejected, the jury should be told that trial rules do not permit some questions to be asked and that the jurors should not attach any significance to the failure of having their question asked.]

. . . .

(d) Verdict, Deliberations and Conduct of Jury; Sealed Verdict; Access to Juror Notes and Notebooks.

1. When the jurors retire to deliberate, they shall be kept together in some convenient place in charge of a proper officer. The court in its discretion may permit jurors to separate while not deliberating, or, on motion of any party, may require them to be sequestered in charge of a proper officer whenever they leave the courtroom or place of deliberation. The court shall admonish them not to converse among themselves or with anyone else on any subject connected with the trial while not deliberating, or to permit themselves to be exposed to any accounts of the proceeding, or to view the place or places where the events involved in the action occurred, until they have completed their deliberations.

2. The court may direct the jury to return a sealed verdict at such time as the court directs.

3. Jurors shall have access to their notes and notebooks during recesses, discussions and deliberations.

(e) Duty of Officer in Charge of Jury. The officer having the jurors under that officer's charge shall not allow any communication to be made to them, or make any, except to ask them if they have agreed upon their verdict, unless by order of the court, and shall not, before the verdict is rendered, communicate to any person the state of their deliberations or the verdict agreed upon.

(f) Admonition to Jurors; Juror Discussions. If the jurors are permitted to separate during the trial, they shall be admonished by the court that it is their duty not to converse with or permit themselves to be addressed by any person on any subject connected with the trial; except that the jurors shall be instructed that they will be permitted to discuss the evidence among themselves in the jury room during recesses from trial when all are present, as long as they reserve judgment about the outcome of the case until deliberations commence. Notwithstanding the foregoing, the jurors' discussion of the evidence among themselves during recesses may be limited or prohibited by the court for good cause.

[Court Comment, 1995 Amendments. Rule 39(f). In exercising its discretion to limit or prohibit jurors' permission to discuss the evidence among themselves during recesses, the trial court should consider the length of the trial, the nature and complexity of the issues, the makeup of the jury, and other factors that may be relevant on a case by case basis.]

(g) Communication to Court by Jury. When the jurors desire to communicate with the court during retirement, they shall make their desire known to the officer having them in charge who shall inform the court and they may be brought into court, and through their foreman shall state to the court, either orally or in writing what they desire to communicate.

(h) Assisting Jurors at Impasse. If the jury advises the court that it has reached an impasse in its deliberations, the court may, in the presence of counsel, inquire of the jurors to determine whether and how court and counsel can assist them in their deliberative process. After receiving the jurors' response, if any, the judge may direct that further proceedings occur as appropriate.

[Court Comment, 1995 Amendments. Rule 39(h). Many juries, after reporting to the judge that they have reached an impasse in their deliberations, are needlessly discharged very soon thereafter and a mistrial declared when it would be appropriate and might be helpful for the judge to offer some assistance in hopes of improving the chances of a verdict. The judge's offer would be designed and intended to address the issues that divide the jurors, if it is legally and practically possible to do so. The invitation to dialogue should not be coercive, suggestive or unduly intrusive.

The judge's response to the jurors' report of impasse could take the following form:

"This instruction is offered to help your deliberations, not to force you to reach a verdict.

"You may wish to identify areas of agreement and areas of disagreement. You may then wish to discuss the law or fact you would like counsel or court to assist you with. If you elect this option, please list in writing the issues where further assistance might help bring about a verdict.

"I do not wish or intend to force a verdict. We are merely trying to be responsive to your apparent need for help. If it is reasonably probable that you could reach a verdict as a result of this procedure, it would be wise to give it a try."

If the jury identifies one or more issues that divide them, the court, with the help of the attorneys, can decide whether and how the issues can be addressed. Among the obvious options are the following: giving additional instructions; clarifying earlier instructions; directing the attorneys to make additional closing argument; reopening the evidence for limited purposes; or a combination of these measures. Of course, the court might decide that it is not legally or practically possible to respond to the jury's concerns.]

(i) Discharge of Jury; New Trial. The jurors may, after the action is submitted to them, be discharged by the court when they have been kept together for such time as to render it altogether improbable that they can agree, or when a calamity, sickness or accident may, in the opinion of the court, require it. When a jury has been discharged without having rendered a verdict the action may be tried again.

. . . .

(m) Advisory Jury and Trial by Consent. In all actions not triable of right by a jury the court upon motion or of its own initiative may try any issue with an advisory jury or, the court, with the consent of both parties, may order a trial with a jury whose verdict has the same effect as if trial by jury had been a matter of right.

(n) Interrogatories When Equitable Relief Sought; Answers Advisory. In actions where equitable relief is sought, if a jury is demanded, and more than one material issue of fact is joined, the court may submit written interrogatories to the jury covering all or part of the issues of fact, and such interrogatories shall be answered by the jury. The interrogatories shall be approved by the court, and each interrogatory shall be confined to a single question of fact and shall be so framed that it can be answered yes or no, and shall be so answered. The answers shall be only advisory to the court.

(o) Arguments. The party having under the pleadings the burden of proof on the whole case shall be entitled to open and close the argument. Where there are several parties having several claims or defenses, and represented by different counsel, the court shall prescribe the order of argument among them.

> [Court Comment, 1995 Amendments. Rule 39(o). The Court has discretion to give final instructions to the jury before closing arguments of counsel instead of after, in order to enhance jurors' ability to apply the applicable law to the facts. In that event, the court may wish to withhold giving the necessary procedural and housekeeping instructions until after closing argument, in order to offset the impact of the last counsel's argument.]

(p) Note Taking by Jurors. The court shall instruct that the jurors may take notes regarding the evidence and keep the notes for the purpose of refreshing their memory for use during recesses, discussions and deliberations. The court shall provide materials suitable for this purpose. After the jury has rendered its verdict, the notes shall be collected by the bailiff or clerk who shall promptly destroy them.

Appendix 7

Suggested Jury Instructions Concerning Juror Questions That Were Not Asked of Witnesses

Reprinted with permission from Warren D. Wolfson, "An Experiment in Juror Interrogation of Witnesses," 1 *CBA Report* 12, 13 (Feb. 1987).

"During the course of this trial, the Court has allowed jurors to prepare questions to be asked of certain witnesses. Some of those questions were not asked. The jury must not concern itself with the Court's reasons for refusing to ask questions. The fact that certain questions were not asked must not affect your consideration of the evidence in any way."

Appendix 8

Sample Preliminary Jury Instructions

SAMPLE A

PRELIMINARY INSTRUCTIONS FROM
TORRES V. ST. JOSEPH'S HOSPITAL,
NO. CV93-06828 (SUPER. CT. ARIZ. 1993)

INTRODUCTION TO PRELIMINARY INSTRUCTIONS

Now that we are about to begin the trial, there are some preliminary matters I would like to share with you so that you will better understand what will happen during the trial. In addition, I have some suggestions about your conduct during the trial.

It is your duty to follow these instructions. These instructions are preliminary only and may be changed during or at the end of the trial. After you have heard all of the evidence I will read the final instructions of law to you. You will also receive a written copy of them. You must follow the final instructions in deciding the case.

IMPORTANCE OF JURY SERVICE

Jury Service is an important part of our system of justice, with a long and distinguished tradition in western civilization.

From its beginning, American law has viewed the jury system as an effective means of drawing on the collective wisdom, experience, and fact-finding abilities of persons such as yourselves. While it may be an occasional inconvenience, or worse, jury service is an important responsibility for you, one which I am sure you will take seriously.

One or more of you is an undesignated alternate juror. We use alternates to avoid the time and expense of starting a new trial in the event one of you becomes sick or detained by some emergency. The alternates will be chosen at random at the end of the case and excused from any deliberations.

<u>WHAT THE PLAINTIFFS MUST PROVE</u>

Plaintiffs' Claim of Medical Negligence

Plaintiffs claim that defendant was at fault for medical negligence.

Medical negligence is the failure to comply with the applicable standard of medical care. To comply with the applicable standard of medical care, a health care provider must exercise that degree of care, skill, and learning that would be expected under similar circumstances of a reasonably prudent health care provider within this state.

Fault is medical negligence that was a cause of injury to plaintiffs. Before you can find defendant at fault, you must find that defendant's negligence was a cause of Amy Olivas' death. Negligence is a cause of death if it helps produce the death, and if the death would not have happened without the negligence.

On the claim of fault for medical negligence, plaintiffs have the burden of proving:

(1) Defendant was negligent;

(2) Defendant's negligence was a cause of Amy Olivas' death; and

(3) Plaintiffs' damages.

Defendant claims that the decedent, Amy Olivas, was at fault for failing to exercise reasonable care for her own health. Defendant has the burden of proving:

(1) Amy Olivas was negligent; and

(2) Her own negligence was a cause of her death.

Expert Witnesses in Medical Negligence Cases

Court rules limit the number of expert witnesses each party can present in a medical negligence case. The rules limit the number of witnesses who can give opinions on the various issues in the case.

Do not speculate on the reasons for these rules. Do not draw any conclusions or inferences from the fact that more expert witnesses did not testify, or from the fact that some expert witnesses who did testify were not asked to give opinions regarding certain issues in the case.

BURDEN OF PROOF

The party who makes a claim has the burden of proof and must persuade you by the evidence that the claim is more probably true than not true. In other words, the evidence supporting a proposition that a party has the burden of proving must outweigh the evidence opposed to it. In determining whether a party has met this burden, you must consider all the evidence, whether produced by plaintiffs or defendant.

NOTE TAKING PERMITTED

Notebooks and pencils have been provided for note taking. No juror is required to take notes. Some of you may feel that note taking is not helpful because it may interfere with the hearing and evaluation of evidence. For example, you need to watch witnesses during their testimony in order to assess their appearance, behavior, memory and whatever else bears on their believability.

Notes are only to help you remember. They should not take the place of your independent memory of the testimony. On the other hand, if you take no notes at all, you run the risk of forgetting important testimony needed for your verdict. Court reporter transcripts of testimony are usually not available during deliberations.

Please remember the number on the cover of your notebook so it can be returned to you after each recess. If you do not take your notebook with you for short recesses, simply leave it on your chair. For longer recesses (overnight and weekends), and if you choose not to take it home with you, the bailiff will store your notebook and return it to the seat when the trial resumes. When deliberations commence you will take your notebook with you. At no time will anyone open or read your notebook. If you take your notebook or instructions home with you, you are not to share the contents with anyone else until the trial is over and you have been discharged.

At the end of the case the notes will be collected, not read, but destroyed by the bailiff, unless you choose to take the notes with you.

QUESTIONS BY JURORS

You may have questions of the witnesses or me from time to time. If one is important to you please write it down, do not sign it, and hand it to the bailiff during a recess or signal if you have a question for a witness about to leave the witness stand. The bailiff will bring it right to me.

If I decide that the question is a proper one, the attorneys and I will provide an answer at the earliest logical opportunity. Keep in mind, however, that the rules of evidence or other rules of law may prevent some of your questions from being answered. I will apply the same legal standards to your questions as I do to questions asked by the lawyers.

Do not speculate as to why your question was not asked, if it wasn't. The failure to ask a question is not a reflection on the person asking it.

INTRODUCTION OF STAFF

I now want to introduce the staff for this division. The bailiff is Peter Powers. He is usually seated at the desk directly across from you. The bailiff assists us in getting into the courtroom on time and helps with many other tasks. He may leave from time to time during testimony to perform some of those other tasks.

The division's judicial assistant is Lori Hughey. She has offices directly across from the jury room. She also doubles as the court's second bailiff. If you need anything during the trial either the bailiff or the judicial assistant would be happy to assist.

The court clerk is Sue Nielsen. She is seated just to my left. Among other things, she keeps the official record of proceedings, handles all the exhibits and swears the witnesses and jurors.

Seated in front of both of us is the court reporter. Her name is Linda Schroeder. She takes down everything said in court so that we can have a word-for-word record.

My name is Michael Dann, Judge of Division 10. This division's phone number is 506-3916.

SCHEDULING DURING TRIAL

The trial is expected to last through Wednesday, December 6. We will all do our best to move the case along, but delays frequently occur. These won't be anyone's fault, so don't hold them against the parties. Delays usually occur because the attorneys and I often need to resolve certain legal matters before these matters may be presented to you in court or because I am busy with emergency matters in other cases.

The usual hours of trial will be from 10:00 a.m. to 4:30 p.m. We will take short recesses about every hour and occasional stretch breaks in place. Unless a different starting time is announced prior to recessing for the evening, you may assume a starting time of 10:00 a.m. for the next day.

At the beginning of the day, please assemble in the jury room for this division. Please do not come back into the courtroom until you are called by the bailiff.

ORDER OF TRIAL

Trials generally proceed in the following order:

First, the plaintiffs' att orney will make an opening statement giving a preview of the case. The defendant's attorney may make an opening statement outlining the defense case immediately after the plaintiffs' statement or it may be postponed until after the plaintiffs' case has been presented. What is said in opening statements is not evidence. Nor is it an argument. The purpose of an opening statement is to help you prepare for anticipated evidence.

Second, the plaintiffs will present their evidence. After the plaintiffs finish, the defendant may present evidence. If the defendant does produce evidence, the plaintiffs may present additional, or rebuttal, evidence.

With each witness, there is a direct examination, a cross examination by the opposing side, and finally a redirect examination. This usually ends the testimony of that witness.

Third, after all the evidence is in, I will read and give you copies of the final instructions, the rules of law you must follow in reaching your verdict.

Fourth, the attorneys will make closing arguments to tell you what they think the evidence shows and how they think you should decide the case. The plaintiffs have the right to open and close the argument since the plaintiffs have the burden of proof. Just as in opening statements, what is said in closing arguments is not evidence.

Fifth, you will deliberate in the jury room about the evidence and rules of law and decide upon a verdict. Once you agree upon the verdict, it will be read in court with you and the parties present.

Finally, you will be discharged and released from the restrictions I will read to you next.

CONDUCT OF JURORS

There are a number of important rules governing your own conduct during the trial. Sometimes these are called admonitions.

First, you should keep an open mind throughout the trial and reach your conclusion only after you have heard all the evidence, the final instructions of law and the closing arguments of counsel and your deliberations have begun.

Second, you may discuss the evidence during the trial, but only among yourselves and only in the jury room. However, you must be very careful not to make up your minds about the final outcome until you have heard everything—all the evidence, the final instructions and the attorneys' arguments—and your deliberations have begun. Obviously, it would be unfair and unwise to decide the case until you have heard everything.

Third, although you may discuss the evidence among yourselves in the jury room during the trial, do not discuss the case with <u>anyone</u> else until after your verdict. Another person might tell you information the parties don't learn about and are unable to prove wrong or explain. To minimize the risk of accidentally overhearing something about the case I ask that you continue to wear the jurors' badges while in and around the courthouse. Should anyone happen to discuss the case in your presence, report that fact at once to any member of the staff.

Fourth, though it is entirely natural to talk or visit with people with whom you are thrown in contact, please do not talk with any of the attorneys, parties, witnesses or spectators either in or out of the courtroom. If you meet in the hallways or elevators, there is nothing wrong with saying a "good morning" or "good afternoon," but your conversation should end there. In no other way can the parties be assured of the absolute fairness they are entitled to expect from you as jurors. If the attorneys, parties and witnesses do not greet you outside of court, or avoid riding in the same elevator with you, they are not being rude. They are just carefully observing this rule forbidding contact.

Next, since this case involves events that occurred at a particular location, you may be tempted to visit the scene. Please do not do so. Important changes may have occurred at the location since the original event. In making an unguided visit without the benefit of an explanation, you might get an erroneous or partial impression.

Last, do not attempt any research, tests, experiments or other investigation on your own. It would be difficult to impossible to duplicate conditions shown by the evidence; therefore, your results would not be reliable. Nor would the parties or I know of your activities. Your verdict must be based solely upon the evidence produced in this courtroom.

If before any break or recess I do not repeat these admonitions word for word, I will simply say, "please remember the admonitions." The rules apply at all times during the trial—24 hours a day, 7 days a week—until you return a verdict in open court and are discharged by me.

FUNCTIONS OF JURY

As jurors, you have two major duties:

First, you must listen to and look at the evidence and decide from the evidence what happened in this case, that is, what the facts are. It is your job and no one else's to decide what the facts are. I intend to preside impartially and not express any opinion concerning the facts. Any views of mine on the facts are totally irrelevant. This includes gestures or frowns or smiles or other body language. Comments to or questions of lawyers or witnesses by me are intended to move the case along or to clarify some evidence.

Second, you must carefully listen to the laws that I will instruct you on at the end of the case. You must follow them in reaching your verdict.

In fulfilling your duties as jurors you must not be influenced by feelings of sympathy or prejudice.

EVIDENCE, STATEMENTS OF LAWYERS AND RULINGS

As I mentioned earlier, it is your job to decide from the evidence what the facts are. Here are six rules that will help you decide what is and what is not evidence:

1. Evidence to be considered:

You are to determine the facts only from the testimony of witnesses and from exhibits received in evidence.

2. <u>Lawyers' statements:</u>

Ordinarily, statements or arguments made by the lawyers in the case are not evidence. Their purpose is to help you understand the evidence and law. However, if the lawyers agree or stipulate that some particular fact is true, you should accept it as the truth.

3. <u>Questions to a witness:</u>

By itself, a question is not evidence. A question can only be used to give meaning to a witness' answer.

4. <u>Objections to questions:</u>

If a lawyer objects to a question and I do not allow the witness to answer, you must not try to guess what the answer might have been. You must also not try to guess the reason why the lawyer objected in the first place.

5. <u>Rejected evidence:</u>

At times during the trial, testimony or exhibits will be offered as evidence but I might not allow them to become evidence. Since they never become evidence, you must not consider them.

6. <u>Stricken Evidence</u>

At times I may order some evidence to be stricken, or thrown out. Since that is no longer evidence, you must not consider it.

<u>CREDIBILITY OF WITNESSES</u>

As jurors, you have to decide which testimony to believe and how much weight to give it.

In making these decisions you should take into account, among other things, each witness' ability and opportunity to observe the events, the witness' memory, appearance and behavior while testifying, any reasons the witness might have to testify as occurred and how the testimony compares to the other evidence in the case.

OPINIONS BY EXPERTS

Ordinarily, a witness may not give an opinion during testimony. However, an expert witness may state an opinion and the reasons for it. An expert witness is a person with special skill or education in a particular field.

Even though expert witnesses may give their opinion, you are not required to accept those opinions. To determine the value of an expert's opinion, you should take into account the expert's qualifications and believability. You should also consider how the conclusions were reached or opinions arrived at.

EXCLUSION OF WITNESSES

The rule of exclusion of witnesses is in effect and will be observed by all witnesses until the trial is over and a result announced.

This means that all witnesses will remain outside the courtroom during the entire trial except when one is called to the witness stand. They will wait in the areas directed by the bailiff unless other arrangements have been made with the attorney who has called them. The rule also forbids witnesses from telling anyone but the lawyers what they will testify about or what they have testified to. If witnesses do talk to the lawyers about their testimony, other witnesses and jurors should avoid being present or overhearing.

The lawyers are directed to inform all their witnesses of these rules and to remind them of their obligations from time to time as may be necessary. The parties and their lawyers should keep a careful lookout to prevent any potential witness from remaining in the courtroom if they inadvertently enter.

CONCLUSION TO PRELIMINARY INSTRUCTIONS

The rules of law I have shared with you in the past few minutes are preliminary only. At the end of the case I will read to you and give you a copy of the final instructions of law. In deciding the case you must be guided by the final instructions.

Sample B

Arizona Suggested Pretrial Instruction on "Conduct of the Jury"

Now, a few words about your conduct as jurors.

First, you are not to discuss the case, or anything about it, with anyone other than your fellow jurors in the jury room. Until you retire to the jury room at the end of the case to deliberate on your verdict, you simply are not to talk about this case with anyone. There is one exception to this rule—during the trial you may discuss with your fellow jurors the testimony of the witnesses and the exhibits so long as that discussion takes place in the jury room when all the jurors are present. In your discussions, you must not attempt to arrive at a conclusion as to the ultimate outcome of the case or what your verdict might be in this case. You must withhold your final decision in this case and keep an open mind until you have heard all the evidence, the court's instructions on the law, final arguments of counsel and after you have deliberated on all aspects of the case with your fellow jurors. This time is solely for you to discuss the exhibits, testimony of the witnesses and evidence in the case among yourselves. When you go home at night during the trial, you may be asked, what happened? Just tell them there is a mean, gray-haired old judge who will skin you alive if you tell, so mum's the word.

Second, do not read, listen to, or watch anything touching this case in any way. If anyone should try to talk to you about this case, tell them you are a juror and that it is improper for them to do so. If they persist, bring it to my attention promptly and I'll take care of it from there!

Third, do not do any research or make any investigation about the case on your own.

If you want to take notes during the course of this trial, you may do so. Many of us have found that taking notes in school or class helps us remember important things that were said. In many ways this trial will be like a class. If taking notes helps you remember, then take notes. Just be sure that your notetaking does not interfere with your listening to all the testimony and carefully observing the witnesses' demeanor while testifying. If you do take notes, do not discuss them with anyone other than your fellow jurors in the jury room before you begin your deliberations, and not be overly influenced by the notes of other jurors. Do not take the notes with you at the end of the day. Leave them in the jury room.

If you choose not to take notes, remember it is your own individual responsibility to listen carefully to the evidence. You cannot give this responsibility to someone who is taking notes. We depend on the judgment of all members of the jury. You must all remember the evidence in this case. We depend not on your individual brilliance, but your collective wisdom.

You will notice that we have an official court reporter making a record of the trial. However, we will not have type-written transcripts of this record available for your use in reaching a decision in this case or to assist you in your deliberations.

One last item: Jurors are allowed to ask questions. If you have a question, please write it out, but do not sign it. The bailiff will collect them at every recess, and I will then determine if they are proper. If it is possible to do so, we will get you an answer to your question before the end of the trial. If your question is not appropriate under the law, I will let you know.

Sample C

Sample Jury Instructions
Before Closing Arguments

A. Opening Instructions

Members of the jury:

Now that the evidence in this case has been presented, the time has come for me to instruct you on the law. My instructions will be in three parts: first, some instructions on general rules that define and control the jury's duties in a criminal case; second, the instructions that define the elements of the offense charged in the indictment, i.e., the elements that the government must prove in order to make its case; and third, some rules and guidelines for your deliberations. A copy of these instructions will be available to you in the jury room to consult if you find it necessary.

Duties of the Jury

In defining the duties of the jury, let me first give you a few general rules:

It is your duty to find the facts from all the evidence in the case. To the facts as you find them you must apply the law as I give it to you. You must follow the law as I give it to you, whether you agree with it or not. And you must do your duty as jurors regardless of any personal likes or dislikes, opinions, prejudices or sympathy. That means, that you must decide the case solely on the evidence before you.

In following my instructions, you must follow all of them and not single out some and ignore others; they are all equally important. And you must not read into these instructions, or into anything the Court may have said or done, any suggestion from the Court as to what verdict you should return—that is a matter entirely up to you.

Three Basic Rules in Criminal Cases

At the beginning of the case, I gave you some general rules about criminal trials. I will now relate them for you in more detail. There are three basic rules.

1. Presumption of Innocence

The first rule is that the defendant is presumed innocent unless or until proved guilty, and this presumption alone is sufficient to acquit him. The indictment brought by the government against a defendant is an assumption, and only that; it is not proof of anything at all. The defendant is presumed innocent unless or until the jury decides, unanimously, that the government has proved the defendant's guilt beyond a reasonable doubt.

2. Burden of Proof on Government

That brings me to the second rule. In a criminal case, the burden of proving guilt is on the government. It has that burden throughout the entire trial. The defendant never has any burden to prove his innocence, to produce any evidence at all, or to testify. The law prohibits you from considering, in arriving at your verdict, that a defendant may not have testified.

3. Proof Beyond a Reasonable Doubt

The third rule is that the government must prove each element of the alleged crime beyond a reasonable doubt. I will explain those elements later in these instructions. A reasonable doubt is a doubt based on reason and common sense. This means that if, after you have considered all the evidence in this case, you have a doubt based on reason and common sense concerning a defendant's guilt, you must acquit. You may not convict on the basis of a mere suspicion. On the other hand, the government is not required to prove guilt beyond all possible doubt. You should return a guilty verdict if, but only if, you find the evidence so convincing that an ordinary person would not hesitate to rely and act on it in the most important of his or her own affairs.

Three Forms of Evidence

Next I want to discuss with you generally what we mean by evidence and how you should consider it.

The evidence from which you are to decide what the facts are comes in one of three forms.

First, there is the sworn testimony of witnesses, both on direct and cross-examination, and regardless of who called the witness.

Second, there are the exhibits that the Court has received into the trial record.

Third, there are any facts to which all the lawyers have agreed or stipulated, or that the Court has directed you to find.

What is Not Evidence

Certain things are not evidence and are to be disregarded in deciding what the facts are:

1. Arguments or statements by lawyers are not evidence.

2. The questions to the witnesses are not evidence. They can be considered only to give meaning to the witnesses' answer.

3. Objections to questions and arguments are not evidence. Attorneys have a duty to their client to object when they believe a question is improper under the rules of evidence. You should not be influenced by the objection or by the Court's ruling on it. If the objection is sustained, ignore the question; if it is overruled, treat the answer like any other answer.

4. Testimony that has been excluded , stricken, or that you have been instructed to disregard is not evidence, and must be disregarded. In addition some testimony and exhibits have been received only for a limited purpose; where the Court has given such a limiting instruction, you must follow it.

5. Anything you may have seen or heard outside the courtroom is not evidence. You are to decide the case solely on the evidence offered and received in the trial.

Direct and Circumstantial Evidence

I have told you about the three forms in which evidence comes: testimony, exhibits and stipulations. There are two kinds of evidence: direct and circumstantial. Direct evidence is direct proof of a fact, such as testimony of an eyewitness. Circumstantial evidence is proof of a chain of circumstances from which you could infer or conclude that a fact exists, even though it has not been proved directly. You are entitled to consider both kinds of evidence.

The word "infer"—or the expression "to draw an inference"—means to find that a fact exists based on proof of another fact. For example, if you see water on the street outside your window, you can infer that is has rained. In other words, the fact of rain is an inference that could be drawn from the presence of water on the street; an inference may also be drawn only if it is reasonable and logical, not if it is speculative. Other facts may, however, explain the presence of water without rain. Therefore, in deciding whether to draw an inference, you must look at and consider all the facts in the light of reason, common sense, and experience. After you have done that, the question whether to draw a particular inference is for the jury to decide.

Deciding What Testimony to Believe

In deciding what the facts are, you must consider all the evidence that has been offered. In doing this, you must decide which testimony to believe and which testimony not to believe. In making that decision, there are a number of factors you may take into account, including the following:

1. The witness' opportunity to observe the events he described.

2. The witness' intelligence and memory.

3. The witness' manner while testifying.

4. Whether the witness has any interest in the outcome of this case or any bias or prejudice concerning any party or any matter involved in the case.

5. The reasonableness of the witness' testimony considered in light of all the evidence in the case.

In considering the testimony of any defendant who chooses to take the stand, you must apply the same standards you apply to any other witness.

If you find that a witness' testimony is contradicted by what that witness has said or done at another time, or by the testimony of other witnesses, you may disbelieve all or any part of the witness' testimony. But in deciding whether or not to believe him, keep this in mind:

1. People sometimes forget things. A contradiction may be an innocent lapse of memory or it may be an intentional falsehood. Consider therefore whether it has to do with an important fact or only a small detail.

2. Different people observing an event may remember it differently and therefore testify about it differently.

You may consider the factors I have discussed in deciding how much weight to give a testimony. Remember that the weight of evidence does not necessarily depend on the number of witnesses testifying on one side or the other. You must consider all the evidence in the case, and you may find the testimony of a smaller number of witnesses on one side more credible than that of a larger number on the other.

All of these are matters for you to consider in finding the facts.

Remember that only this defendant is on trial here, not anyone else. You should consider evidence about the acts, statements, and intentions of others only as they bear on the charges against the defendant.

And remember that this defendant is on trial only for the offenses charged in the indictment, not for anything else.

B. Conspiracy

In this case, the defendant is accused of having been a member of a conspiracy. A conspiracy is a kind of criminal partnership, an agreement or combination of two or more people to do something unlawful. The crime is the making of the agreement or combination; it does not matter whether it was successful or not.

For you to decide whether the government has proved its charge against the defendant, you must answer these four questions:

First, did the government prove beyond a reasonable doubt that there was a conspiracy to import cocaine as charged, starting sometime before (date)?

Second, did the government prove beyond a reasonable doubt that defendant became a member of that conspiracy sometime on or before (date)?

Third, did the government prove beyond a reasonable doubt that one of the members of the conspiracy did one of the overt acts described in the indictment?

Fourth, did the government prove beyond a reasonable doubt that whatever overt act was done by one of the members of the conspiracy was done to accomplish the purpose of the conspiracy, i.e., the importation of cocaine?

I will discuss with you briefly the law relating to each of these four questions.

Concerning the first question, you must decide whether the evidence shows beyond a reasonable doubt that A and B, alone or with defendant, entered into an agreement or a joint plan to import cocaine.

It is not necessary that they a formal agreement or that they agreed on every detail of the conspiracy. On the other hand, it is not enough if you merely find that they associated together, discussed matters of common interest, acted in similar ways, or perhaps helped one another. You must find beyond a reasonable doubt a joint plan to import cocaine.

Concerning the second question, if you find A and B entered into a conspiracy you must then decide whether the evidence shows beyond a reasonable doubt that defendant joined them. To find against defendant here, you must find that he became a member of a conspiracy knowing of the unlawful plan and intending to help accomplish it.

Bear in mind that defendant is charged with a serious crime. He cannot be convicted unless you are satisfied beyond a reasonable doubt that he had a specific intention to join in an unlawful conspiracy. So it is not enough for you to find, for example, simply that defendant helped unload a crate containing cocaine or that he was present when the crate was opened and cocaine unloaded. To convict defendant you must in addition find that he actually and deliberately jointed with A or B or both in a plan to import cocaine.

Since you cannot look into a defendant's mind to ascertain his intent, you must infer his intent, from what the evidence shows about his acts and words, both on and before (date) and from all the surrounding circumstances. Only if those acts enable you to find beyond a reasonable doubt that defendant did these things, but that he did them with the intent to join in the conspiracy can you find him guilty.

Unless you have answered yes to the first two questions, you will not reach the third. If you do, you must then decide if the evidence shows beyond a reasonable doubt that one of the overt acts charged in the indictment was committed.

An overt act is simply any act done to achieve the purpose of the conspiracy. It does not have to be unlawful by itself. And it does not matter whether defendant was himself involved in that act, because once you have found him to have been a member of the conspiracy he then becomes responsible for what the other conspirators said or did to carry out the conspiracy, whether he knew about it or not.

Finally, if you have answered the first three questions yes, you must decide whether the evidence shows beyond a reasonable doubt that the overt act was done for the purpose of carrying out the conspiracy. By way of example, picking up a crate at the airport, although innocent itself, may be an overt act if it is shown to have been done for the purpose of carrying out an unlawful plan. To return a guilty verdict you must find that the evidence establishes beyond a reasonable doubt that one such overt act was done by some member of the conspiracy for that purpose.

C. Closing Instructions

I will now say a few words about your deliberations.

First, keep in mind that nothing I have said in these instructions is intended to suggest to you in any way what I think your verdict should be. That is entirely for you to decide.

When you retire, it is your duty to discuss the case with your fellow jurors for the purpose of reaching agreement if you can do so. Each of you must decide the case for yourself, but should do so only after considering all the evidence, listening to the views of your fellow jurors, and discussing it fully with the other jurors. It is important that you reach a verdict if you can do so conscientiously. You should not hesitate to reconsider your own opinions from time to time and to change them if you are convinced that they are wrong. However, do not surrender an honest conviction as to the weight and effect of the evidence simply to arrive at a verdict.

Remember that your verdict must be unanimous on each count and as to each defendant.

Remember also that your verdict must be based solely on the evidence in the case and the law as the Court has given it to you, not on anything else. Opening statements, closing arguments, or other statements or arguments of counsel are not evidence. If your recollection differs from the way counsel has stated it, then your recollection controls.

And finally, bear in mind that the government has the burden of proof and that you must be convinced of defendant's guilt beyond a reasonable doubt to return a guilty verdict. If you find that this burden has not been met, you must return a verdict of not guilty.

Some of you have taken notes during the trial. Remember that the notes are only for the personal use of the person who took them. They are not to be read or given to others.

It is very important that you not communicate with anyone outside the jury room about your deliberations or about anything touching this case. There is only one exception to this rule. It if becomes necessary during your deliberations to communicate with the Court, you may send a note through the Marshal, signed by your foreman or by one or more members of the jury. No member of the jury should ever attempt to communicate with the Court except by a signed writing; and the Court will never communicate with any member of the jury on any subject touching the merits of the case other than in writing, or orally here in open court. If you send any notes to the Court, do not disclose anything about your deliberations. Specifically, do not disclose to anyone—not even to the Court—how the jury stands, numerically or otherwise, on the question of the guilt or innocence of the defendant, until after you have reached a unanimous verdict or have been discharged.

Appendix 9

Suggestions for Juries About Deliberations

Sample A

Prepared by Hon. Janet Kintner (San Diego, CA) and Prof. Herman Gadon

You are free to manage your jury deliberations in any way that seems most suitable to you. However, I will offer a few suggestions, and you are free to accept or reject them, that may make it possible to proceed more smoothly with your deliberations.

1. When you return to the jury room to begin your deliberations, you should elect one of your group as presiding juror. The presiding juror should preside over your deliberations and will speak for the jury when you are brought back to the court-room.

It will be important who your presiding juror is. Give the selection careful thought. Don't select someone for some arbitrary reason, for example, on the basis of age or gender. Rather, select a juror the majority feels will be fair and efficient at managing the deliberations. I suggest that you choose the presiding juror by secret ballot.

2. All of you have been prohibited from discussing this case and are probably bursting to say something. First, each of you should be given a couple of minutes to express how you are feeling about the case in terms of what things you want to hear discussed, what questions you have, and so forth. Say anything you feel, but at this point do not give your opinion as to a guilty or not guilty judgment. In addition, each juror should repeat for the others the kind of basic background information given in court during jury selection.

Start with one juror, and proceed clockwise or counter-clockwise around the table. One important ground rule to observe to make this meaningful is that no juror is to respond to or answer in any way what each individual says. This is only a period for each person to hold the floor alone, to get some feeling out, without getting into an open discussion or dialogue—otherwise you will never get around the table.

3. Immediately following the completion of the above circle, elect by private ballot the individual you wish to be your presiding juror—the person receiving the most votes is elected. The presiding juror will preside over your deliberations and speak for the jury in open court.

4. Jury deliberations include the examining and weighing of evidence and the consideration of the law. At some point, make a list on the board of the evidence or law you wish to discuss. Any person can add an item to the list at this point. If you make a complete list before discussing any one piece of evidence or any one instruction, you will have a better feeling for how you wish to proceed with your discussions.

5. Try free and open discussion for as long as the process is moving well. However, if too much confusion arises or if some use more than their share of the air time, a member might be appointed to keep a list of who wishes to talk, e.g., you go to the bottom of the list and when your name rises to the top, you're on.

6. Use whatever voting procedure you wish. However, if you use the secret ballot (some people who have not made up their minds may feel most comfortable with this privacy) remember that you will all have to give your decision openly before the jury process comes to a conclusion and the verdicts are signed.

7. Each of you must decide the case for yourself, but you should do so only after you have considered all the evidence and the law, discussed the case fully with the other jurors, and listened to the views of your fellow jurors.

Do not be afraid to change your opinion if the discussion persuades you that you should. But do not come to a decision simply because other jurors think it is right. Each of you must make your own conscientious decision. Do not change an honest belief about the weight and effect of the evidence simply to reach a verdict.

8. Here are some of the values which will help your deliberations:

a. Give respect and consideration for the honestly held views of others. We all perceive the world differently. Regard differences in views as healthy—differences bring the evidence into focus, and bring out facts not previously considered.

b. Make sure each person has the opportunity to have a share of the air time. Every person's opinion is important. Each person should go home with the feeling: "I had my opportunity to fully express my views on the case."

c. Listen for understanding. Ideally, at the end of the session, you should all be able to summarize what the views of each other were, if you have listened well.

d. Give the defendant and the State the same complete consideration you would wish to have if you were the defendant or the prosecutor—that is the essence of the trial by impartial jurors.

e. Appreciate the positive feelings of regard that generally arise when twelve people are thrown together in a close encounter to complete this most responsible task. Appreciate this rare opportunity to learn how others perceive important aspects of this case and the jury process.

9. Your verdict must be based solely on the evidence and on the law as I have given it to you in these instructions. Nothing that I have said or done is intended to suggest what your verdict should be—that is entirely for you to decide.

SAMPLE B

From Judicial Council of California, "Report of the Blue Ribbon Commission on Jury System Improvement" (1996)

Appendix O
Suggested Instruction for Jury
Deliberation Procedures

The following comments are suggestions to aid your procedure in the jury room, and it is not mandatory that you follow them.

When you first get in the jury room, take some time to get acquainted before you select a presiding juror. This helps you in choosing a presiding juror and in speaking more freely when you start your work, which saves time. Each of you might take a few minutes to introduce yourselves with your name, what you prefer to be called, and how you feel about being in the room together. All the jurors should feel free to comment, give feedback and ask questions. That prevents others from being bored and lets the speaker know he or she is heard. It also energizes the group and that helps everyone concentrate.

Then look for a presiding juror who is (1) a good listener and observer of who isn't participating, (2) who can organize the evidence and tasks, (3) who can be certain everyone is heard fairly, and (4) who can help jurors understand why different persons have different opinions.

Discuss the case before you take any vote on a verdict to avoid people feeling committed or defensive.

Remember there are no experts in the jury room. Each of you is to reach your own decision.

Some suggestions to assist jurors, especially the presiding juror, are as follows:

(1) Make a list of things the jury must decide. Make summaries as you proceed in a complicated case. Have someone take notes to keep track of the process.

(2) Be certain everybody gets heard and nobody monopolizes the time. Discuss jurors' concerns and questions.

(3) Be certain everybody is respectful of each other and nobody gets unduly pressured.

(4) If you have a disagreement, with majority and minority viewpoints expressed, do not automatically assume the majority is correct, but use that as an opportunity to re-examine your assumptions.

(5) Remind jurors to follow the Court's instructions if they forget, for example, if they want to base a decision on inadmissible evidence or want to testify as an expert or want to bring in legal advice or evidence from sources outside the courtroom.

(6) If you reach a deadlock, you may wish to make a chart with two sheets of paper on the wall. List the evidence and reasoning supporting each position, not just to find the longer list, but the better decision under the Court's instructions on the law.

If the Court has given you a special verdict, each juror should keep track of that juror's answers in case the Court wants to know how each juror voted on each issue.

SAMPLE C

SUGGESTIONS TO JURORS ABOUT USING JURY INSTRUCTIONS

Reprinted with permission from Christopher N. May, "'What Do We Do Now?':
Helping Juries Apply the Instructions," 28 *Loyola L.A. L. Rev.* 869, 884-885
(1995).

In a few minutes you will retire to begin your deliberations. Before you do so, I
want to make a suggestion that you may find helpful in using these instructions.

As you know, the plaintiff in this case has asserted three claims against the
defendant. These claims are for breach of contract, libel, and assault. I explained to
you earlier in these instructions that each of the plaintiff's claims is made up of
certain elements or requirements. In order for the plaintiff to win on any of these
claims, the plaintiff must prove each element of that claim by a preponderance of
the evidence.

My suggestion to you is this. When you are ready to use these instructions, you
might take up the plaintiff's claims one at a time. As you consider each claim, look
at the instructions to see what the specific elements or requirements for proving that
claim are. You should then discuss each of these elements one at a time, in the
order that they are listed in the instructions.

If you find that the plaintiff has proved all of the elements of a claim by a
preponderance of the evidence, then the plaintiff is entitled to win on that claim. If,
on the other hand, you conclude that the plaintiff has failed to prove one or more of
the elements of a claim by a preponderance of the evidence, the plaintiff loses on
that claim.

After you have finished considering the plaintiff's first claim, go to the next
claim and discuss it in the same way, one element at a time. Continue in this manner
until you have decided upon all of the plaintiff's claims.

Appendix 10

Sample Verdict Forms

Sample A

See *Watson v. Navistart International Transportation Corp.*, 121 Idaho 643, 827 P.2d 656 (1992).

Question No. 1   Was there negligence on the part of the defendant, INTERNATIONAL HARVESTER COMPANY, which was a proximate cause of the accident?

ANSWER   Yes _____   No _____

Question No. 2   Was there negligence on the part of the defendant, BOKKEN IMPLEMENT CO., INC., which was a proximate cause of the accident?

ANSWER   Yes _____   No _____

If you answered either of the above questions, "Yes", then please answer Question No. 3.

If you answered both of the above questions "No", you will not answer the remaining questions, but will simply sign the verdict.

Question No. 3   Was there negligence on the part of the plaintiff, LARRY W. WATSON, which was a proximate cause of the accident?

ANSWER   Yes _____   No _____

You are now to compare the negligence of the parties. If you answered "No" to Question 3, then insert a zero (0) in answer to Question No. 4(c). If you answered the previous question "Yes", then insert in the answer to Question No. 4 the percentage of negligence you find attributable to each party. Your percentage must total 100%.

Question No. 4   We find that the parties contributed to the cause of the accident in the following percentages:

a) The defendant, INTERNATIONAL HARVESTER COMPANY   _____
b) The defendant, BOKKEN IMPLEMENT CO., INC.   _____
c) The Plaintiff, LARRY W. WATSON   _____
    TOTAL   100%

If the percentage of the negligence attributed to the plaintiff is equal to or greater than the percentage of negligence attributed to each defendant, then you will not answer any further questions, but will sign the verdict.

If the percentage of negligence to the plaintiff is less than the percentage attributed to any defendant, then you will answer Questions 5 and 6.

Question No. 5   What is the total amount of damages sustained by the plaintiff, LARRY W. WATSON, as a result of the accident?

ANSWER   __________

Question No. 6   What is the total amount of damages sustained by the plaintiff, SHERRY WATSON, as a result of the accident?

ANSWER   __________

Sample B

See *Myers V. Reading Co.*, 331 U.S. 477, 481 n.5 (1947).

1. Was the brake in question an efficient brake?

2. If you find that the brake in question was not an efficient brake, did that fact contribute to or cause any injuries to the plaintiff [plaintiff's version of events]?

3. Was the plaintiff thrown from a moving train [defendant's version]?

Sample C

See *Floyd V. Kellogg Sales Co.*, 841 F.2d 226, 228 n.1 (8th Cir. 1988), *cert denied* 109 S. Ct. 501 (1988) (promissory estoppel claim).

1. Did Mr. Harper promise Mr. Floyd that if he requested an investigation of his claim of race discrimination he would not be terminated during this investigation?

2. Did Mr. Harper expect or should he have reasonably expected Mr. Floyd to request the investigation in reliance on his promise?

3. Did Mr. Floyd reasonably rely on Mr. Harper's promise when making the request for an investigation?

4. Did the employee of Kellogg Sales Company who made the decision to terminate Mr. Floyd do so because he requested an investigation?

5. Did the investigation conducted by Mr. Harper fail to conform to the investigation he promised Mr. Floyd?

Sample D

See Pope Lowerre, "Revised Rule 288—A Better Special Verdict System for Texas," 27 *Sw. L. J.* 577, 591 (1973).

1. On the occasion in question, was Don Davis negligent in his speed, in the application of his brakes, or in his lookout? Answer "Yes" or "No" on each line in Column 1. If any of your answers in Column 1 are "Yes", was any such negligence a proximate cause of the occurrence in question? Answer "Yes" or "No" on the corresponding line of Column 2.

	Column 1/Negligence	Column 2/Causation
a. Speed	_________	_________
b. Brakes	_________	_________
c. Lookout	_________	_________

Appendix 11

Suggested Concluding Jury Admonition

From Jury Committee of the Ninth Circuit,
A Manual on Jury Trial Procedures 154 (1993).

Now that you have concluded your service on this case, I thank you for your patience and conscientious attention to your duty as jurors. You have not only fulfilled your civic duty, but you have also made a personal contribution to the ideal of equal justice for all people.

You may have questions about the confidentiality of the proceedings. Because the case is over, you are free to discuss the case with any person you choose. However, you do not *have* to talk to anyone about the case if you do not want to. If you tell someone you do not wish to talk about it and they continue to bother you, let the Court know, for we can protect your privacy. If you *do* decide to discuss the case with anyone, I would suggest you treat it with a degree of solemnity, so that whatever you say, you would be willing to say in the presence of your fellow jurors or under oath here in open court in the presence of all the parties. Also, if you do decide to discuss the case, please respect the privacy of the views of your fellow jurors. Your fellow jurors fully and freely stated their opinions in deliberations with the understanding they were being expressed in confidence.

Again, I thank you for your willingness to give of your time away from your accustomed pursuits and faithfully discharge your duty as jurors. You are now excused.

Appendix 12

Suggested Procedures for Judges Conducting Juror Debriefings

Prepared by Thomas L. Hafemeister, Ph.D., J.D.

1. Make the session as informal as possible. It is often recommended that the judge remove his or her robe and conduct the session in a conversational manner. Generally the judge will emphasize that the trial is over and that this conversation is not on the record. Anything that can be done to minimize the psychological distance between the judge and the jurors will help jurors relax, open up, and view the judge as a compatriot, rather than an authority figure. At the same time, the session needs to be conducted in a manner with which the judge is comfortable. Some judges find it very natural to be informal. Other judges do not. The session should be conducted in a manner that allows the judge to come across as sincere about the value of the jurors and what the jurors have done.

2. There are three main settings used for these sessions:

(a) Some judges will send the jurors back to the deliberation room while they finish up business in the court, and then clear the courtroom and bring the jurors back into the courtroom. The courtroom has the advantage of being a relatively open area. Generally it is recommended that the judge not conduct the session from the bench, but come down and conduct the session at the juror's eye level, thereby minimizing the psychological distance between the judge and the jurors.

(b) Other judges will send the jurors back into chambers where the judge will meet with them. This setting has the advantage of impressing jurors with being invited into the inner sanctum and allowing these discussions to take place in a relatively pleasant setting. Disadvantages may include that there is not enough room or the jurors feel intimidated by being in the judge's private office.

(c) Some judges will hold the session in the jury deliberation room. The advantage of this setting is that the jurors may be relatively comfortable in this room, which they see as essentially their domain. A potential downside of this setting is that after a long trial or deliberation, the jurors may be sick of this room.

3. A key component of this session is that it allows the judge to personally thank the jurors for their hard work. One judge stands at the jury box as the jurors are brought back into the courtroom for the session, shakes each juror's hand, looks them in the eye, and thanks them by name for their help. Some jurors might find this a little overwhelming, but the point is that by personally thanking them, the judge affirms the value of their contribution and helps them walk out of the courtroom feeling positive about themselves, their job, the judge, and the judicial system.

4.   Generally these sessions are held with only the judge and the jurors present, with everyone else dismissed. Sometimes the judge will include his or her clerk or a bailiff or someone who has been very close to the jurors throughout the trial. To the extent that a large number of people are present, the setting becomes more intimidating and it is more difficult for jurors to relax, ask questions, or express their emotions.

5.   Sometimes it takes a bit of time to engage the jurors (although some juries will just naturally bubble over). It may be necessary to allow some time for the jurors' emotions to run their course. They may simply need to spend some time crying or hugging or expressing their emotions in other ways, which are normal reactions to a long or stressful trial. Some jurors may be so overwhelmed by their feelings that they literally will not be able to participate in the session for a period of time. One judge said he generally "babbled" about anything that came to his mind during this time just to give the jurors a chance to regroup. He said that it really didn't matter what he said; the important thing was that he was talking and that he was there for the jurors. Generally, it just takes one juror to say something to get most of the jurors talking. Asking a question of a relatively outspoken or gregarious juror may do the trick.

6.   There is some danger that a few jurors may dominate the session. If left to its own course, the conversation during this session may take on the same pattern that predominated in the deliberation room. To the extent that high levels of stress were induced by the deliberations themselves with some jurors alienated from other jurors, allowing the conversations to continue along this same course may actually enhance the frustrations of the nonparticipating jurors. One signal to watch for is whether some jurors are avoiding eye contact with jurors who are doing a lot of talking (although some jurors may just be naturally slow in joining in the conversations). It may be necessary for the judge to actively engage all members of the jury and perhaps draw out some jurors. However, some jurors may be reluctant to disclose their feelings in front of those jurors who are the source of their frustration and anxiety. Such jurors may have to be addressed individually subsequent to the group session.

7.   The judge should expect complaints about delays and breaks in the proceedings, probably the most frequent source of frustration for jurors, and questions about why they occurred and why the trial took so long. Most judges seem to have few problems discussing these matters once the verdict is returned. A frank discussion of trial procedures, the rationale for the rules of evidence, and why certain matters are heard outside the presence of jurors can help fill in troubling information gaps and reassure jurors that their time was not being wasted unnecessarily. These discussions also tend to be a good ice breaker.

8. Relatedly, jurors will often have questions about the trial. For example, they may ask why certain individuals didn't testify or why certain evidence wasn't presented or was excluded. Some judges are reluctant to speculate, but many judges seem relatively comfortable answering these questions but may frame their answers as being just their own speculations. Answering such questions can resolve a lot of the uncertainty of the jurors. One question often raised in a criminal trial is whether it's permissible for the jurors to attend the sentencing. For some jurors, attendance at the sentencing provides important closure. In this case, if a sentencing does occur, jurors should probably be warned that the media is likely to note their presence and reaction at sentencing.

9. Asking the jurors what the court should have done differently or what the court could have done to make jury service a more positive experience is also a good ice breaker and helps affirm for the jurors the importance of their role and their contribution. Many judges use exit surveys that do exactly this.

10. Another good ice breaker and a particularly important issue for this jury is how to deal with the media. These jurors may be unaware of and unprepared for what awaits them. They are likely to be deluged by requests for interviews from the media, and the members of the media are going to be very reluctant to take no for an answer. To induce jurors to grant interviews, they will probably play the jurors off of one another (e.g., Juror X said such and such or that you said so and so, don't you want to respond?). Some jurors think they have to talk to the media (e.g., because it is a public trial). Telling the jurors what their rights are with regard to the media can be very reassuring to the jurors (e.g., their right to say "no comment" or refuse to respond). Suggesting to the jurors that they might want to designate a spokesperson is sometimes helpful (it can at least allow the other jurors to get a head start down the back stairs). Some judges tell the jurors to contact them directly if they are harassed in any way after the trial and provide their phone number.

In this case, I'm afraid that none of this is going to completely shield a juror who wants to have absolutely no contact with the media. They should probably be prepared to expect the worst (e.g., that the media will print their names and even their addresses). A more realistic approach may be for the jurors to agree among themselves what they will talk about. For example, some judges suggest that jurors should repeat only what they personally said during deliberations and not try to repeat what some other juror said, which should be left to that juror who is the better source of that information and which also respects that juror's privacy. Juries often come out of a trial feeling extreme loyalty to one another (as well as being very solicitous of their fellow jurors' welfare). Emphasizing the likelihood of such feelings and the virtue of this loyalty may provide them needed guidance and support in their subsequent contacts with the media. Some juries will make a pact with one another regarding these contacts, although that may be very difficult to maintain and may cause pressures of its own. It may be best for the jurors to simply agree to meet en masse with the media and to get it over with.

11. A similar issue concerns whether jurors have to talk to the attorneys or should talk to the attorneys and, if so, what they should talk about. Judges sometimes warn jurors that they may not want to discuss the deliberations because the attorneys may use this to attack the verdict. Judges also sometimes say that attorneys have a legitimate interest in learning how they could have done a better job, and thus these types of conversations are not inappropriate. However, again, the judge may emphasize that the juror is advised to provide only his or her own opinion on attorney behavior and not attempt to speculate about the opinions of other jurors or what impact the attorneys' behavior had on the verdict, which was a group decision.

12. Not surprisingly, jurors often want to talk about the attorneys' behavior. Judges seem to consider this subject to be very safe common ground with the jurors and find it both easy and enjoyable to join in this critique. This type of conversation also has the virtue of helping the jury further coalesce and even heal after a difficult deliberation. The attorneys may serve as a common "enemy" or "target." There are also often some characteristics of the attorneys that allows for the interjection of levity in these sessions, which tends to be very helpful for relieving stress. The timely interjection of humor throughout these sessions can be very helpful.

13. The judge can expect to be "pumped" for what the judge thought about the verdict or whether the judge thought it was a correct verdict. Indeed, the jurors will be looking closely for any signs (verbal or nonverbal) that the judge has an opinion about the verdict. This is a delicate matter. Often what the jurors are really looking for is affirmation that they did a good job rather than an honest opinion by the judge. The judge may be the most important person in the jurors' world at this point, being held in high respect and seen as the most natural ally and affiliate of the jury. For the judge to criticize the verdict can be very troubling for the jurors.

    Usually jurors approach this question very gingerly, and some judges say its easy to see it coming and to head it off by saying that they will not or cannot comment on the verdict. Some judges will say they are too busy during a jury trial to try and predict the outcome. Other judges will say that having a jury takes the burden off them to reach a verdict and thus the judge is thinking about other things (e.g., ruling on motions) and not thinking about what an appropriate verdict would be. Some judges will say that the value of a jury determination is that it allows for the pooling of a collective wisdom and that any opinion of the judge under these circumstances is irrelevant. Some judges will say that juries are almost always right, but if a jury should make a bad decision, it is the fault of the attorneys, the evidence, or the judge.

Other judges feel no qualms about affirming the jury and will do so in a very direct fashion. In a civil case, the judge may note a prior Workmen's Compensation judgment along the same lines. In a criminal case, the judge may note the existence or lack of prior convictions or may note excluded evidence that confirms the jury's verdict. If a conviction occurs, some judges will talk about the information likely to be raised at sentencing that confirms the verdict. One judge says, "I can't comment on the verdict but you'll notice I'm smiling."

A particularly difficult situation may arise when the judge disagrees with the verdict. One judge simply issues a terse thank you and tries to leave the courtroom before his feelings show through. Some judges seem to be able to suspend their own opinions or are able to accept almost any verdict.

Regardless of the approach, almost all judges emphasize to the jurors that they recognize how tough it is to be a juror and to reach a verdict. They may note that cases don't usually go to trial unless they are sharply contested and thus difficult to decide. Some judges will say that they are very grateful for the jury system because it relieves the heavy burden of deciding from their shoulders.

14. Some judges encourage jurors to contact them directly if they have any questions that arise after they leave and describe how the jurors can contact them. Some judges will look for signals that a given juror is having troubles and suggest or insist that the juror call the judge or someone else within a given period of time. Some judges will warn jurors that they may feel out of sorts for a few days (e.g., depressed, tense, fatigued, unable to sleep, flashbacks), but that this is not unusual after a difficult trial and that these feelings will usually go away in a few days. The judge may suggest that if they don't go away within a few days, the juror should then seek professional help. Some courts are preparing referral lists for jurors, and some courts even offer to pay for needed services.

15. Particularly in cases involving violent crimes, jurors are sometimes concerned about their personal safety or that of their family after the trial (e.g., concerns

courts are preparing referral lists for jurors, and some courts even offer to pay for needed services.

15. Particularly in cases involving violent crimes, jurors are sometimes concerned about their personal safety or that of their family after the trial (e.g., concerns about possible attacks by the defendant or the family/friends of the defendant). Some judges directly address these concerns, often by emphasizing that threats to personal safety tend to be extremely rare and telling jurors to contact the court if a threat or reprisal does occur. This discussion can help ease such concerns and enhance jurors' sense that the court is concerned about their well-being. In your case, you are probably preparing additional security contingencies. You will not want to induce dread or panic in jurors, but discussing these contingencies in an objective and confident manner should enhance their confidence in and appreciation for the court.

APPENDIX 13

LETTER FROM A JUROR IN A HIGH-PROFILE CASE

In Frederick County, Maryland, jury service is a 30-day obligation. You need not be present every day, but you must check in every night and be available every day. You may serve on several trials in that month, or none at all. Several of us had already served our month-long "tour" when they recalled us for the Horn trial which lasted about five weeks or so. That amounted to nearly three months we had to put our lives on hold for the state.

Some common pre-selection stressors include:

- Threats of loss of pay, promotion, and even employment if we did not make every effort to avoid jury service.
- Immediate monetary loss from loss of work time.
- Family pressures and child care problems.

Many of us who felt it our responsibility to serve risked "standing our ground" with our employers to do so. For those who are not supported, it begins as a choice and a commitment, and stress is inherent long before selection.

Entering a jury box for the first time is entering unknown territory with different rules, limitations and expectations. The jury process is separate and distinct from the trial process. It is a most peculiar isolation. It has no familiar cues and it can be an uneasy experience. Experiencing it is the only possible preparation. The burden of the responsibility is something else you cannot prepare for. Additionally, you are immediately aware that you are very much part of the "show" as you are watched by the principals in the case while being scrutinized by the attorneys so they can get a "read" on how their case is being accepted, so you try to be neutral in your responses, which effectively eliminates all avenues of expression since we are not permitted to discuss it.

Our jury is a unique group. Some are not as outspoken as others, but most of us have strong assertive personalities tempered by a sense of humor and governed with patience for each other's quirks. Age, status, and education were never issues. I suppose it was our shared burden of deciding a capital murder case that we started bonding the first day. We maintained that bond throughout the trial and some of us are still in touch. It took us about a week, but once we discovered the trick of discussing the trial without discussing the case we could relieve a good bit of pressure. Aside from the obvious, there is also a sense of loss when your little community that carried the profound burden of deciding life or death for another human being is dissolved and you attempt to get back to where you were.

We are all still processing the experience. Some are having a more difficult time than others. We all agree it has changed us in some way. Most feel that once digested, it will translate into a positive experience. In the end, it is all in the learning and the individual lessons that await each of us.

Bottom Line

If there is one key element to the successful melding of a group of strangers into a resonant orchestra, it is, in my opinion, the judge. Judge Ann S. Harrington of the Sixth Judicial Circuit of Maryland was a pleasure to work with and conducted the trial with graceful dignity, and relaxed authority. Her demeanor and control of the court, and her genuine interest in, and immediate responses to our needs and requests were communicated to us on a daily basis both by her and her clerk Julie Sippel. I was fascinated by the complicated role the judge plays in simultaneously balancing all aspects of the trial so we can have the optimum climate to do our respective tasks well.

Judge Harrington had someone from your office speak with us, but to do so immediately afterward when jurors are numb and so deeply emotionally exhausted, you just don't hear very much. Discussion so soon after the trial is premature because it takes a few weeks for some reactions to surface. Some have been uncomfortable and expressed concern about what they are feeling. Something that might be helpful to exiting jurors is information they can take with them to read at their leisure about what they might expect, what is "normal," and why they might be reacting in such a manner. Ideally, there would also be a number they can call. All coping skills are not equal, and if the state can ask people to make the sacrifices we must make to serve, then it seems appropriate that they have something in place to assist those who don't carry the burden as well as others.

Appendix 14

**"Tips for Coping After Jury Duty,"
Brochure Distributed by the Maricopa
County (Arizona) Superior Court**

FINAL THOUGHTS

◆ Remember that jury service is the responsibility of good citizens.

◆ Resist negative thoughts about the verdict.

◆ No matter what others think about the verdict, your opinion is the only one that matters.

◆ You don't have to prove yourself to anyone.

◆ Sometimes it takes a lot of courage to serve on a jury. Some cases are very violent and brutal and hard to deal with. The case is now over and it is important for you to get on with your life.

◆ If you are fearful of retaliation or if you are threatened after the trial, tell the court and/or law enforcement immediately.

If signs of distress persist for two weeks after jury service has ended, you may wish to contact your primary care physician, a counselor, or one of the following agencies for a referral.

MENTAL HEALTH ASSOCIATION
OF ARIZONA
(602) 994-4407
(800) 642-9277

ARIZONA PSYCHIATRIC SOCIETY
(602) 898-3314

ARIZONA PSYCHOLOGICAL ASSOCIATION
(602) 675-9477

7/96

TIPS FOR COPING AFTER JURY DUTY

The techniques in this brochure may be helpful in understanding your experience as a juror.

Superior Court of Arizona
in Maricopa County
101 W. Jefferson
Phoenix, AZ 85003

THE JURY DUTY EXPERIENCE

Thank you for serving your community. Being on a jury is a rewarding experience which in some cases may be quite demanding. You were asked to listen to testimony and to examine facts and evidence. Coming to decisions is often not easy, but your participation is appreciated.

Serving on a jury is not a common experience and may cause some jurors to have temporary symptoms of distress.

This booklet reviews ways to cope with symptoms of distress. Not everyone feels anxiety or increased stress after jury duty. However, it may be helpful to be aware of the symptoms if they arise.

Some temporary signs of distress following jury duty include: anxiety, sleep or appetite changes, moodiness, physical problems, (e.g. headaches, stomach aches, no energy, and the like), second guessing your verdict, feeling guilty, fear, trouble dealing with issues or topics related to the case, a desire to be by yourself, or decreased concentration or memory problems.

Symptoms may come and go, but will eventually go away. To help yourself, it is important to admit any symptoms you may have and deal with any unpleasant reactions.

COPING TECHNIQUES AFTER SERVING ON A JURY

• Talk to family members and friends. One of the best ways to put your jury experience in perspective is to discuss your feelings and reactions with loved ones and friends. You may also want to talk with your family physician or a member of the clergy.

• Stick to your normal, daily routines. It is important to return to your normal schedule. Don't isolate yourself.

• Before you leave the court, you may wish to get the names and numbers of at least two of your fellow jurors. Sometimes it is helpful to talk to people who went through the experience with you. This can help you to remember that you were part of a group (jury) and are not alone.

• Remember that you are having normal responses to an unusual experience.

• You can deal with signs of distress by cutting down on alcohol, caffeine, and nicotine. These substances can increase anxiety, fatigue and make sleep problems worse.

COPING TECHNIQUES AFTER SERVING ON A JURY (CONT.)

• Relax with deep breathing.

Breathe in slowly through your nose.

Breathe out through your mouth.

Slow your thoughts down and think about a relaxing scene.

Continue deep breathing until you feel more relaxed.

• Cope with sleep problems.

Increase your daily exercise, but do not exercise just before bedtime.

Decrease your caffeine consumption, especially in the afternoon or evening.

Do "boring" activities before bedtime.

Listen to relaxation tapes or relaxing music before bedtime.

Appendix 15

Sample Jury Exit Questionnaires

From Jury Committee of the Ninth Circuit,
A Manual on Jury Trial Procedures, Appendix 6 (1993).

JURY SERVICE EXIT QUESTIONNAIRE

Your answers to the following questions will help improve jury service. All responses are voluntary and confidential. (Please circle answers where appropriate.)

1. Approximately how many days did you report to the courthouse? _________

2. What percent of your time was spent in the jury waiting room? _________

3. How many times did you report to a courtroom for jury selection? _________

4. How many times were you actually selected to be a juror? _________

5. How would you rate the following factors? (Check all)

	Good	Adequate	Poor
A. Initial Orientation	______	______	______
B. Treatment by Court Personnel	______	______	______
C. Physical Comforts	______	______	______
D. Personal Safety	______	______	______
E. Parking Facilities	______	______	______
F. Scheduling of Your Time	______	______	______

6. After having served, what is your impression of jury service? (Check one)

    A.   The same as before — Favorable
    B.   The same as before — Unfavorable
    C.   More Favorable than Before
    D.   Less Favorable than Before

7. AGE: 18-20   21-24   25-34   35-44   45-54   55-64   65-Over

8. SEX: Female   Male   9. Occupation: ______________________

10. RACE: Black   White   Other

11. Did you lose income as a result of jury service?   YES   NO

                                        Amount $ _________

12. Have you ever served on jury duty before?   YES   NO

13. (a) Are you a registered voter in the county?   YES   NO

    (b) Do you have a driver's license and/or identification
         card issued by the Department of Motor Vehicles?   YES   NO

14. In what ways do you think jury service can be improved? (Use reverse side if necessary)

____

____

____

JURY SERVICE EXIT QUESTIONNAIRE   Judge _______   Panel _______

Date of Panel _____________

Your answers to the following questions will help us to improve jury service for those who will follow you. Please try to make your comments helpful and constructive in nature. You may use the enclosed postage paid envelop. All replies are confidential.

1.   How many days did you spend on jury duty? ___________

2.   Were you selected to participate in a jury selection process? ___________

3.   During your term as jurors, two different procedures for challenges have been used. The first procedure required each attorney to orally express his challenge of a juror. The second procedure required each attorney to indicate in writing who he wishes to challenge. Please indicate which procedure you prefer:

Oral Challenges ______   Written Challenges ______

Comments:____
____
____

4.   Did you actually sit as a juror on a case?   ___________

5.   How would you rate the following aspects of your stay here?

	Good	Adequate	Poor
A. Orientation Instructions Given to You	______	______	______
B. Treatment by Court Personnel	______	______	______
C. Physical Comforts	______	______	______

6.   Should anything be added or changed about your orientation session to better prepare you for jury service? ________   If "yes," comment under #17 below

7.   Did you find your juror handbook to be of value? ___________

8.   Do you feel a jury lounge should be provided? ___________

9.   Did the payment you received adequately cover your expenses while serving?

____

10. What major inconveniences, if any, did you experience due to jury duty?

____

____

____

11. What was your attitude toward jury duty when you first received your summons? ____

____

____

12. Since having served, have your feelings remained the same, or have they become more positive or more negative toward jury duty? _______________

____

____

13. Now that you have served, what impression would you convey to your friends concerning jury service? ____

____

____

14. Did you experience any difficulty in receiving notice to appear? If yes, please comment and make any suggestions as to how we can improve our notification system. ____

____

____

15. For those jurors who were required to call the code-a-phone, did you find the use of this service helpful? If not, would you prefer to be notified in some other way? Please explain. ____

____

____

16. For those jurors required to use the code-a-phone, were the instructions you received clear and understandable? _________________________________

____

____

17. Please use the remaining space to indicate constructive measures that could be implemented so that jury duty may be improved. You may also comment on any of the above matters. We welcome your ideas and suggestions. (You may continue on the reverse.) ____

____

____

JUROR'S EVALUATION FORM

Please rate the following persons by circling a number for each trait using the scale below.

THE JUDGE

	Excellent	Good	Neutral	Poor	Very Poor
Attentiveness	1	2	3	4	5
Competence	1	2	3	4	5
Courtesy	1	2	3	4	5
Courtroom Demeanor	1	2	3	4	5
Patience	1	2	3	4	5
Punctuality	1	2	3	4	5
Fairness/Impartiality	1	2	3	4	5

Did the judge appear to favor one side or the other? _____________

If so, which side? ____

Comments: ____

WAS THE COURTROOM STAFF COURTEOUS AND PLEASANT

	Yes	No
Court Clerk	___	___
Court Reporter	___	___
Bailiff	___	___

THE PROSECUTING ATTORNEY (CRIMINAL) OR THE PLAINTIFF'S ATTORNEY (CIVIL)

	Excellent	Good	Neutral	Poor	Very Poor	PLAINTIFF'S CO-COUNSEL, IF ANY Use appropriate number (1 - 5)
Competence	1	2	3	4	5	_____
Courtroom Demeanor	1	2	3	4	5	_____
Preparedness	1	2	3	4	5	_____
Sincerity	1	2	3	4	5	_____
Opening Statement	1	2	3	4	5	_____
Evidence Presentation	1	2	3	4	5	_____
Closing Argument	1	2	3	4	5	_____

Comments: ____

<u>THE DEFENSE ATTORNEY</u>

	Excellent	Good	Neutral	Poor	Very Poor	PLAINTIFF'S CO-COUNSEL, IF ANY Use appropriate number (1 - 5)
Competence	1	2	3	4	5	______
Courtroom Demeanor	1	2	3	4	5	______
Preparedness	1	2	3	4	5	______
Sincerity	1	2	3	4	5	______
Opening Statement	1	2	3	4	5	______
Evidence Presentation	1	2	3	4	5	______
Closing Argument	1	2	3	4	5	______

Comments: ____

____

GENERAL COMMENTS/SUGGESTIONS FOR IMPROVEMENT (USE BACK, IF DESIRED).____

Selected Bibliography

Jeffrey Abramson, *We, the Jury: Justice and the Democratic Ideal* (1994).

Stephen Adler, *The Jury: Trial and Error in the American Courtroom* (1994).

Albert W. Alschuler, "Racial Quotas and the Jury," 44 *Duke L. J.* 704 (1995).

Albert W. Alschuler, "The Supreme Court and the Jury: Voir Dire, Peremptory Challenges, and the Review of Jury Verdicts," 56 *U. Chi. L. Rev.* 153 (1989).

American Bar Association, *Standards for Criminal Justice: Trial by Jury* (1986).

American Bar Association, Commission on Mental and Physical Disability Law and Commission on Legal Problems of the Elderly, *Into the Jury Box: A Disability Accommodation Guide for State Courts* (1994).

American Bar Association, Commission on Mental and Physical Disability Law and Commission on Legal Problems of the Elderly, *Opening the Courthouse Door: An ADA Access Guide for State Courts* (1992).

American Bar Association, Committee on Jury Standards, *Standards Relating to Juror Use and Management* (1993).

American Bar Association, Project on Standards for Criminal Justice, *Standards Relating to Fair Trial and Free Press* (1983).

Arizona Supreme Court Committee on More Effective Use of Juries, *Jurors: The Power of 12: Report of the Arizona Supreme Court Committee on More Effective Use of Juries* (1994).

Leigh B. Bienen, "Helping Jurors Out: Post-Verdict Debriefing for Jurors in Emotionally Disturbing Trials," 68 *Ind. L. J.* 1333 (1993).

Dennis Bilecki, "Efficient Method of Jury Selection for Lengthy Trials," 73 *Judicature* 43 (June-July 1989).

Lisa Blue, Ted A. Donner, and Jane N. Saginaw, *Jury Selection: Strategies and Science* (1986).

Martin J. Bourgeois, I. A. Horowitz & Lynne Forster Lee, "Effects of Technicality and Access to Trial Transcripts on Verdicts and Information Processing in a Civil Trial," 19 *Personality & Soc. Psychol. Bull.* 220 (1993).

Jeffrey S. Brand, "The Supreme Court, Equal Protection and Jury Selection: Denying That Race Still Matters," 1994 *Wis. L. Rev.* 514.

Mark S. Brodin, "Accuracy, Efficiency, and Accountability in the Litigation Process—The Case for the Fact Verdict," 59 *U. Cin. L. Rev.* 15 (1964).

Brookings Institution, *Charting a Future for the Civil Jury System: A Report from an American Bar Association/Brookings Symposium* (1992).

Pamela Casey & Shelley Gable, *Judicial Benchbook on Juror Stress* (National Center for State Courts, forthcoming 1997).

Joe S. Cecil, Valerie P. Hans, and E. C. Wiggins, "Citizen Comprehension of Difficult Issues: Lessons from Civil Jury Trials," 40 *Am. U. L. Rev.* 727 (1991).

Robert P. Charrow and Veda R. Charrow, "Making Legal Language Understandable: A Psycholinguistic Study of Jury Instructions," 79 *Colum. L. Rev.* 1306 (1979).

Committee on Federal Courts, New York State Bar Association, "Improving Jury Comprehension in Complex Civil Litigation," 62 *St. John's L. Rev.* 549 (1988).

Susan Crump, "Jury Misconduct, Jury Interviews, and the Federal Rules of Evidence: Is the Broad Exclusionary Principle of Rule 606(b) Justified?" 66 *N.C. L. Rev.* 509 (1988).

B. Michael Dann, "'Learning Lessons' and 'Speaking Rights': Creating Educated and Democratic Juries," 68 *Ind. L. J.* 1229 (1993).

Shari S. Diamond & Judith N. Levi, "Improving Decisions on Death by Revising and Testing Jury Instructions," 79 *Judicature* 224 (1996).

Phoebe C. Elsworth, "Are Twelve Heads Better Than One?" 52 *Law & Contemp. Probs.* 205 (1989).

Amiram Elwork, Bruce D. Sales & James J. Alfini, "Juridic Decisions: In Ignorance of the Law or In Light of It?" 1 *Law & Hum. Behav.* 163 (1977).

Amiram Elwork, Bruce D. Sales & James J. Alfini, *Making Jury Instructions Understandable* (1982).

David L. Faigman & A. J. Baglioni, Jr., "Bayes' Theorem in the Trial Process: Instructing Jurors on the Value of Statistical Evidence," 12 *Law & Hum. Behav.* 1 (1988).

Michael J. Farrell, "Communication in the Courtroom: Jury Instructions," 85 *W. Va. L. Rev.* 5 (1982).

Theodore B. Feldmann & Roger A. Bell, "Crisis Debriefing of a Jury After a Murder Trial," 42 *Hosp. & Community Psychiatry* 79 (1991).

Jeffrey T. Frederick, *Mastering Voir Dire and Jury Selection* (1995).

John Guinther, *The Jury in America* 49 (1988).

Thomas L. Hafemeister & W. Larry Ventis, "Juror Stress: What Burden Have We Placed on Our Juries?" 56 *Tex. B. J.* 586 (1993).

Valerie Hans & Neil Vidmar, *Judging the Jury* (1986).

Reid Hastie, Steven D. Penrod & Nancy Pennington, *Inside the Jury* (1983).

Larry Heuer & Steven D. Penrod, "Instructing Jurors: A Field Experiment with Written and Preliminary Instructions," 13 *Law & Hum. Behav.* 409 (1989).

Edward J. Imwinkelried & Lloyd R. Schwed, "Guidelines for Drafting Understandable Jury Instructions: An Introduction to the Use of Psycholinguistics," 23 *Crim. L. Bull.* 135 (1987).

Susan E. Jones, "Judge- Versus Attorney-Conducted Voir Dire," 11 *Law & Hum. Behav.* 131 (1987).

Judicial Conference of the United States, Subcommittee on Pattern Instructions, *Pattern Criminal Jury Instructions* (1988).

D. Nolan Kaiser, "Juries, Blindness and the Juror Function," 60 *Chi.-Kent L. Rev.* 191 (1984).

H. Kalven & Hans Zeisel, *The American Jury* (1966).

Saul M. Kassin & Lawrence S. Wrightsman, *The American Jury on Trial: Psychological Perspectives* (1988).

Saul M. Kassin & Lawrence S. Wrightsman, "On the Requirements of Proof: The Timing of Judicial Instruction and Mock Juror Verdicts," 37 *J. Personality & Soc. Psychol.* 1877 (1979).

Robert E. Kehoe, Jr., *Jury Instruction for Contract Cases* (1995).

James E. Kelley, "Addressing Juror Stress: A Trial Judge's Perspective," 43 *Drake L. Rev.* 97 (1994).

J. Clark Kelso, "Report of the Blue Ribbon Commission on Jury System Improvement" (Judicial Council of California, 1996).

Nancy J. King, "Nameless Justice: The Case for the Routine Use of Anonymous Juries in Criminal Trials," 49 *Vand. L. Rev.* 123 (1996).

Nancy J. King, "Nameless Justice: The Case for the Routine Use of Anonymous Juries in Criminal Trials," 49 *Vand. L. Rev.* 123 (1996).

Nancy J. King, "Racial Jurymandering: Cancer or Cure? A Contemporary Review of Affirmative Action in Jury Selection," 68 *N.Y.U. L. Rev.* 707 (1993).

Nancy J. King & G. Thomas Munsterman, "Stratified Juror Selection: Cross-Section by Design," 79 *Judicature* 273 (1996).

Koenig, Kerr & Hoeck, "Michigan Standard Criminal Jury Instructions: Judges' Perspectives After Ten Years Use," 4 *Cooley L. Rev.* 347 (1987).

Kramer & Koenig, "Do Jurors Understand Criminal Jury Instructions? Analyzing the Results of the Michigan Juror Comprehension Project," 23 *U. Mich. J. L. Ref.* 401 (1990).

Elissa Krauss & Beth Bonora, eds., *Jurywork: Systematic Techniques* (2d ed. 1995).

Richard O. Lempert, "Civil Juries and Complex Cases: Let's Not Rush to Judgment," 80 *Mich. L. Rev.* 68 (1981).

Robert E. Litan, ed., *Verdict: Assessing the Civil Jury System* (1993).

Nancy S. Marder, "Beyond Gender: Peremptory Challenges and the Roles of the Jury," 73 *Tex. L. Rev.* 1041 (1995).

Shaun P. Martin, "Rationalizing the Irrational: The Treatment of Untenable Federal Civil Jury Verdicts," 28 *Creighton L. Rev.* 683 (1995).

Christopher N. May, "'What Do We Do Now?': Helping Juries Apply the Instructions," 28 *Loyola L.A. L. Rev.* 869 (1995).

Robert L. McBride, *The Art of Instructing the Jury* (1969).

G. Thomas Munsterman, *Jury System Management* (National Center for State Courts, 1996).

G. Thomas Munsterman, *Reduced Terms of Jury Service in the Federal Courts* (National Center for State Courts, 1986).

Janice T. Munsterman, *The Relationship of Juror Fees and Terms of Service to Jury System Performance* (National Center for State Courts, 1991).

Timothy R. Murphy, Genevra K. Loveland & G. Thomas Munsterman, *A Manual for Managing Notorious Cases* (National Center for State Courts, 1992).

Michael T. Nietzel & Ronald C. Dillehay, "The Effects of Variation in Voir Dire Procedures in Capital Murder Trials," 6 *Law & Hum. Behav.* 1 (1982).

Nancy Pennington & Reid Hastie, "Evidence Evaluation in Complex Decision Making," 51 *J. Personality & Soc. Psychol.* 242 (1986).

Harvey S. Perlman, "Pattern Jury Instructions: The Application of Social Science Research," 65 *Neb. L. Rev.* 520 (1986).

Robin Reed, "Jury Simulation: The Impact of Judge's Instructions and Attorney Tactics on Decisionmaking," 71 *J. Crim. L. & Criminology* 68 (1980).

Michael J. Saks, "Judicial Nullification," 68 *Ind. L. J.* 1281 (1993).

Bruce Sales, ed., *Perspectives in Law and Psychology: Volume I, The Criminal Justice System* (1977).

Leonard B. Sand & Steven A. Reiss, "A Report on Seven Experiments Conducted by District Court Judges in the Second Circuit," 60 *N.Y.U. L. Rev.* 423 (1985).

Susan R. Schwaiger, "The Submission of Written Instructions and Statutory Language to New York Criminal Juries," 56 *Brook. L. Rev.* 1353 (1991).

William W Schwarzer, "Communication with Juries: Problems and Remedies," 69 *Cal. L. Rev.* 731 (1981).

Laurence J. Severance, Edith Greene & Elizabeth F. Loftus, "Toward Criminal Jury Instructions That Jurors Can Understand," 75 *J. Crim. L. & Criminology* 198 (1984).

Laurence J. Severance & Elizabeth F. Loftus, "Improving the Ability of Jurors to Comprehend and Apply Criminal Jury Instructions," 17 *Law & Soc. Rev.* 153 (1982).

Vicki L. Smith, "Impact of Pretrial Instruction on Jurors' Information Processing and Decision Making," 76 *J. Applied Psychol.* 220 (1991).

V. Hales Starr & Mark McCormick, *Jury Selection: An Attorney's Guide to Jury Law and Methods* (2d ed. 1993).

Walter W. Steele, Jr. & Elizabeth G. Thornburg, "Jury Instructions: A Persistent Failure to Communicate," 67 *N.C. L. Rev.* 77 (1988).

David U. Strawn, Raymond W. Buchanan, Albert Pryor & K. Phillip Taylor, "Reaching a Verdict, Step by Step," 60 *Judicature* 383 (1977).

David Suggs & Bruce D. Sales, "Juror Self-Disclosure in the Voir Dire: A Social Science Analysis," 56 *Ind. L. J.* 245 (1981).

J. Alexander Tanford, "The Law and Psychology of Jury Instructions," 69 *Neb. L. Rev.* 71 (1990).

William C. Thompson, "Are Juries Competent to Evaluate Statistical Evidence?" 52 *Law & Contemp. Probs.* 9 (1989).

H. P. Weld & E. R. Danzig, "A Study of the Way in Which a Verdict is Reached by a Jury," 53 *Am. J. Psychol.* 518 (1940).

Elizabeth C. Wiggins & Steven J. Breckler, "Special Verdicts as Guides to Jury Decision Making," 14 *Law & Psychol. Rev.* 1 (1990).

Jamison Wilcox, "The Craft of Drafting Plain-Language Jury Instructions: A Study of Sample Pattern Instructions on Obscenity," 59 *Temp. L. Q.* 1159 (1986).